ALSO BY JANE

Novels

THE THREE LIVES TRILOGY:
Parallel Lines
Triangles in Squares
Full Circle

The Brini Boy

THE RAWLINGS TRILOGY:
The Strange Year of E G Rawlings
A Year of Trials for E G Rawlings
Quo Vadis E G Rawlings

Verse

Between Sanity and Madness
Saint or Monster

Children's Books

Sir Edward and Nimrod
Diggory Loppet
Do's it Have a Hamster?

JANE McCULLOCH

You Won't Believe This, But ...

A Memoir

AUSTIN MACAULEY PUBLISHERS®
LONDON • CAMBRIDGE • NEW YORK • SHARJAH

Copyright © Estate of Jane McCulloch 2024

The right of Jane McCulloch to be identified as author of this work has been asserted in accordance with sections 77 and 78 of the Copyright, Designs and Patents Act 1988.

All rights reserved. No part of this publication may be reproduced, stored in a retrieval system, or transmitted in any form or by any means, electronic, mechanical, photocopying, recording, or otherwise, without the prior permission of the publishers.

Any person who commits any unauthorised act in relation to this publication may be liable to criminal prosecution and civil claims for damages.

Uncredited photographs appearing in this book are from the author's personal collection. Photographs not owned by the author are published with kind permission of their respective owners, as credited in the accompanying captions.

All of the events in this memoir are true to the best of the author's memory. The views expressed in this memoir are solely those of the author.

A CIP catalogue record for this title is available from the British Library.

ISBN 9781035862535 (Paperback)
ISBN 9781035862542 (ePub e-book)

www.austinmacauley.com

First Published 2024
Austin Macauley Publishers Ltd®
1 Canada Square
Canary Wharf
London
E14 5AA

For Toby's children and grandchildren.

ACKNOWLEDGEMENTS

So many people encouraged and helped me with this book it will be impossible to name them all, but there are some I must acknowledge.

First, my family, for continually encouraging me with this project.

Dr Stephen Carver has been my invaluable mentor and guided me perfectly through yet another book, so great thanks to him.

I am hugely grateful to James Reeve for saving our correspondence and sending the letters to me, which proved a wonderful source of material.

There are also two friends I want to mention, who always helped and supported me, but sadly are no longer with us: Rosemary Say, war heroine and drama critic, and Simon Raison, who encouraged me for over forty years.

Lastly, huge thanks to all at Austin Macauley Publishers.

CONTENTS

1 Dunkirk Baby 13

2 Family Life 32

3 Towards Adulthood 48

4 The Incidents Begin 69

5 Engagement, Wedding and Honeymoon 86

6 And Then We Were Six 96

7 A Manic Decade of Activity 113

8 Russia and the Aftermath 123

9 A Momentous Meeting 135

10 The Wilderness Years 155

11 The Great Jessye Norman 168

12 The Great and the Good 183

13 Towards the Millenium 200

14 Life as a Single Woman 210

15 Calmer Waters 221

16 Something's Gotta Give 243

The Final Chapter: Winter 254

Postscript 259

Index of Names 280

The web of our life is a mingled yarn, good and ill together...
                               WILLIAM SHAKESPEARE

Sometimes there are clouds of gloom,
But these are transient all,
If a shower will make the roses bloom,
O why lament its fall?
                               CHARLOTTE BRONTË

Life is pure adventure, and the sooner we realise
that, the sooner we will be able to treat life as art.
                               MAYA ANGELOU

Chapter One
DUNKIRK BABY

TO BEGIN AT the beginning...

I was a Dunkirk baby. At least, I've always presumed I was. In any case, it's something of a miracle I ever made my way into the world at all. My mother had been advised not to have more children because two bouts of rheumatic fever left her with a seriously weakened heart. I can only presume I was conceived in the euphoria after Dunkirk and nine months later, on 4 February 1941, I made my troubled way into the world during one of the worst air raids of the war. I was named Teresa Jane: Teresa after the saint and Jane after Jane Welsh Carlyle. It was hoped I would have the spiritual qualities of the first and the brains and wit of the latter. A tall order for anyone.

My brother Christopher was six when I was born, and my sister Gabriel four. They looked on my arrival as a definite intrusion into their lives, especially Gabriel, who throughout my childhood found me a constant irritation. It was now made clear to my mother, having endured a long and difficult labour, there could be no more pregnancies. In those days, with no birth control, the only safe way to avoid pregnancy was for there to be no sex, which must have put an impossible strain on their marriage.

My parents gave me a scattering of interesting godparents. One of them was Lady Margaret Douglas Home (formerly Spencer, and aunt of Princess Diana). Another was an eccentric Cambridge don, who always started his letters to me, 'Oh what a knave [sic.] and peasant slave am I, my dear Teresa Jane...' This would be by way of an apology for neglecting me, and then he would enclose a crisp ten-shilling note. Other than that, my birth was rather ignored. There was a war on, and nobody had time to make a fuss over a baby. It set the tone for my early childhood, which was mainly one of isolation and loneliness.

During the war, my father was an army chaplain and when I was two, he became Rector of St Mary's Chatham, with responsibility for the large and busy naval dockyard. There was no rectory with this living, so my parents took a house in Prospect Row, Old Brompton, a once-elegant row of Georgian houses, most of which had sadly become slum dwellings. Old Brompton was then a village, a mile up the hill from Chatham Town and the Church. My memories of the Chatham years are few. Our house was at the top end of the Row and next door to the Royal Marine barracks.

JM, aged three

I became used to the bugle calls night and morning and would spend hours watching from my nursery window as the marines paraded in their smart white helmets. Various events were arranged by the resident Admiral at the dockyard, who inevitably became a great friend of my father. I say inevitably, because my father, from his Oxford days, had made a habit of collecting famous and influential people. We would regularly be taken to the Admiral's house for tea, where there would be chocolate biscuits and iced cakes, a rare luxury. Special events were thrown around Christmas and Easter, when parties would be given for children of the navy personnel, and we were included.

I clearly remember one fancy dress party. Gabriel, who had recently been a bridesmaid, wore her pretty bridesmaid's dress of yellow organdie, to which had been added some green leaves to represent Spring. I was consumed with envy and resentment, being dressed in a hastily put-together costume representing Autumn. It consisted of my father's old khaki army shirt, which was scratchy, with a lot of dingy brown leaves sewn onto it. In contrast to Gabriel, I was sadly drab. Worse was to follow a year later. Gabriel and Christopher were away staying with friends because my mother was ill again. I was on my own, being looked after by various helpers. It meant there was nobody around to organise party clothes for me. When I inquired, I was told to go in whatever I was wearing, which was an old skirt with a jumper with holes in it. On arriving at the party, one of the mothers called out, 'Oh look, how sweet. Teresa Jane has come as a refugee.' My humiliation was complete.

My mother's two brothers were both in the navy. Peter was on Russian convoys and Anthony, the younger brother, was in the Fleet Air Arm and already decorated for dropping the first direct hit on the battleship Bismarck. There was great excitement when they occasionally arrived back at Chatham dockyard and came to visit us on leave, looking very dashing in their uniforms. On one occasion I was presented with a banana. Having never seen one before, I attempted to eat it with the skin on, and everyone laughed. I've disliked bananas ever since.

The war came to an end when I was four. I can vaguely recall the celebrations at the Prospect Row street party with plenty of flags and bunting. After this brief excitement, the family settled down to a few difficult years. My mother was recovering from another bout of rheumatoid arthritis and was invited to stay with the Bishop of Rochester and his wife while she regained her strength. Gabriel and Christopher were at boarding school, and in the holidays whatever nanny was now looking after me was given the added work of the other two. Gabriel was the ringleader in our minor rebellions, particularly with Nanny Walker, who started out over-strict and consequently suffered Gabriel's revenges. We would slip out and hide behind the tombstones in a disused churchyard near to us and then watch as Nanny Walker rushed up and down the street in total panic, trying to find us. Poor Nanny Walker. She finally had a nervous collapse and spent a week in hospital. After that, we had a series of young and much less qualified girls to look after us. On one occasion there was a Swedish girl called Gunborg. She was not the beautiful, blonde variety, but a plain, lumpy girl who gave few utterances and wore an expression of permanent gloom. On one occasion she was instructed to take the three of us to the Bishop's Palace in Rochester to visit my mother. She had been given directions how to get to the Palace once we had left the bus but became completely lost and seemed incapable of asking anyone for help. I remember the panic I felt as we went round in circles, my legs worn out, with Gunborg dragging me along, getting increasingly desperate. I think it was Gabriel who finally took charge and asked for directions. We turned up very late, with my poor mother in a state of agitation. This incident left me with a fear of being lost, something which has remained with me throughout my life.

In the Prospect Row house there was a large room on the top floor where we would spend most of our time in the holidays. This room contained a piano and one Christmas we were given the *Observer Book of Folk Songs*. Soon we knew most of the songs by heart, working our way through the entire volume. The moment I hear 'The Ashgrove' or 'There is a Tavern in the Town' or 'Barbara Allen', it takes me straight back to that room. One holiday, we ambitiously

McCulloch family group, 1946

decided to write a children's opera. Christopher composed the music; Gabriel directed proceedings and wrote the lyrics, and I took the main part. The story for this opera was taken from a book I'd been given, which quite frankly terrified me, but Gabriel insisted was an ideal subject. It told of an evil witch who lived on Carauntowhil Mountain in Ireland, who was destroying the lives of everyone who lived in the village nearby. Our hero was a young boy who lived with his grandfather. Out walking one day, he met an old man and told him he longed to destroy the witch and save the people in his village. The old man said he would help the boy by giving him three wishes, but adding he could only use the wishes once. The boy first wished for the witch to be burnt by fire, but the witch blew the fire down the mountain, and it was in danger of destroying the village and had to be put out. The boy then wished for the witch to be drowned, but the witch just laughed and diverted the mighty roar of water and again threatened the village. In desperation the boy turned the witch into a small piece of bread and ate it. But the bread stuck in his throat, with the witch screaming he would be choked to death. The grandfather was powerless to help the boy who had no more wishes left, but the old man arrived, fished the bread from the boy's throat, threw it on the fire and with a terrible scream the witch was destroyed. I took the part of the boy and Gabriel played the witch with rather too much venom and was quite terrifying. I don't remember much about any performances but one of the lyrics stuck in my head because Christopher set it to a beautiful melody:

> *Oh Carauntowhil, dreamy mountain,*
> *Mountain where we live with dreams,*
> *Light of the morning, light of the evening,*
> *Beautiful mountain, our Carauntowhil home.*

Until I was eight, my father was a remote character, and we hardly ever saw him. He remained in his study, with a 'not to be disturbed' sign because he was in the white heat of writing. His books had provocative titles like *A Parson in Revolt*. Consequently, he quickly became known as the '*enfant terrible*' of the Church. He was an intellectual socialist, of the Fabian Society variety, and had many friends at the top of the new post-war Labour Government. On one occasion he invited Sir Stafford Cripps, the then Chancellor of the Exchequer, to look at the post-war slum conditions in Chatham. As they walked together up our street, my father pointed out that there were children forced to play in the

Cartoon of my father by Coia

gutter. When he looked further, he saw, to his embarrassment, that one of those children was me.

Sir Stafford was not the only distinguished visitor. The Archbishop of Canterbury was another. I was four years old when I first met him, being brought to the drawing room to be introduced to the great man. He was in full Trollopian dress, complete with gaiters. Apparently, I stared and then poked him in the leg and asked, 'Why are you wearing leggings?'

He benignly answered, 'Those are gaiters, my child.' I think I was quickly removed.

Looking back, it seems astonishing that my father, then a young man in his early thirties, should know so many great and famous people. But he did, and he continued to collect them throughout his life. It was therefore typical that his batman during the war should have been Jestyn Phillips, Viscount St Davids. Jestyn's family seat was Roch Castle, a spectacular Norman keep rising dramatically from the top of a rocky mound and overlooking the Pembrokeshire coast. One summer holiday, Christopher, Gabriel and I were despatched to the castle, in the care of Mary Mares, who had been a nanny when I was a baby and was now a trained midwife. She'd offered to look after us as neither of my parents could. Mary was pretty and gentle, certainly no match for the sharp tongue of Gabriel, but I loved her and was relieved she was with us, as life in the castle was for me a frightening ordeal. Jestyn had three children: Colwyn, the same age as Christopher, Rowena, the same age as Gabriel and Myfanwy, known as Miffin, who was three years younger than me and who attached herself to Christopher. I don't remember being fazed when the servants called them Lord Colwyn and Lady Rowena, while we were plain Master and Miss, but once again I was left on my own. We were lodged in the battlements right at the very top, with slit windows from where hung the horrible bats, who occasionally would flap around the room with Gabriel and Christopher leaping about, trying to force them outside. It was always damp and cold, even in summer. On our first morning we trailed down to the dining room, a vast gothic room hewn out of rock, with water dripping down the walls. It was here we found the severe-looking Dowager Duchess, sitting at the top of the long table. She didn't acknowledge our arrival and as far as I remember never spoke to us, and only a few times to her grandchildren. There were no parents around, only the servants. We were served bowls of grey porridge, which I immediately rejected. After two days, Mary managed to find eggs at the local farm and suggested we had those instead. Most days were spent on the vast sandy beach, a short walk down a leafy lane, smelling of meadowsweet and other wildflowers – Gabriel of course knew all their names. I was happy on the beach, keeping to myself, making sandcastles and swimming when it wasn't rough. The breakers could be huge, and I once found myself hurled around underwater as if in a washing machine, until I was thrown in a ragged heap onto the beach. Consequently, the fear of being underwater has never left me. The only other real drama that occurred was when Christopher was stung by a jellyfish and passed out with the pain.

Towards the end of the holiday, we were asked to join the haymaking. This was 1947, and there were still some German prisoners of war working on the farm. I thought they were like gods, bronzed and handsome. They made a great fuss of me, throwing me up onto the haycarts and then catching me on the way down. It was the highlight of the holiday. Recently, I visited Roch Castle. It is now a smart hotel, owned by a Japanese firm I believe, and sadly no longer surrounded by farmland and leafy lanes, but rows of holiday bungalows.

Soon after this, I caught measles and had to lie in a

darkened room to preserve my eyesight. To my surprise and delight, my father paid me short daily visits. This was a rare event. He bought me a book called *Groundsel and Necklaces* and would read it to me because I wasn't allowed to use my eyes. I loved that book. The author, Cicely M Barker, was famous for her illustrations, and the pictures were as beautiful as the story. I recently purchased an expensive copy in a shop for rare books and was surprised the story could still move me to tears.

Gabriel and Christopher were at boarding school and when term ended were farmed out to various friends in the holidays. With my mother still unwell, once I'd recovered from the measles, it was decided to send me to stay with my uncle Anthony and his wife Brenda. Anthony had become a master at Bedales, a progressive co-educational boarding school, and the family had a house, Five Oaks, in the village of Steep, close to the school. My mother, although still an invalid, was determined to see me off at Waterloo Station, where I was placed in the charge of the guard. As the train drew out, I realised my bear was no longer with me. I had dropped it somewhere on the platform.

I wailed loudly, 'I've lost my bear. I don't have my bear!'

My mother called out, 'Don't worry, darling, I'll find it and send it to you.' And she did. It was typical of her tenacity and determination. It took her three weeks to trace it, during which time she even wrote to the station master. Finally, it turned up in a porter's locker. He hadn't had time to take it to lost property and forgotten about it, until a notice was put up about my lost bear. There were no further dramas on the journey, and I arrived at Five Oaks, to start my long stay. I was taken up to the large nursery which I was to share with my younger cousins Jane and Sarah. It was a very forlorn six-year-old who sat on the bed without her bear. Tears started to trickle down my cheeks.

Poor Brenda. She already had two small children and was

pregnant again. Now she had me as well. Looking back, I think she tried to be kind, but her tone was often stern and offhand, and there were no outward signs of affection. I was told briskly to cheer up, as I was probably just feeling homesick. Having no idea what this meant I was alarmed at the mention of being sick. It surely meant I was ill and only increased my fears and unhappiness.

I spent over a year at Five Oaks, during which time my cousin Stephen was born. Brenda also had a miscarriage, the result of which I unfortunately found in a bucket in the bathroom before it was removed, a shocking memory which has never left me. The house was bleak and the regime strict, and I was permanently cold. I craved for affection, but none was given, except by Anthony, which must have been noticed by Brenda. Anthony became an adored father figure for me. He was a handsome man, in a piratical, Gregory Peck sort of way. He was also something of a hero. I learned later he'd run away from Eton to the Spanish Civil War to fight on the Republican side. After being fetched home by my grandfather, he went up to Oxford, but no sooner had he obtained his degree than war broke out. He survived five years of the war in the Fleet Air Arm and was decorated along the way. Anthony possessed the most beautiful baritone voice. Had he returned from the war unmarried, he might well have made a career in music. As it was, with a growing family, he became a teacher. Bedales was the ideal school, where he could use his musical talents to the full. Unlike his own two children, who were fair and looked like their mother, I bore an uncanny resemblance to Anthony. So much so that when we were out walking together a woman stopped us and said, 'Easy to see whose little girl this is!' Maybe it was for this reason there was an immediate bond between us. He was always indulgent towards me, whereas with his own two children, he was stern and strict.

Brenda's mother, Mrs Gimmy, came to stay while Brenda

was recovering from the birth of their third child. I know Mrs Gimmy was looked on as a kind grandmother, but with the sensitivity of a small child, I felt she resented me. She probably did, worried an extra child in the house was too much for her exhausted daughter. She may also have noticed Anthony's great affection for me, which didn't help. Mrs Gimmy wasn't exactly unkind, but perhaps more severe than she needed to have been. One day I was sitting in the garden and had picked a few blackcurrants which I was eating. Crossly she informed me I was stealing and as punishment I wasn't to have jam for a week. I was bewildered by this – after all, we ate blackberries from the hedgerows – and felt this was grossly unfair. Since then, I have always reacted badly if I think I have been misjudged or treated unfairly.

My time at Five Oaks seemed to pass unbearably slowly and I suffered constant bouts of homesickness. The days had a strict routine, broken by mealtimes, which I often found a struggle. The food in these post-war years appeared grey and unappetising, especially the whale meat. I was made to sit in front of my plate of food until I'd finished it. This could take a long time and would often leave me feeling sick. I still panic if I'm given a large helping, knowing it to be too much. Most days we were taken for walks up the wooded hills around Steep. There was an artistic community living in the area. Roger Powell, the bookbinder, and the furniture-maker Edward Barnsley both had their workshops nearby, and occasionally, to my great delight, we would visit them. When Anthony returned from school, there was always music in the house. I would lie listening to it at night when unable to sleep. Anthony ran a madrigal group and had a vast repertoire of songs. Sometimes I joined him in the singing, and he taught me many sea shanties. He also owned a large collection of classical records. At the weekends we would often listen to *Peter and the Wolf*, which I loved, although I always worried about the fate of the poor duck! The only composer I didn't enjoy was Benjamin Britten. For some odd reason, his music gave me instant feelings of nausea. Anthony was a great admirer of Britten, so his music was played a good deal. It was certainly a strange reaction to have, but looking back, I realise I was a child prey to many anxieties, fears, and extreme emotions. I also had what my mother referred to as a 'nervous stomach'. It took little to bring on feelings of nausea. The worst of these was when I was taken to the cinema. Films often made me physically sick, and we would have to leave, much to Gabriel's fury. I still haven't seen the last half of *Bambi*. As soon as Bambi was told, 'Bambi, your mother is no more,' I started vomiting. I was well into my teens before I recovered from this condition, and when films were shown at boarding school, I was always terrified I would throw up. (In later years, when I suffered from migraines, the doctor thought the flickering images in the films could have had something to do with this early reaction.) I also couldn't bear sadness and unhappy endings. The first time I was read 'The Lady of Shalott' I burst into tears. As for *Romeo and Juliet*, it was just too much to bear, even the watered-down version in *Lamb's Tales of Shakespeare*.

It was during my time at Five Oaks that I became an avid reader. Reading was my chief comfort in my loneliness. At some point my father sent me *The Margaret Tarrant Story Book*, which I read repeatedly. It came with the inscription:

> *A book for our Teresa Jane*
> *It is not likely she'll complain*
> *For now she's just begun to read*
> *A book is a great joy indeed.*

It is curious to remember what simple things gave me pleasure during my Five Oaks days. One incident that sticks in my mind is when I needed new shoes and was bought a pair of bright blue sandals. I could not get over the beauty of these shoes and lay in bed just staring at them for hours. I had very few possessions. Apart from my books, my bear, and one doll who I strangely named Myrtle, I had nothing. I can't help reflecting how different it is today, when I see my grandchildren over-loaded with toys and gadgets.

I was finally returned to Chatham, and it was then I decided I no longer liked the name of Teresa and from now on was to be called Jane. Thankfully, no fuss was made, and it was immediately accepted. My father may have liked the fact it was his mother's name. Anyway, I have been Jane since then, although Teresa has remained the name on all legal documents, including my passport, which has occasionally caused problems. The return to Chatham meant at last I was able to spend time with my mother, although she was still frail, and these moments were limited. She had very high standards of behaviour and always demanded the truth, sometimes putting me through endless questioning if she thought I had done something wrong. On one occasion, I was accused of having stolen some chocolate biscuits from the pantry. The inquisition went on and on, until I became so tired I admitted to it, even though I was innocent. I was immediately forgiven and praised for finally owning up, and then two days later the maid was caught stealing more chocolate biscuits and admitted the original deed. I think my mother had some remorse over this and after that, if I said I hadn't done something I was believed without further interrogation.

One of the great joys of being in my mother's company were her dramatic renderings of books and poems. She had after all trained at RADA. I can still hear her terrifying tones reading *Lorna Doone* at the moment when Carver Doone made his appearance. Her singing was also dramatic, especially in her rendering of 'The Raggle Taggle Gypsies O'.

She was a great romantic, and in her mind this song had a happy ending, with the heroine giving up her life of finery to run off and find freedom with the gypsies. I remember wondering privately if this lady had really made the right choice. I rather favoured the life of finery.

My education up to the age of eight was extremely erratic, mainly because of the difficult circumstances of our lives and being moved around to so many different places. This resulted in going to many schools and never staying in any of them for long. For two terms I went to a small private school in Chatham, with a smart uniform in silver grey and emerald green which I thought heaven, probably because for once it was new and not a cast-off from Gabriel. This school was called Throwley House and run by a rather eccentric couple who insisted on being called Sir and Madam. I would return home and announce firmly, 'Sir says this', or 'Madam says that', much to everyone's amusement. I wasn't unhappy at these many schools, but the constant changes meant I never had time to settle, make friends, or indeed learn anything. My happiest moments were reserved for when my mother and I were doing some activity together. She would often remark, 'Aren't we busy, Jane?' One day when asked what I was doing I replied, 'I'm being busy-Jane,' which was immediately adopted as a family saying.

My poor mother still had regular bouts of illness and during these times friends would rally round and take me in, but I never became used to being away in unfamiliar surroundings. These kind people did their best to make me happy. One of them took me to a performance of *Swan Lake*, but the entrance of the evil Von Rothbart so terrified me I had nightmares for days afterwards. One of the happier visits was to Oxford, where I stayed with two elderly sisters who lived in a splendid house in Holywell (later described in my novel *Parallel Lines*). The younger of the two sisters,

Toby, was a doctor. She was odd to look at, gnomish with a misshapen frame, but wonderfully kind, insisting on checking me over on each visit and always declaring me undernourished. I was clucked over and pampered by them both. The elder sister, Jan, had met my father while he was up at Oxford and had fallen under his spell, as so many did. She was a war widow and had no children and was only too happy to thoroughly spoil me. One of the great joys of staying in the Holywell house was the short walk to Blackwell's Children's Bookshop, where they provided small chairs, and I spent many happy mornings just sitting and reading. Apart from all the good food and supply of vitamins, I was also given a new wardrobe and for the first time in my life found the joy of having beautiful clothes. I'm afraid I was aware of being a pretty child, with a mass of chestnut curls and large brown eyes. My looks were often commented on, so it is unsurprising I became rather vain, but this was quickly stamped on once back with Gabriel.

Despite these occasional diversions, the Chatham years remained lonely. For most of the time I had no friends, until one day, while playing in the garden, a small boy popped his head over the wall. His name was John Gummer, and from then on, we spent all our spare time together. His father was also a clergyman, being the Rector of Old Brompton parish church, but I hardly saw him. Their rectory garden backed on to ours, and as we became acquainted, I was introduced to his two brothers, John being the eldest. His mother, who was sweet and gentle, always made a great fuss of me, telling me I was the daughter she'd always wanted. My recollection is I wasn't always very kind to John, who was a shy and sensitive boy. One time I even broke a gramophone record over his head, but somehow, he remained devoted to me. This friendship was brought to an abrupt end when my father was offered the living of St Mary's Warwick, and we departed the Medway towns for Warwickshire. John

Gummer later became a Conservative MP and was in the government of Margaret Thatcher and after her departure was John Major's Minister for Environment. He is now Baron Deben, and we meet occasionally, when he charmingly refers to me as his first girlfriend. His brother Peter also became a Lord, Baron Chadlington. Strange to think of those gangly boys elevated to the House of Lords.

The family now moved to the Old Deanery Warwick, a large, rambling, mainly Regency house, with a Tudor wing reputed to have been Henry VIII's stables. It had beautiful gardens with a fountain in the middle of the lawn and an adjacent tennis court, all far grander than Prospect Row.

The garden led directly into the churchyard and enabled my father to make a quick last-minute dash to the vestry. Around the churchyard was a paved path called the 'Tinkatank', supposedly because of the noise it made when you walked. The main joy for me was that this path led directly to the public library, where I spent most of my time.

My mother's health had improved, so it remains a puzzle to me why I should have been sent away again when the school in question, the Kingsley School Leamington Spa, was mainly a day school and only took in a few boarders. I have since concluded my father wished to write undisturbed and a small child around the house would have been a distraction. I was therefore despatched to Dilke House, the junior boarding house for children between the ages of eight and ten. Here I encountered the fierce housemistress, Miss Moss. She was an unhappy spinster, who almost never smiled, but there was one moment when she unbent, and it happened on a night when I couldn't sleep. I crept out onto the landing and sat cross-legged on the cold linoleum floor, listening to the music coming from her room. Miss Moss suddenly came out and found me. I must have looked frightened, but unexpectedly, she picked me up and took me to her room, where I sat on her lap until the music ended.

She told me it was composed by a man called Sir Edward Elgar, and I told her I found it beautiful. Her gesture that night was a small act of kindness, but in some way, it was as if she recognised in me a loneliness that matched her own.

The Kingsley School was a private school, with pupils drawn mainly from wealthy, middle-class homes. The parents were generally Conservatives, and their daughters talked endlessly of their ponies, their new cars and their houses fitted with every possible gadget including a TV (a rare luxury then) and of course, their glamorous holidays abroad. It was all totally alien to me. I came from a bohemian, disorganised household, with eccentric, intellectual parents who were staunch socialists and who at that time owned neither a television nor a car. I couldn't discuss or talk about my home life, so as a defence mechanism I began to invent a different background for myself. This soon became a habit, as I found it far easier to live in my imaginary world than to talk about something I instinctively knew they wouldn't understand. This world of make-believe became so real it led to one occasion when my fantasy life was horribly exposed. I had lent our music teacher a much-loved children's book about the life of Mozart. The book included some short piano pieces and in my enthusiasm for the book, I foolishly boasted I could play all these pieces, which in my mind of course I could. When she had finished reading the book, the teacher, another mealy-mouthed spinster, who must have known my boast was untrue but seemed determined to publicly shame me, called me up, sat me on the piano stool and told me to perform one of the pieces. I sat with head hung and hands by my side for what seemed like an eternity, until the school bell rang. The class filed out and the teacher handed me the book, telling me coldly that in future I shouldn't tell lies. Too late. I was branded a liar, a name that stuck until I left the school a year later.

There was one positive note in all this gloom. Apart from

that music teacher, I had quickly learned I could charm adults and soon became a favourite with many of the other members of staff. This continued into my next, more permanent school, but it was never something which endeared me to my fellow pupils.

It was in the holidays, during the Warwick years, I began to know better, not only my brother and sister, but also my father. This new life was very different from the Chatham days, when Gabriel and Christopher had hardly been home, and I had rarely seen my parents. In Warwick, I experienced what could loosely be termed as 'family life', even if it was a rather eccentric variety and not altogether a happy one.

Chapter Two
FAMILY LIFE

THERE IS SOMETHING about 'family life' which I find endlessly fascinating. Why on earth should a combination of different characters, of varying ages, be expected to live in a constant state of happiness? It seems ridiculously optimistic, and in general it just doesn't happen. Underneath the seemingly contented outward appearance run layers of discontent and resentment. Moments of calm are often shattered by an unexpected row or revelation, which can destroy a family's united front. It's all the sadder because family life usually starts so promisingly, with young children bringing pride and joy to their parents. But children grow up and develop characters of their own, and parental relationships fail. Consequently, the thin fabric of a happy family life can quickly disintegrate. It is a topic which has provided writers with endless fodder, even me, and I didn't have to look far for inspiration or material. Few families live in blissful harmony. Some do manage it, but they are rare. Most have the obligatory 'skeletons' in the cupboard and few can escape the endless character clashes which prove so destructive. It's even worse for the rich and famous, who have their family failures made public, with all the gossip and speculation that involves.

Given the personalities that made up my own family, it is hardly surprising our family life should have been difficult, verging on the dysfunctional. Our childhoods were dominated by my father, Joseph McCulloch, a complex and difficult character, who really needs a whole book to himself to do him justice. He was born in 1908, in Liverpool, to a working-class family. His father, William, was a ship's carpenter who had left Aberdeen to come south in search of work. He married Jane Davis, a Welsh girl who had worked in the music halls. They had five sons, my father being the youngest and something of an afterthought. He was not in the best of health for the first years of his life but was exceptionally bright, doted on by his mother and extremely spoiled. After attending Liverpool Cathedral Choir School, he won a scholarship to Liverpool College and from there went up to Oxford as a scholar of Exeter College. It was at this point his life completely changed. He cut himself off

My father, Joseph McCulloch

from his family and his Liverpool roots, to completely re-invent himself. In this metamorphosis, there were several assets he used to his advantage. Already languid, witty, charming, with striking looks (many commented on his likeness to the actor Leslie Howard), he now cultivated a beautiful speaking voice, which was decidedly upper class. Oxford suited him. It was the Oxford of the 'twenties, as described in Evelyn Waugh's *Brideshead Revisited*. My father made his immediate mark and could easily have become a successful actor, or entered politics, or the legal profession, but it was a chance meeting with the great William Temple, the then Archbishop of Canterbury, which persuaded him to enter the Church and take Holy Orders.

Sadly, Archbishop Temple died before he could greatly help my father's career. His candid criticisms and reforming zeal were alarming to many, and he was regarded with suspicion by future archbishops and the Church establishment. Consequently, his preferment was slow and disappointing, and certainly did not match his talents. It was hardly surprising. He was outspoken in his views, and his radical ideas for reform were made clear in both his books and frequent broadcasts. 'Who will rid me of this turbulent priest?' must have frequently crossed the minds of his superiors. Looking back, it is easy to see he was ahead of his time, supporting women priests, re-marriage for divorced people, and disestablishment of the Church of England. He also made it abundantly clear how much he despised the watering down of the language of the Bible and Book of Common Prayer, with their ghastly modern versions. Quite early on he was interviewed to become Head of Religious Broadcasting at the BBC, but when he informed them he would be supporting all faiths, including Muslim, Jewish and Buddhist beliefs, the management had panicked, and the offer was withdrawn. This left him with a bitterness and anger from which he never recovered.

Even his early career in the Church had a rocky start. To clear his Oxford debts, he'd written a blockbuster novel, which he described as his 'bosoms and bathrooms' fiction. This racy book was a great success and certainly cleared all the money he owed, but it quickly landed him in further trouble. Although he'd written it under another name, many of the characters were cruelly based on people in his first parish, where he was a curate. Inevitably, some of them were recognised, and it produced an immediate outcry and demand for him to be defrocked. His bishop at the time, recognising his potential, decided to give him a second chance and had him transferred to Blackheath, London, putting him under the charge of the one man the bishop felt could deal with him, my grandfather, Canon F H Gillingham, known by all as Gilly.

Wedding of my Gillingham grandparents, 1910

Gilly was a larger-than-life personality. He'd been a cricketing hero in the years before WW1, a brilliant batsman playing for Essex, and, when his clerical duties allowed, for

England. In those days cricket was revered in the way football is now. Gilly was a star of the game. I have inherited a book full of press cuttings with headlines like 'A double century for Gillingham' and 'Gillingham takes five catches and makes a century'. He later became the first radio cricket commentator. Early on, Gilly had been appointed a Royal Chaplain, later to become Senior Royal Chaplain, which often meant trips to Sandringham to see King George V, giving him even more kudos. Being landed with a troublesome curate can't have been ideal. Worse was to follow. When my father walked into the room to be introduced to Gilly's very beautiful daughter Betty, there was what my father described as a *coup de foudre*. They fell instantly and passionately in love and, despite my grandparents' misgivings, were married in 1934 with a large society wedding. Interesting to note, not a single member of my father's family was present, his side of the Church being filled with his Oxford friends and influential people he'd met.

Nothing had prepared my father for having a family, and his knowledge of babies and small children was nil. Before we arrived in Warwick, he'd been a distant figure, mainly because we were away so much while my mother was ill. This all changed in Warwick when he became a visible presence in our lives. At this time, I was eight, Gabriel twelve and Christopher fourteen. We called him Joseph, another oddity my contemporaries found difficult to understand, but as Gabriel pointed out, he was never a 'Daddy', 'Dad' and definitely not a 'Papa'. His attitude towards his children was complicated and affected each of us in different ways. Until I was eighteen, I escaped the worst of his erratic behaviour, except to observe it. Christopher and Gabriel were damaged more directly. Quite simply we had to accept my father had two personalities, a sort of Jekyll and Hyde. On the one side he was the witty, charming, and amusing man his public adored. On the other, he was a cruel, selfish, self-centred man who could crush you with his withering remarks and cut you off completely if he didn't approve of something you had said or done. As he often remarked, 'If I'm not number one in your life, I'm not interested in you.' I suppose today he would have been put in category, or given a label – a narcissist, with a personality disorder, or some such thing. Back then we just accepted his moods and cruel behaviour, without expecting any explanation for it.

Joseph's relationship with my mother was also complicated. I think he loved her deeply and admired her, for she had both beauty and brains. It was noticeable in public he was positively uxorious, but in private his treatment of her was often cruel and uncaring, and she suffered because of this. He must have known his behaviour fell below her own high standards. My mother was something of a Puritan and had a saint-like quality. It can't have been easy, living with

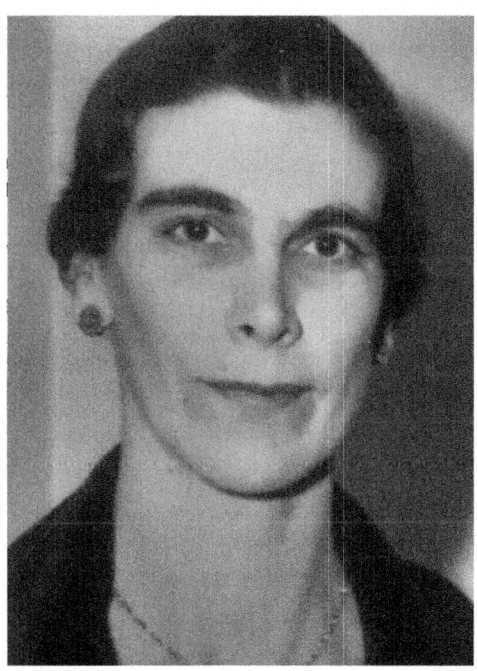

My mother, Betty Gillingham/McCulloch

a saint, especially with Joseph's many faults and weaknesses. From the Warwick years on, the situation was further aggravated by Joseph having a mistress, Sonya. Sonya had followed him from Chatham, where she was among a group of young followers from his congregation, most of them women, who quite simply adored him. Sonya became obsessed with Joseph. He was a Svengali to her, and she soon became a permanent fixture in our lives. I was very naïve and for many years accepted her constant presence just as a family friend. It was Gabriel who enlightened and informed me otherwise.

In many ways, I suppose it was inevitable that the Sonya situation should have happened. Joseph was an attractive man and always surrounded by adoring women. After my birth, to avoid another pregnancy, sexual abstinence had been demanded. Despite this, my mother would never have strayed. My father did, and Sonya was the inevitable result. In appearance she was the complete opposite to my mother, who was a classic beauty. Sonya was certainly pretty, petite, with a childlike quality, always neatly dressed and with perfect hair and manicured nails. She was also gifted, highly artistic and becoming proficient in design and calligraphy. I think what attracted her most to my father was that she never challenged him intellectually, nor was she ever critical of him. She was often frivolous and silly, making him laugh. He would relax in her company in a way he never could with my mother. It was an odd *ménage à trois*, but my mother accepted it, however much it hurt, so we children did the same.

My mother we called Ma, again thanks to Gabriel. I had referred to her as Mummy when I was little, but was told firmly by G this was babyish, so my letters from boarding school were always addressed to Ma. She was the only daughter of Gilly and Molly. Gilly had married Molly Matthews when both were on the rebound from failed love affairs, so it was not surprising their marriage was destined to be an unhappy one. Molly was an exceptional beauty, one of three Matthews sisters, all lovely and all married well, but Molly was temperamental, mercurial, subject to moods and migraines. She was totally unsuited to be the wife of a clergyman, however famous, and she quickly became bored. Their sex life must also have left her deeply dissatisfied, because as soon as she became pregnant Gilly left the marriage bed, his duty done. After the youngest of the three children was born, they were confined to separate beds, which must have put a strain on the passionate Molly. To compensate, she surrounded herself with adoring young men, who, according to my mother, were expected to write sonnets dedicated to her beauty. She had a beautiful singing voice and had taken lessons from Gustav Holst. I am told when she auditioned for him, she chose a song which ended with a top A. 'Very nice dear, but vulgar,' was Holst's comment, adding, 'The song is always more important than the singer.' She remained a troubled woman, not only a hopeless wife but also a hopeless mother and their family life was punctuated with her hysterical tantrums.

The boys were educated well but my mother's education, although she was the cleverest and most academic of the three siblings, was shamefully neglected. She was sent to a few select girl's schools, where the concentration was on flower arranging and deportment, rather than academic work. To my grandmother's horror, her daughter was a blue-stocking, devouring the English poets, including the Metaphysicals and the Romantics. Her reading was extensive, but despite her obviously brilliant mind, at seventeen she was packed off to France to a finishing school. A mild compensation was she became a talented linguist, not only in French and Italian, but the Slav languages as well, after staying with a Czechoslovakian family for several months. Back in England it was made clear university was not an option, so instead she went to RADA. Among her contemporaries were Stephen Haggard, Michael Redgrave, Rachel Kempson (who went on to marry Redgrave), Anthony Quayle, and her greatest friend of all, Valerie Hobson (who played Estella so brilliantly in *Great Expectations* among her many other film roles). My mother won a gold medal and had the makings of a successful classical actress. On leaving RADA her first job was to understudy Gwen Frangcon-Davies in *Richard of Bordeaux* at the Old Vic, with John Gielgud playing Richard. But her acting career ended abruptly when she married my father, and like her mother before her, she was destined to live the life of a clergyman's wife. However, unlike her mother, she didn't become bored and frustrated, but used her endless talents wherever she could. She acted in and directed my father's religious plays, which were performed with regularity in the church. She wrote a modern version, from Medieval English, of the Chester Miracle Plays and despite her struggle with ill-health, she was a constant support to Joseph, correcting his work and proving an expert proof-reader. In the Warwick years, by sheer personality she became a Labour Councillor, an astonishing feat in a solid Conservative town, and later a JP, which she greatly enjoyed. She painted beautiful watercolours and taught herself the piano, as far as her arthritic hands would let her. I have a memory of her playing the slow movement of the *Moonlight Sonata*.

She was tenacious to a degree. It wasn't in her nature ever to give up. One of her more unnerving achievements was learning to drive at the age of forty. A grateful parishioner had presented us with a car, and so she set about it. She was an erratic driver, to say the least, and on the hills in Cornwall would often run out of gears. However, over the years her confidence grew, and she became positively intrepid and took on long journeys both here and in Europe. Her classic beauty and tall figure – she was five foot ten – made her rather intimidating. In many ways, like my father, I found her high standards rather difficult to live up to.

Despite her sophisticated and elegant appearance, she remained something of an innocent. When I was at drama school, I had to explain what being gay meant. Apparently, my grandmother had always referred to a gay man as '*uno de quello*' ('one of them'), and any mention of Oscar Wilde had been forbidden during my mother's childhood, so her ignorance on these matters was hardly surprising. Ma loved to laugh, but always at other people's wit, especially my father's. On the rare occasion she told a joke she would quickly admit she could only remember the punchline, leaving her helpless with laughter, but her audience bewildered. She had a dramatic way of speaking but with certain oddities. She would say 'hark' instead of 'listen' and 'motor' instead of 'car'. Despite her frequent absences due to ill-health, I think she tried to be a good mother, and in many ways she was. She adored Christopher and did her best to shield him from the worst of Joseph's treatment. My father expected his children to reflect well on him; sadly, the withdrawn and sensitive Christopher failed miserably in this respect. Christopher was a brilliant, if eccentric, academic scholar, quietly immersed in his books, unable to match Joseph's flamboyant wit. But my mother understood him. In Gabriel she also found an academic equal. Their minds were similar, and they would converse for hours, mainly about poetry, but sharing a mutual knowledge of other topics, especially wildflowers and writers. Joseph also admired Gabriel's academic abilities, and for some time he became almost obsessed with her, demanding her entire attention. Sadly, he never understood her fierce and independent nature and never became the number one in her life, as he would have liked, but for a few years they managed to get on. To my annoyance they would converse in Latin, and I immediately felt an outsider again.

For most of my teenage years I had a rather surface relationship with Joseph. He liked my appearance and the way I charmed his friends. But for the most part he ignored me, and this hurt. I was left admiring and hating him in equal measure. Being the youngest, and least academic of the three, I had a slightly different relationship with my mother. I realise she may have found me rather frivolous and irritated by my obsession with wanting to be like other people. I was often ill, mainly with tonsillitis, and I never understood why they weren't taken out at this time. My frequent illnesses were maybe the reason Ma became over-protective, an over-protectiveness which continued until I left home, much to my frustration and annoyance. One thing that stands out in my memory is how endlessly brave and stoical she was, even though suffering terrible pain from rheumatic diseases most of her adult life. I remember the shock of watching her roll out her gnarled and curled fingers with a pencil to straighten them. She never complained and expected us not to complain either, about anything. If we told her the milk was sour when it was nearly solid, she would tell us sharply, 'Nonsense, it's fine.' Similarly, the bread could be covered in grey mould, but we were told to scrape it off and stop moaning. Her constant refrain was: 'Think of the starving poor in India.'

Ma hated spending money on anything she thought was unnecessary, and her economies were legion. One of her more bizarre actions was to save the tissue paper wrapped around oranges and have it put in the loo to save on loo paper. At one point my father exploded about this, furiously telling her that although we were still only in February, the calendar by the loo was now down to September!

Joseph was also strict on savings. We were reprimanded severely if we left lights on. The Old Deanery was an ancient and draughty house, with no central heating, and in the winter we simply froze. 'Put on more clothes' was Ma's constant refrain. Joseph's study was the only room that was permanently warm, where he not only had an open fire, but also an oil stove, and both were on all day. My bedroom, in the Tudor wing, was the coldest part of the house, where the icy winds whistled through the old beams. After my third bout of tonsillitis, the doctor insisted I had some heat in the room, so I was reluctantly given a small electric fire with strict instructions never to use more than one bar. As I lay in yet another cold bed, in yet another freezing room, I made a silent vow that when I was an adult, I would make sure I was never cold again.

I never quite understood these extreme economies. Although not rich, we certainly weren't poor. As well as his stipend from the Church, my father earned a good deal from his broadcasting, books and lectures. He did not have to pay for the Deanery, which went with the living. I know my mother had private money. Her family were like the Forsytes in *The Forsyte Saga*, solid, upper middle class, with a certain amount of wealth. This might explain her sudden extravagances. Her smarter clothes were expensive, being purchased from Woollands in Knightsbridge, or Harvey Nichols. On our holiday trips she would pay for everything. She was also generous with theatre tickets, and our many visits to the Stratford Memorial Theatre were the highlight of the holidays. In contrast she baulked at paying for quite ordinary things which she easily could have afforded. I never had the right school uniform, and school lists were ignored. I was made to wait two years for a bicycle, which made my school life difficult as I had to walk the distance from my house to the main school instead of making the short bike ride. I never understood her reason for this.

My brother and sister were very different in character. Christopher was a beautiful boy, with a young Rupert Brooke appearance. He was gentle, a dreamer, introverted and, looking back on it, almost certainly autistic, probably with Asperger's. His brainpower was astonishing. At the age of ten he could cope with an Oxford Maths paper. But his abilities were one-sided and didn't fit into any normal school curriculum. Consequently, his school reports were dismal with his masters expressing their frustration. His interest lay in making up codes or solving them. In the holidays he spent hours in his room filling up notebooks with weird signs and figures. He loved his music and from an early age had rather esoteric tastes, especially enjoying the early music of Purcell or Dowland, and having a great knowledge of more obscure Baroque music. My experience of listening to classical music came entirely from Christopher and he took great care to introduce me to his latest discoveries.

About the time he was eight he had developed a bad stammer, and my mother diligently took him to several specialists, one of whom suggested his brain was working too fast for his speech and to calm things down he should build card houses. For a time, he did, but he would reach a certain point, and then Gabriel would knock them down. I never once saw Christopher lose his temper. He would just quietly take himself off to his room to avoid confrontation. His stammer later improved but even when an adult there was always a trace of it, especially when he was trying to make a point. As for his relationship with my father, it was a disaster. I would dread the moment his school report arrived, and he would be summoned to my father's study. After an hour or two he would emerge, pale and shaking, and shut himself away in his room.

Apparently, on one occasion Joseph said witheringly, 'You should be rubbed out and done again.'

For once Christopher stood up to him and said, 'And you should be rrr-rubbed out and nnn-not done again.'

My mother did her best to protect him from the worst of Joseph's vituperative comments, but there was little she could do and she was constantly torn between her passionate love for Joseph and her protective love for her children. Joseph always became hostile if she showed the latter. The fact is, with Christopher, Joseph just did not understand him. He recognised he was brilliant, but it was not a brilliance he understood. Instead, he took out his disappointment in the worst possible way by bullying him. Had Christopher's Asperger's been diagnosed, things might have been different, but sadly it wasn't. Apart from his music, Christopher found consolation in walking. He had been given a small corgi, Rusty, by one of his godparents, and he would set off with Rusty and walk for miles, losing all track of time. The result was he often arrived late for meals, another source of annoyance for Joseph. Christopher kept his distance from Gabriel as far as possible. She became impatient with his stammer and apparent slowness, and he avoided her biting tongue and barbed comments, although they did share a love of music, particularly Bach.

Gabriel, from the moment she was born, was a determined, strong-willed and formidable character. This inner strength was just as well, because at the age of eight months she became gravely ill with double Mastoiditis. For weeks my parents feared she wouldn't survive. This was 1937, before penicillin, and no other drugs were as effective. Against the odds Gabriel did make it through, but it left her totally deaf in one ear. Nobody realised how much this affected her, until she was an adult, when she admitted she'd missed a great deal through lack of hearing. This could have contributed to her somewhat prickly character. Despite her deafness, she was brilliant academically, but unlike Christopher she coped easily with the school curriculum and excelled in all her work, gaining glowing reports. Socially, maybe again due to the deafness, she was difficult, impatient, and scornful of anyone she felt was being slow or stupid, which was often me. Her relationship with Joseph only developed after we arrived in Warwick, when he began to take a real interest in her, finding she shared his love of the classics, both Latin and Greek. Sadly, as Gabriel became more independent, this relationship didn't last and later broke down entirely.

I was at the bottom of the pack academically. We were generally known as 'clever children', and I suffered from this, never feeling I could adequately keep up, although I found early on I could act intelligent, fooling many, and would often come out with precocious remarks. I was bright but scatter-brained, and I lacked the ability to retain facts. Also, unlike the other two, I'd had no early education, so I didn't take part in the many lively conversations, feeling I had nothing to contribute. One holiday there was a great deal of discussion about various psychoanalysts, and the names of Jung, Freud and Adler dominated the conversation. At some point I suddenly burst out with, 'I'm a jung, freud, adled egg!' There was a moment's silence and then everyone laughed. At last, I had found my place in the family, which was to amuse and make them laugh. In this way I often managed to break the constant tension. Gabriel and Christopher could not compete with me in this, and never tried. Unlike either of them I was always socially at ease, happy in the company of my parents' friends. This especially pleased Joseph. Other than that, I was on my own, in my private world of imagination and books. During the school holidays I spent most of my time in Warwick Library. I soon exhausted the children's books and was allowed to move on to the adult section, where I found the Mills & Boon and other romantic novels greatly to my liking. The librarian remarked to my father she was concerned about the books I was now reading, feeling they were not appropriate for a child of nine. Joseph was unworried by this news, telling her if I read a lot of dross now it would stand me in good stead for sorting out the wheat from the chaff in the future.

Unaware of this conversation until it was reported to me later, I lived in a world of romance, with dreams of passionate love and a handsome hero filling my every waking hour and some of my sleeping ones as well. I became increasingly convinced something wonderful would eventually happen to me and my life would take a happier turn. Meanwhile, I had a few tough years ahead of me.

Chapter Three

TOWARDS ADULTHOOD

THE WARWICK YEARS lasted from when I was eight until I was eighteen, and in contrast to what was to come, these were moderately uneventful times. However, this decade greatly shaped my character and is therefore of importance to my story.

Most of the year was spent away at boarding school. In the shorter Christmas and Easter Holidays we generally stayed at the Old Deanery, but in the summer, Joseph tended to take a locum, when he swapped places with another member of the clergy. The result was we found ourselves in some interesting locations. I must have been about ten when we set off for Iona. Joseph wasn't with us in the car but came on later. Ma had not been driving long and the journey was something of an ordeal. There were very few dual carriageways, and we were often stuck behind lorries for hours, unable to overtake. During the tedious parts of the journey, we would pass the time by singing, and to add to our extensive repertoire of folk songs we now added my mother's curious collection, drawn from the music hall and early musicals. Two of these we sang raucously, one of them being 'Molly the Marchioness':

> *Molly married the Marquis*
> *What a thing to do!*
> *She hurried him up to London Town*

And hurried the service through.
The Star, *the* Sun *and the* Echo, *and all the evening press*
Came out with the heading,
'The Wonderful Wedding
Of Molly the Marchioness!'

The other I most remember had to be sung very quickly:

I think it's going to be a very, very lovely day
Very, very fine for May,
80 in the shade they say,
Just fancy!
I think it's going to be a very, very lovely day
Oh what very lovely weather!

There were a lot more verses, and it certainly helped to pass the time. To Gabriel's annoyance I had to sit in the front because I was prone to car sickness. When the Scottish roads became ever more winding, several stops were required, irritating her even further. At one point my mother went into a pub and came out with a glass of 'horse's neck', a brandy and ginger ale, which she poured down me. Whether it was the brandy or the ginger I don't know, but I certainly felt better after drinking it.

There was a strange moment when we had just driven past Glencoe. My mother, needing a break, parked at the side of the road. There were some castle ruins and as we walked up towards them, we saw a sign creaking in the wind which read 'This is the Ancestral Home of the Wild and Warlike McCullochs'. The fact our ancestral home was a complete ruin felt significant somehow. The car journey ended at Oban and the rest of the journey was made by boat, a trip via Tobermory and Fingal's Cave. We were staying in Lord Macleod's large house just above the

Abbey. George Macleod was the head of the Macleod clan, and another friend of Joseph's. He'd been the founder of the Iona Community and organised the restoration of the Abbey. I found Iona a truly magical place. There were a few houses grouped round the harbour, but no cars or transport of any kind, and the island so small you could walk round it in a day. Each night it became a ritual for us to climb to the highest point and watch the sun go down, giving a rosy hue to the white sands below. Joseph only came for a short time and while with us he seemed unsettled, surly and uncommunicative, probably missing Sonya. He upset Ma by being very rude to some friends of hers who had visited us. For once his behaviour didn't worry us, as we spent our days away from the house exploring. Once his duties in the Abbey were done, Joseph quickly departed, a great relief.

Christmas and Easter were spent in the Deanery, because Church duties meant Joseph couldn't leave. It was at this time I started loathing Church services and would try to make up excuses not to go. I disliked being the vicar's daughter and being marched up to the front pew with the congregation staring at me, only to make comments later like, 'Jane's growing up fast', 'Jane's looking quite the little lady today' and so on. I found the tedium of the services unbearable. I never understood a word of Joseph's sermons and judging by the bewildered faces of his congregation, few did. He found greater success in London where he was preaching to a more sophisticated audience. The Bible readings I found obscure, and they had little relevance to me, and although I liked the hymns, the rest of the various rituals seemed a waste of time and some of them made me feel uneasy. I think the children of clergymen are often regarded as a little odd. It's interesting to note that so many of them become writers or find a career like acting where they can escape.

I always felt we were outsiders and aware other people thought we were different too.

Because of my father, we would be invited by various Warwick families to join their children for tennis parties and dances. Gabriel and Christopher, being a good deal older, now led independent lives and managed to escape these ordeals, but Joseph insisted on my going. I would know nobody and sit on the sidelines, just longing to go home. I didn't belong to their set. However, one boy did take an interest in me and would sometimes invite me to his house for tennis. It was all rather grand. His father was high up in the military and consequently his son's great aim was to go to Sandhurst. His name was Guy Blenkinsop and Gabriel referred to him as the 'blinking sap' and mocked me heavily when I was summoned to put on my tennis whites. Guy apart, I was aware boys at the dances had to be persuaded by their parents to ask me to dance. I was a stranger and usually would be left like the proverbial wallflower watching proceedings. I had no small-talk, and found it an ordeal, uncomfortable for them, embarrassing for me. In my mid-teens, boys of my own age held absolutely no interest for me; I found them callow and boring and longed for more adult company.

In the holidays I was happiest when left to my own devices. When I wasn't in the library, I would spend hours in the large dining room, only used for special occasions, where the collections of *Punch* were kept. These volumes, dating from 1896 to 1934 – two large volumes a year – filled an entire bookcase. I would peruse them for hours and they provided endless amusement and delight. I also spent time in the snug, the most comfortable room in the house, which had a coal fire occasionally lit on very cold days. Mostly I was on my own, but sometimes the other two would join me for a game of Monopoly, Scrabble or Mah-jong, the last being my favourite, the other two games often ending in arguments with someone storming off.

The main asset of this room was the wind-up gramophone with a very esoteric collection of records, probably Joseph's from his Oxford days. These included César Franck's *Variations Symphoniques*, Bach's 'Air on a G String', Holst's 'Jupiter' from the *Planet's Suite*, Vaughan William's *Variations on a Theme of Thomas Tallis*, Stravinsky's *Rite of Spring*, Elgar's 'Nimrod' from the *Enigma Variations,* and my personal favourite, Kathleen Ferrier singing 'What is Life to Me without You?' from Gluck's *Orpheus and Eurydice*. The only record I personally owned was Danny Kaye's 'Tubby the Tuba', given to me on my eighth birthday. Gabriel and I knew this by heart, and it became our party piece.

These holidays were a mixture of great contrasts, highs, and lows, entirely depending on Joseph's moods. He was at his best when we had visitors, and among the most frequent of these were Valerie Hobson, whom I adored, and Nancy Spain, who apparently adored me. Nancy Spain was a renowned journalist and broadcaster and lived with her partner, Joan Werner Laurie, a publisher and founder of *She* magazine. I had no idea they were lesbians, having no idea what lesbians were until being informed by Gabriel some years later. I found Joan and Nancy fascinating, especially as they knew most of the famous people of the time and provided sparkling company for Joseph. He revelled in being the centre of attention once again. Even when the visitors were gone, the glow would hang over the house for a few days and Joseph would continue at his most charming, even joining in with word games, which he always won, and sometimes playing the odd game of tennis. Then, without warning, his mood would change. Something, maybe a chance remark, would upset him and after an initial rage, he would shut himself away in his study, all his meals being taken in on trays. Ma tried to reason with him, and I would sit on the stairs listening to her endless pleas. The stress and tension were felt by everyone, and it was particularly upsetting watching the effect it had on Ma and worrying about her health. On one occasion I went in and sobbed for him to return to us, but I was just told to go away, and I never tried again. These black moods happened regularly every holiday and I would dread the moment when for a week our lives would become so hellish. Once returned to us he behaved as if nothing had happened, but we were all left shaken, treading on eggshells in case we set him off again.

Mealtimes were also a challenge. For breakfast there was only Gabriel and Christopher, and they would play various games, most of them too difficult for me. One of these was when they took it in turns to sing a few bars of classical music and we were expected to know which work it was from. Bach's Brandenburgs presented a problem because the six concertos were so similar, but I became quite good at the Beethoven symphonies and concertos. Joseph would join us for lunch armed with *The Times* crossword, from which he would read out clues. I hated this and was never quick with the answers. The odd quotation I could sometimes manage, especially if it was Shakespeare, but otherwise I sat through the meal in silence.

On one memorable occasion there was an argument over one of the answers and Christopher was despatched to the study for a dictionary. He came rushing back and stammered out, 'The room is on fire!'

Everyone sprang into action and the fire brigade was called. Gabriel and Ma put out the worst of the fire with buckets of water and then Joseph tried to stop the fireman from hosing down the room, which would have ruined his books and manuscripts. A great row ensued, but Ma finally managed to reach an agreement with them. The fire, thanks to Christopher, had been caught early and not much damage was done. While all this uproar was going on, I went into the road and gave a dramatic running commentary to the small crowd who had gathered outside. The final verdict was a smouldering cigarette butt must have dropped into Joseph's armchair and after that he was supplied with even more ashtrays. Suppers were my least favourite meal. Lively conversation at the start would often turn into violent argument, generally between Joseph and Gabriel or Christopher, with Ma trying to mediate. When the shouting started, I would ask to leave the table.

The Easter of 1952 was a particularly memorable one. Once again, the house was filled with people and I was sent to share a room with Gabriel, mine being used as an extra spare room. The sparkling conversation was all rather beyond me and my mother, realising this, asked Mary, now a midwife in Warwick, to take me out for the afternoon. I don't remember much of this expedition except it was to a country house with a large topiary. It was while we walked round the gardens, I began to feel very ill and was violently sick behind one of the elegant topiaries. Mary decided it would be best to take me straight home. Ma, busy with the house party, had little time for sympathy and told me to lie down until I felt better. This I did and was then forgotten about. It must have been some hours later Gabriel was despatched to see how I was. By this time, I had a high fever and was apparently delirious. Even Gabriel became alarmed and reported back. The doctor was quickly summoned, and I remember him pulling pins across my stomach. The verdict was acute appendicitis, and I was to be rushed to hospital. When told I needed an operation I became greatly alarmed and sobbed hysterically. My parents decided they couldn't leave their guests, so Christopher was despatched to go with me in the ambulance. His stuttering sympathy somehow calmed me, and he held my hand all the way to the operating theatre.

A week later I was sent home and a week after that I was due to start my new school, St Swithun's Winchester. Gabriel had been at this school for two years and made no bones about loathing it. She had been happy at her previous school, Cranbourne Chase, and a major row had ensued when told she had to leave. But her protestations did little good and St Swithun's became her final school, and I now joined her. (There was a financial reason for this choice. We were both on bursaries; there was a reduction for the daughters of clergymen and a reduction for sisters, so the fees were heavily reduced. This didn't stop my father moaning when the bill came in each holiday.) My departure for the new school was another typical example of my bizarre childhood neglect.

Joseph and Ma were due to go on holiday a few days before term was to begin, and nothing had been organised for me. In any case Ma never took the slightest notice of uniform demands, or school lists, which were the normal procedure for all public schools. She couldn't see the importance of them and regarded them as a waste of money. The matron looked horrified as she unpacked my trunk – not even a trunk but my father's old army kitbag – and muttered she would have to find everything for me in the second-hand school shop. I felt humiliated and ashamed. To make matters worse, I didn't have a silk eiderdown like other girls, but instead had my father's old grey army blanket. Gabriel scorned my worries and positively revelled in being eccentric and different. Instead of a dressing gown she proudly wore one of Joseph's old black cassocks, but unlike her I hated being regarded as an oddity.

The main school was a bleak building, high on the downs above Winchester. Some of the houses were at least a mile from the school, and I was in one of these. We would make the journey four times a day and I found this tiring until a few years later, when Ma finally agreed to let me have a bicycle. The school doctor, when first examining me, found me under-nourished and prescribed extract of malt to be taken daily. He then looked at my lurid appendix scar with horror. Why had no letter been sent telling them of the operation? I explained my mother was in Austria on holiday. On then being told I'd only had the operation two weeks previously, there was much tutting, and I was forbidden all games and gymnastics for four weeks, leaving me feeling an outsider yet again.

From the outset, my life at St Swithun's was not a happy one, at least until I reached the sixth form. Unlike Gabriel, the academic work didn't come to me as easily, partly due to my lack of education thus far. It was automatically assumed I would do as well as my brilliant sister. I didn't and was in an almost permanent state of panic. Where I was happiest was in the music and singing classes and I also took part in any plays that were being put on. I quickly gained a reputation for having a good voice for verse speaking and would be asked to take part in the morning lesson or poetry recitals. For these I often suffered from stage fright and would develop a lump in my throat which sometimes made it difficult for me to get the words out. This induced panic and I dreaded being asked to do these solo readings. Far happier were the few occasions I was allowed to direct plays. One year, I created quite a stir, putting on a pantomime, *Cinderella*, for the domestic staff and their families. I wrote and directed, also playing Buttons. At one point I had the two sides of the hall competing to see who could sing 'How much is that doggie in the window?' the loudest. The annual domestic staff party was usually a very dull affair, so this one was considered a great success.

However, this success was frowned on by some of the elderly spinster teachers, who considered it far too raucous and vulgar and sadly, there was to be no repeat. I would have thrived so much better at Bedales, or any school where the arts were encouraged. St Swithun's at that time was very conservative and set in its ways, having not recovered from the war years. Its focus was on religion and sport, consequently the academic standards weren't high either. Gabriel was one of very few who made it to university. Most leaving girls went to domestic science colleges or took secretarial courses and were then expected to make good marriages and become respectable pillars of the local community. (I hasten to add St Swithun's is very different now and is regularly in the top ten of girls' public schools for their academic achievements.)

For the first few years I was terribly bullied and left miserable, often sobbing long into the night. Gabriel was no help. She already disliked this school, and my arrival was one more aggravation for her, so she ignored my existence. I longed for her to behave as other sisters did, supportive and affectionate with their siblings. But this just wasn't in her nature. This did change once she left and went up to Cambridge. She became much kinder, even supportive, and wrote the most wonderful and amusing letters, but at the school she wanted nothing to do with me. I never understood why I was quite so bullied, except I was a bit quaint, childish for my age and obviously vulnerable. Maybe for the same reason I was a favourite with the older girls and many of the teachers, which probably antagonised my peer group even further. The situation changed once I reached the sixth form when I had more freedom. For the last two years life became almost enjoyable. I was made a prefect and gained kudos through my drama and music exploits and to my surprise suddenly found myself popular.

Another of my mother's bizarre economies was that she refused to have us home for half term, because she thought the train fares a ridiculous extravagance for so short a time. Instead, Gabriel and I sometimes went to stay at Five Oaks, only a short bus ride away. At other times I stayed on alone in the house, except for the housemistress, who had no great liking for me. Another instance of my mother's rather heartless behaviour was when my nose was badly broken by a lacrosse ball, and I was whisked off to Winchester Hospital for an immediate operation. She never visited me. I couldn't help thinking most parents would have rushed to the hospital bedside. I don't think she meant to be uncaring, but just presumed I would be looked after. This did give me a stoical attitude to all future problems, so perhaps it was a good thing, but at the time I was left feeling lonely and neglected.

One unexpected and joyful event was the week-long holiday we were given for the Coronation in 1953, when Gabriel and I joined Ma in London. This was because my grandfather and uncle were both royal chaplains, and we were given seats in the Royal Household Stand. My memory is of a long, rainy, and cold day, despite it being June. But there was a lot of cheering and waving of flags, and the gold coach was spectacular. The greatest cheer was reserved for the Queen of Tonga, who went by in an open carriage braving the rain. Maybe the most memorable moment was nothing to do with the Coronation, but the announcement Everest had been climbed, which seemed to me far more exciting. While in London we were also taken to the Festival of Britain, with its Dome of Discovery.

The 'fifties didn't offer much in the way of excitement, so these events were an unexpected diversion.

Winchester Cathedral played an important role in our school lives. Each Sunday we would trail down the hill in crocodile to attend morning service in that vast nave. My attitude to church services didn't change in the least; nevertheless, like everyone else in my peer group, I was confirmed in the Cathedral. Greatly to my alarm, I developed violent hiccups before my first Communion and was terrified in case I hiccupped while the clergy were dispensing the wafers and wine. Privately I found the whole idea of eating a body and drinking blood rather cannibalistic, however symbolic, and avoided it from then on. In contrast, the most joyful experiences in the Cathedral were when the school choir sang in regular performances of oratorios. The Winchester Choral Society was an impressive one and famous singers would be invited to take part. I particularly remember a performance of Beethoven's *Missa Solemnis*. The sheer volume of sound was overwhelming, and to this day I can recall the pure joy and exhilaration I felt while taking part in that performance.

St Swithun's was an all-girl's school and the only males we ever saw were one ancient groundsman and an occasional visit from the school doctor. It therefore came as a surprise to me that I seemed to have the power to attract older men. An incident occurred when, as a prefect, I had the task of introducing and then thanking a male lecturer. I don't remember the subject of the lecture but afterwards, as instructed, I kept him company with tea and biscuits. The next day a large box arrived with a note, 'To the enchanting Jane who I very much hope to see again.' (Joseph would have quickly pointed out he should have used 'whom' instead of 'who'.) The box contained 'Plain Jane' chocolates and he had crossed out 'plain' and in large black pen written 'beautiful'. Someone stupidly reported this to my housemistress, who, greatly alarmed, reported it to the headmistress, and I was summoned to see her. She gave me a mild ticking off, telling me I should be more careful when talking to men I didn't know, as I might rue the consequences. I thought the whole thing ridiculous but was secretly flattered by the lecherous lecturer's attention.

There was one other mildly sexual occurrence when I was in the sixth form, and the only lesbian feelings I ever experienced. On this occasion it was with one of the younger members of staff. She had a sports car, which greatly added to her glamour; I was never quite sure whether I had feelings for her or the sports car. One thing is certain, it soon became evident she had feelings for me. One weekend she took me out and we went to her house for tea. I remember she played Schumann's piano concerto, and it was all rather romantic, but innocent, and ended with nothing more than a hug and brief kiss as she delivered me back. But we were seen, and once again I was summoned to see the headmistress. I was told I was wrong to allow myself to be drawn into an unhealthy relationship and I was forbidden to speak, or be alone, with that teacher again. I found this a bit ripe as the headmistress was herself a lesbian. Looking back, I think nearly all the teachers were either lesbians, spinsters, or, like my housemistress a war widow. This was the 'fifties, and sex was basically a taboo subject. We had absolutely no sex education. An aged, unmarried Biology teacher even informed us that all copulation between humans was conducted standing up. At the age of eighteen, I left school with no sexual knowledge at all and thought an erection was a building. This was even more bewildering because I came from a bohemian household, where Gabriel and I were continually summoned to talk to Joseph while he had his bath, and he would be given to walking from bathroom to bedroom totally naked. Another of his seemingly strange habits was his demand to take nude photographs of Gabriel and myself. I think this may have affected Gabriel more, as his demands for the photographic sessions were mainly with her. I just found them boring. Gabriel obviously knew there was something odd about this and forbade me to mention it to anyone, especially at school. She also told me not to mention any of the famous people we'd met during the holidays, as this would be considered showing off. It was all very confusing.

Outside school, there was one mildly sexual incident, which did upset me. It occurred when I was about sixteen.

It was during the annual summer fête, held every year in the Deanery Garden. I had been given a floaty dress for the occasion and was aware I looked pretty. My happiness was further increased when the film star Joan Fontaine – a friend of Valerie's, who Joseph had brought in to open the fête – paid me a compliment. Joseph had instructed me to be particularly kind to a man with only one arm, after he was badly wounded in the war, and had also recently lost his wife. I immediately felt a surge of sympathy and did my best to pay him a great deal of attention. At some point he suggested we walk to the far part of the tennis court where there was a tree to give us shade. Nobody was about, and he suddenly grabbed me and with his body pinned me back against the tree, proceeding to kiss me violently and rub himself against me in an alarming way. This was accompanied by heavy breathing and sexual murmurings. With only one arm he was surprisingly strong, and it took me a while to finally push him away, catching him off balance. I ran back into the house, hot with shame and disgust and tore off my dress. The day was ruined. Later, Joseph said the Major had expressed a great affection for me and invited me to go to tea with him. I was horrified and shouted, probably hysterically, I never wanted to see the man again. Joseph was annoyed and said I was being typically difficult, but my mother, noting my reaction, realised something must have happened. Thankfully she may also have said something to Joseph in private and the subject was never mentioned again.

One of the advantages of living in Warwick was being only eight miles from Stratford and the Shakespeare Memorial Theatre. During the winter months the D'Oyly Carte were brought in for a season of Gilbert and Sullivan, which we loved. We saw all the productions and knew many of the songs by heart, but I think *Patience* was our favourite because of its witty lyrics. In the summer it was the turn of Shakespeare. These were glory days for the Shakespeare Memorial Theatre Company, and my mother arranged for us to see every play each season. The most memorable for me was the season of History Plays, with Richard Burton playing Prince Hal and then Henry V. Anthony Quayle was Falstaff and the whole company was a brilliant ensemble. The following season was with the Oliviers, the best play being *Twelfth Night*, with Laurence Olivier brilliant as Malvolio. To my annoyance the one play I didn't see that year was *Titus Andronicus* as it was felt it would be too violent for me. Gabriel of course went to see it and reported with glee at how many people had fainted and had to be carried out during the gory bits. She then went on to describe them in graphic detail. Quite frankly, I would have preferred to see it for myself. The large souvenir programmes brought out for each season were greatly treasured. I would write comments beside the photos of the actors, and it is interesting to note that one of these was my future husband, Toby Robertson (before he became a director). Beside his photo I had written, not a review of his acting talents, but 'very good looking'! These many visits to Stratford finally confirmed my obsession with the theatre and my determination to go to drama school.

One of the best summer holidays was when Joseph took a locum in Monte Carlo. Christopher was by this time doing his National Service, so it was just the four of us. Joseph spent most of his time writing, but Ma, Gabriel and I found a great spot near the harbour for sunbathing, where there were concrete slabs to dive off and swim. We called this 'slabbing' and from there we had a great view of the millionaire yachts. After two weeks we left Monte Carlo to embark on the long meander back, a route Joseph had proudly planned. We progressed up into the Alps and then back through Burgundy, visiting the monasteries and churches, including the spectacular Vézelay Abbey and Autun Cathedral.

Almost at the end of the journey, Ma developed a bad attack of food poisoning and we had to stay an extra two days in a remote village, to give her time to recover enough to drive. Unfortunately, during this time Joseph was bitten by some insect on the leg and had an allergic reaction. Gabriel and I watched with alarm as both our parents began to fall apart. By the time Ma felt she was just well enough to drive again, Joseph's leg had become lurid and swollen. We arrived back in Warwick, and both went straight to their beds. Ma was still not fully recovered, and the effort of the

JM in Monte Carlo, 1956

long drive had left her suffering from exhaustion. Joseph was given massive doses of penicillin, but nobody realised he was allergic. I was despatched to his room to see if he needed anything and found him shaking violently. I learned later this was a rigor. An ambulance was called, and he was taken to hospital where he remained seriously ill for several days. It was a sad end to what otherwise had been one of the better holidays.

The last of the family holidays, again without Christopher, was to Stornoway on the Isle of Lewis, which we reached by car ferry (there was no airport until later). Although surrounded by beautiful countryside, Stornoway was a strangely dour town and on Sundays everyone dressed in black. Dominating the town was the port area with the fishing boats, where the fishwives would wait for the deliveries from the overnight haul, and then set about gutting the fish, with the seagulls dive-bombing for scraps. Gabriel immediately became friendly with the fisherman and persuaded the skipper on one of the boats, the Ivy Rose, to let her go out with them. They were dubious at first, but she was persistent, and they finally agreed. She survived the trip but described it as a rough experience in every way. She especially loved the puffins, who, she reported, became unsteady on an overdose of fish and kept toppling over. Having the car meant we drove all over the island, up to the farthest tip of the British Isles, then visiting the Callanish stones, a sort of mini-Stonehenge, but mostly travelling South to the many lochs. In one of these I am convinced I saw a large serpent creature in the water. I imagine it's how the Loch Ness Monster must have looked, but sadly didn't manage to take a picture and Gabriel scornfully dismissed it as my imagination running riot again.

Towards the end of the holiday the final crisis between Gabriel and Joseph came to a head. Their relationship had been deteriorating for some time with endless disagreements and arguments and they were continually at loggerheads. On this occasion I was inadvertently the cause of the trouble. We were visiting Loch Seaforth to have a picnic. At this time, I was deep in *The Forsyte Saga*, so when a walk was suggested, I declined, saying I'd rather stay by the loch and read. Joseph then told me sharply to put the damned book away and take some exercise. Gabriel unexpectedly came to my defence and said, 'I don't think she should be coerced.' It seemed an innocent enough remark, but something about it made Joseph react violently. Within minutes they were both shouting angrily at each other, and it became increasingly out of control as Ma and I looked on helplessly. Finally, Gabriel ran up into the hills, and we could hear her howling with rage. It was as if she was giving vent to years of pent-up anger and resentment. Then she disappeared. We waited a long time for her to return and were all getting cold. Joseph finally said she would just have to make her own way back to Stornoway, about fifteen miles away. We drove back in silence and with sinking heart I knew this would trigger one of his moods. Gabriel returned late that night and, to my alarm, started packing. The next day she left, telling me she would stay with friends until she was due to go up to Cambridge. Her relationship with Joseph never really recovered. Neither would give in or make any attempt to be reconciled. Once Gabriel had her degree, she left England, married happily, but again against Joseph's advice, and settled in Canada.

Once again, I became the only child. I kept to myself, although I let it be known I intended to make a career in the theatre as soon as possible. Joseph called in Valerie Hobson and asked her to try and deter me. This was rather a fruitless exercise as I had idolised Valerie ever since being taken to see her at Drury Lane in *The King and I* when I was six. The performance had dazzled me, but even better was being taken backstage to see Valerie in her glamorous dressing room. I can remember vividly the smell of greasepaint and the dresser coming in to collect her costumes. Even more exciting was when Valerie arranged for me to be taken onto the stage. They had just finished setting up for the opening boat scene, but it wasn't the scenery that impressed me, but staring out into that vast auditorium. It hit me in the solar plexus. From that moment on I was stagestruck, and the theatre became my obsession. Poor Valerie. There was little she could have done because this obsession had increased over the years, further helped by continual visits to Stratford. However, she did say something that remained with me. To give Valerie her due, she did try and point out what a precarious profession I was choosing, and then she said, 'The best advice I can give you, in this very over-crowded line of work, is to find a "gimmick", something that is entirely yours. There will be many, all trying to do the same thing – far too many Hamlets and Ophelias! You will need to find something special to you, your own "gimmick".' I considered this and then asked her what her gimmick was. She laughed and said, 'My hair!' Although it was an unexpected reply, I understood. She was wonderfully glamorous and had long, wavy, chestnut hair that perfectly framed her face. My mother told me that straight after RADA Valerie was snapped up for films and her career had never looked back.

When we weren't on some special locum locations, we most often went to North Cornwall and these holidays were without Joseph. It is a part of the country which has always held a special place in my heart. We started in Trebetherick and then moved up the coast when my mother bought a cottage in Port Isaac, The Windlass. However, in my late teens my favourite holidays were spent in the house of one of Joseph's greatest friends, Peggy Thomas, the extremely attractive wife of the headmaster of Repton. The Thomas's house, White Horses, was on the cliff, just above Daymer

Bay, between Trebetherick and Polzeath. Peggy would fill the house with friends of her younger son, Mike, who was up at Oxford, and she always invited me to join them. Mike was three years older than me, and I adored him, and why not? He was charming, good-looking, artistic, a wonderful athlete especially at tennis, and kind. On those holidays he treated me like a favourite sister. I was in the last two years of school, gauche and unsophisticated, compared with all Mike's witty, clever Oxford friends, but despite this, they were golden times. One of the party, Paul Betjeman (son of John), had a battered car and we would pile in each day and go off to one of the bays for rock diving, swimming, and hunting for cowry shells. Often, we would repair to a pub for lunch and Mike treated me as an equal, handing me a cider, or lager and lime, my first taste of alcohol.

A great friend of Peggy's who always joined us was Edward Hornby, a charming, amusing, extremely wealthy (coming from the W H Smith family) and generous man, paying for all the outings and I suspect a good deal more. He took a special interest in Mike, and they had a close relationship, but he was good to us all, including me. After the holidays, I would always receive a glamorous present of some kind, usually from Asprey in Mayfair. One of the best of Edward's actions was to buy a daily bottle of Pimm's, and it became a ritual to gather on the terrace for 'Pimm's time', which I remember as being full of banter and much laughter.

A frequent visitor to White Horses, and another great friend of both Peggy and my father, was John Betjeman, who had a cottage nearby. He was never happier than when he was with a young, admiring audience who would hang on his every word. Sometimes, for our amusement, he would resort to baby language, 'Johnny wanttee choccy biccy' and one of us, usually me being the youngest, would be sent off on frequent errands. On one occasion he set a competition, telling us to write something during the day and he would then judge the winner in the evening. Inevitably, all the Oxford pieces were light, witty and amusing. In contrast I wrote a rather turgid poem. I can't remember who won, but I felt my failure keenly and took myself off to sit on the cliff, staring out at the sea, depressed and dejected. After a while, John came and sat beside me. We sat in silence for a short time, until I suddenly burst out how terrible my poem had been. John gave a long sigh and shook his head, saying, 'It never does to try too hard. If the words don't flow, put them away and wait until they do.' A little later he added, 'People think, quite wrongly, writing poetry is easy. It isn't.' Then he broke the serious moment by saying something trivial and silly, which made me laugh. He was one of the loveliest men I ever met.

At the age of eighteen, my childhood came to an end. It had been a strange one, certainly not conventional, often lonely, and although leaving me with little self-confidence and extreme naivety, it provided me with a heightened intuition into the behaviour of human beings and a definite stoicism with which to cope with the various 'slings and arrows' thrown my way. I also learned to be contented with my own company, which is a rare asset. I began to look on life as a series of events needing to be managed, some joyful, some difficult and distressing, but all necessary on this journey for which I was so little prepared. It was to be – as my husband Toby later put it – 'a life not without incident!'

Chapter Four
THE INCIDENTS BEGIN

MY ADULT LIFE began with a sudden and unexpected occurrence, straight out of Restoration Drama. I was asked to become an older man's mistress. Given my sheltered upbringing, this came as something of a shock. The incident occurred on the last holiday I took with my parents. Joseph had taken a final locum, in Viareggio near Pisa, where we were to stay for two weeks, before travelling across Northern Italy and finishing with a week in Venice. Gabriel and Christopher had left home by this time, so I was told I could bring a friend with me. I asked Ann Rawlings, a friend who had left St Swithuns before me. Despite her early departure we remained close. She was far more mature than I, and her guidance was welcome as I struggled to emerge from school life into adulthood. Joseph once again didn't come with us in the car but took the train to Viareggio, along with Sonya. Our large family car had been swapped for a Morris Minor, and this small vehicle was not entirely suitable for such a long journey, but after a couple of breakdowns, one where the wife of a garage mechanic provided us with a nylon stocking to improvise as a temporary fan belt, we finally made it.

Viareggio itself was a holiday resort and of no historical interest. It consisted of a long beach and a series of hotels. Ann and I didn't mind this at all. We were set on acquiring a suntan and happy to lie on the beach all day. I had recently been given a dress allowance, and again with the help of Ann, bought a wardrobe designed to catch the eye. Ann, who was later to become a great beauty, was still rather plump, but I was tall and skinny and revelled in my new clothes. My mother proclaimed my bikinis far too skimpy, but I wore them all the same. It was no doubt this that first attracted Enrique Arias, who came and sat beside me, politely asking if I was English. I said yes, introduced myself, told him how we came to be here, and he instantly became interested. Ann was soon bored and wandered off, but Enrique and I remained deep in conversation. I am sure I flirted, finding it flattering to have so much attention paid to me by this elegant and sophisticated man. I learned he was from Colombia but travelled all over the world as a concert pianist and he was now in Italy planning a series of concerts. His appearance was one of neatness; small and delicate in build and immaculately dressed, even on the beach. That evening I introduced him to my parents, and he asked if he could take me to the opera the following night. Ma, knowing my love of music, immediately said yes. Ann didn't share this passion and was happy to opt out. It was my first opera and being *La Bohème* I was suitably overcome by emotion, Enrique lending me his perfectly laundered handkerchief to mop up my tears.

For the next three days he continued to give me his full attention. My mother found him charming. Joseph didn't and was suspicious of his motives, making this plain whenever Enrique appeared. He needn't have worried. Enrique's behaviour towards me was as impeccable as his appearance. Before he left, I told him we were going on to Florence and then would be in Venice. In my innocence I even told him where we would be staying in Venice. I also gave him my address in Hampstead. Enrique thanked me, politely kissed my hand and I rather presumed that was that. Sonya now departed for England, but Joseph came with us for the next part of the journey. Ma took sightseeing seriously and I found this particularly tiring in Florence, being dragged off to see everything on her extensive list. It was August and very hot and we arrived in Venice in a dramatic thunderstorm. On the first morning we were marched firmly to the Academia but after that Ma seemed happy to leave us to our own devices. Just as well, because on the second morning, Enrique arrived at the Pensione where we were staying. He said he was in Venice for two days and wanted to devote his entire time to me. Ma and Joseph were busy with their own sightseeing and Ann was quite happy to explore on her own.

Joseph seemed annoyed by the reappearance of Enrique but there was little he could do. He was mollified by the fact 'the irritating little man' was only in Venice for a limited time. During this second meeting our relationship became more serious. I didn't let this worry me. I revelled in my new freedom and found his company fascinating. Enrique wined and dined me, always punctiliously delivering me back early enough to satisfy my parents. We talked endlessly. I told him about going to drama school, and he told me of his plans to settle in Spain. He especially talked of an amazing Moorish village called Mojacar, near Almeria, which he planned to develop as an artistic community.

After he kissed me for the first time, I remember wondering whether I found him physically attractive. My entire experience of love and romantic heroes was drawn from reading novels. Enrique was not a Heathcliff, or Mr Rochester, or indeed Nancy Mitford's Fabrice. Too clearly, I remembered Marianne in *Sense and Sensibility* saying, 'to love is to burn'. I was certainly not burning, but I was flattered by his attention and the many compliments that flowed my way. For me it was an exciting experience which had an end in sight. He left, and a week later we returned to England.

A month went by, and I was preoccupied with my audition for the Central School of Speech and Drama, chosen mainly for its proximity to Hampstead, where we now lived. Then, out of the blue, Enrique's letter arrived. It was a long, convoluted, outpouring of passion, and looking back on it, very flowery and un-English. The gist was he had fallen passionately in love, could not think of a life without me in it, further adding I needed to forget the idea of drama school and move on to the exciting future that lay in front of me. As love letters go, it was a full-blown declaration, and he finished with a flourish offering me an apartment in Madrid, and, as I had expressed a love of sports cars, one of my own. The latter was very tempting, but I found it all rather bewildering. I put the letter away for a day, and then bravely decided to ring him. As I remember, it was a rather stilted conversation that went something like this:

'Thank you for your letter, Enrique.' Long pause.

'So, what have you decided? Will you come to Madrid?'

'I'm not sure. I need to think about it.' Long pause and then, 'What colour is the sports car?'

This produced a short laugh. Was he shocked or amused? I wasn't sure. He finally said, 'Any colour you like, sweet girl.' He called me 'sweet girl' a great deal. Another long pause.

'It does all sound lovely. Can I let you know in a bit? I have my audition for drama school this week. I will ring you after that.'

With that poor Enrique had to be satisfied. I tried not to think about it and concentrate on the audition, but Enrique's proposition was never far from my mind. Marriage was never offered, and I later learned he was married, albeit in a rather detached way. I felt torn between the excitement of a grown-up life in Madrid or embarking on a theatre career. As I continued to dither, matters were brought to a swift conclusion. I had stupidly left Enrique's letter open on my desk and my mother, going into my room, had noticed it, given it a glance and then, with alarm bells ringing, had read the whole thing. Thankfully, she didn't tell Joseph, who would have blown a gasket, but she was obviously both horrified and shocked. I was told firmly to inform Enrique the whole idea was absolutely out of the question, forbidding me to have any further dealings with the man. I wrote to Enrique, full of apologies, explaining how my mother had found his letter and my parents were adamant I should not join him. Enrique was rather graceful about this, probably alarmed at the thought of a confrontation with Joseph, and in the circumstances wrote an understanding letter back, saying he wasn't giving up on me, but would wait to see me again once I had finished at drama school. The one adverse result of this whole adventure was that my mother became extremely over-protective, and until I left home made sure I was never left alone with anyone of the male sex.

We were now living in a spacious flat at the top of Redington Road, very near the Heath. Joseph had finally been offered a London living, the bombed church of St Mary le Bow, which needed complete rebuilding and restoration. I think the C of E establishment felt he couldn't do much harm from a building that didn't exist! However, it was just the challenge Joseph needed. He set off on a world tour of English-speaking peoples to raise sufficient funds to rebuild. It took him nine months, the last stop being New York. St Mary le Bow was not only the famous Cockney church that housed Bow Bells, but as my father brilliantly discovered, it was the sister church of Trinity Church, Wall Street. Joseph, always charming, was also a brilliant speaker. By the time he left Wall Street he had sufficient funds, not only to rebuild St Mary le Bow, but also to restore the Norman crypt and build a penthouse to live in over the roof of the church. This took two years to complete, so meanwhile we were installed in the Hampstead flat.

My audition to Central was a rather curious event. As we walked up the steps to the Embassy Theatre my mother let out a shriek of 'Darling!' and rushed across to embrace Rachel Kempson, mother of Lynn Redgrave, who was also auditioning. They hadn't seen each other since RADA days, and Lynn and I were abandoned while they caught up. After performing my audition speeches, I was interviewed by the aged Principal, Gwynneth Thurburn. She gave the impression of being almost Edwardian. Very grand, she spoke with a rather querulous voice, reminding me of Edith Evans.

'And what makes you want to be an actress?'

I plunged in. 'Well, more than acting, I would really like to be a theatre director.'

This produced a shocked silence. The great lady spoke in chilling tones. 'My dear girl, women do *not* direct.' I immediately realised I'd made a great mistake and felt increasingly depressed as I sat around with the other candidates waiting for results. The verdict was I would need a rounded theatre experience and should start out on the stage management course. I often wonder what would have happened if I hadn't mentioned I wanted to be a director. At that juncture my life could have gone in several directions. I could have gone to Madrid to live with Enrique, I could have gone to a further educational establishment and crammed for university, or I could have done the acting course and become an actress. In the event I agreed to the suggested course. Little did I know it, but it was to be the best possible foundation for my future professional life. Valerie Hobson would have been pleased, because it enabled me to follow her advice of finding a 'gimmick', that special niche for myself. However, at the time I found my life at Central often frustrating and inadequate.

On the plus side, I became acquainted with every aspect

of theatre – lighting, music, design and stagecraft. Most of all, I learned by watching and working with the professional directors who were brought into the school. It was fascinating to observe the different approaches used during the rehearsal process in order to bring the play to fruition for opening night. I also began to understand the problems actors experienced, how easily confidence could be lost, or how a wrong approach taken to a character could leave the interpretation muddled and confused. Maybe the most important lesson of all was observing how a good director could make or break a performance. Ironically, after that original interview, one of the first directors I worked with was a woman, Ann Jellicoe, also a distinguished playwright, who had been brought in for a production of John Arden's *Live Like Pigs*.

The most memorable thing about this production was it almost managed to make Julie Christie look dowdy, but not quite. My father, who very rarely came to see the shows but on this occasion was in the audience, picked her out as being 'startlingly beautiful'. Meanwhile, I found Ann Jellicoe fascinating, attaching myself to her like a limpet and hanging out with her in the pub after rehearsals. She was certainly striking to look at, with a black patch over one eye, and she was patient and kind, seemingly never irritated by my endless questions.

Another director I greatly admired was Harry Moore, who undertook the production of *The Witch Boy*, with James Bolam giving a superb performance in the leading role. (Jimmy Bolam became quickly famous after leaving Central as one of *The Likely Lads*, and he later played Beethoven for me. I've always considered him a brilliant actor, although not always easy to work with.) From Harry Moore I learned the important role music plays in productions. He was meticulous in his choices for this play, which greatly contributed to its success. The other useful lesson learned was the realisation directors need endurance, particularly during technical and dress rehearsals, which tend to go disastrously wrong. Somehow, it usually turns out to be 'all right on the night' but not before the stress levels have gone sky-high. A director can easily lose confidence at this stage. So many decisions have been made, not just with the acting performances, but all the other aspects of the production. The question remains, will all the elements of a production come together, or have bad decisions been made during rehearsals, when it is too late to put them right? It all falls on the director's shoulders, and the critics can be merciless.

I learned from bad directors as well. It's not always easy managing the many egos that emerge during rehearsals and patience is an asset, which many did not have. A director should never bully or be overbearing, which could have disastrous results. I also quickly learned directors are the outsiders and not part of the company, who become a close, self-contained unit. There is the need to develop a thick skin and not mind criticism, something I never found easy. However, my future directing career was some years away.

Meanwhile, my social life had picked up. I made many friends at Central but my boyfriend at this time was up at Cambridge. Ben Pierce Higgins' father was also a clergyman and we met through mutual friends of our parents. He was a gifted musician and, despite being mainly self-taught, went on to study piano at the Royal College of Music. I seem to have been particularly susceptible to pianists, because, apart from Toby Robertson, all the important relationships in my life have been with men who played the piano.

During my second year at Central, Ben arranged for me to join a university skiing party. He was most persuasive and, against my better judgement, I went along, a further temptation being a beautiful ski suit bought for me by Nancy Spain: white with purple edging, ridiculous, and far too grand for a beginner. I do recall the train journey out to

Austria was long and tedious, so Ben read me *Lady Chatterley's Lover* to help pass the time. The trip turned out to be a disaster. I had no time to enjoy the parties, or the skiing, because on the second day, the safety-catch on my boots snapped – it was later found to have been faulty – and my right leg shot under the left one with a deafening crack. The ski instructor immediately announced I had a break and would need the hospital. A tin bath was summoned, and I was ignominiously bundled in and taken down the slopes. A tearful Ben skied down behind me, and I remember saying crossly it was me who should be crying not him. I was taken by ambulance to the hospital and met Herr Doctor, an extremely attractive, bronzed man, probably in his early forties. The verdict was I had a compound, complex spiral fracture and would need six weeks of traction. To add to my woes, I lost the Nancy Spain ski suit, which had to be cut off me. It would have been a miserable ordeal if I hadn't shared a room with a charming German girl who spoke excellent English and who became an instant friend. Nobody else spoke any English at all. Ben came to visit once, but it was a difficult journey from the resort, and he was so full of anguish and apologies I was relieved when he returned to England. I wasn't comfortable and often in pain but inevitably fell in love with the handsome doctor, and his daily visits made life bearable.

When my companion left, I was once more on my own and boredom hovered. Gabriel brilliantly came to the rescue and sent me a strange collection of books, ranging from Walt Whitman to P G Wodehouse, which I devoured. The latter made me laugh so much I fell out of bed, taking my traction with me. No damage was done, but Herr Doctor was not best pleased. For the last week my mother came out to oversee my journey back to England. Joseph had given her strict instructions not to ski herself, cursing what he called 'upper-class sports', which in those days I suppose skiing was. Ma immediately became alarmed by my noticeable attachment to Herr Doctor and did her best to see we were never left alone together, which I found infuriating, but he occasionally made late visits after she had returned to her hotel.

The day before I was due to leave, I was taken off the traction and manipulation began to put the bones back together, without anaesthetic. This was before the days of quick operations and metal plates and pins. It was a long, painful process but I was determined not to cry. Herr Doctor afterwards told my mother how impressed he was by my bravery and stoicism. Now, in a huge plaster, I was given a pair of crutches and the following day left for the long train journey home. My adventures were not over, because approaching Munich station our train went off the rails. It was also my 20th birthday. My mother, whose German was fluent, now resembled a Wagnerian heroine as she shouted out that her daughter had a broken leg. At least I think that is what she said, but it had an instant effect. Two burly officials appeared and carried me to a replacement train. Ma must have been exhausted by the whole ordeal, but our troubles continued. As we boarded the boat for the Channel crossing, we were informed it would be extremely rough. My balance on the crutches was not good, so Ma insisted we made our way to the first-class lounge where we could comfortably sit. An official came in and informed us we couldn't stay in first, because nobody was allowed to be ill in this lounge, and it was obvious with my crutches I couldn't make a quick exit. My mother haughtily assured him that neither of us had any intention of being ill. And we weren't. I don't think I would have dared. Joseph met us at the station and didn't appear overjoyed at seeing us, annoyed by the whole escapade. I hobbled for the next two months, unable to put my right leg on the ground, so I didn't make it back to Central until the start of the summer term.

This incident was one of many that caused me a change of direction. It soon became apparent I had missed too much at Central for it to be worth continuing without doing an extra year. I rejected this idea and decided to leave. Ben felt huge guilt at this outcome, being responsible for the disastrous skiing trip which he thought had ruined my time at Central. I told him this was nonsense; it had just sent my life off in a different direction. I left Central with no real regrets, having learned a great deal about working in the theatre and making many good friends, including Fiona Walker (who married Herbie Wise, the director of the brilliant *I Claudius*), Julie Christie, Jennie Heslewood (who later married the wonderful Freddie Jones), and Timothy Carlton, father of Benedict Cumberbatch.

One of the directors at Central, Peter Streuli, who for some reason felt I had potential, arranged for me to go to Frinton for their summer season. It was the first job for many students straight from drama school, and being a weekly rep, was a baptism of fire. I was an acting/ASM, which meant I did small parts and assisted in the stage management. I don't think I distinguished myself in either department, but again learned a great deal from watching, and I loved being part of a company. There was a funny moment when I was playing an Italian au pair girl, and an Italian member of the audience came up afterwards and told me I had a Viareggio accent! I must have picked it up lying on the beach listening to all those ice cream and brioche vendors shouting out their wares.

After Frinton I returned to the Hampstead flat, only to find the situation was not happy.

Joseph was at a loose end while St Mary le Bow was being restored and spent most of his time with Sonya, now installed in a flat at the other end of Redington Road. I was increasingly worried about Ma's health. She had taken a job with the Citizen's Advice Bureau, which was in Wandsworth, a long way from Hampstead. She would arrive home completely exhausted and then start making Joseph supper. I tried to escape the rows and depressing atmosphere by picking up my social life again. One of the most memorable parties was at Nancy Spain and Joan Werner Laurie's house in South Kensington. Inevitably, it was filled with wall-to-wall celebrities. I did say nervously to Nancy I wouldn't know anyone, but she replied with a breezy, 'Nonsense darling, just stand around looking decorative.' Not easy to do, but I did watch as the celebrities poured in. Most of them were from the theatre, but I was introduced to a famous radio presenter, a well-known author, the editor of Vogue, and even a dress designer who worked in the house of Dior. John Mills and his entire family entered, and a great fuss was made of daughter Hayley, who'd just opened in a film. Then the whisper went round the room that 'the Master' had arrived, and a few minutes later Noël Coward walked in.

Everyone crowded round him, and the poor man was forced to the piano and begged to perform. He started on 'The Stately Homes of England' but when he reached the second verse, he dramatically removed his hands from the piano and declared, 'I've dried.' He stood up and looked across the room to where I was standing alone. To my astonishment, he walked over and said, 'I don't know who you are, but you look quite charming. Would you care to take a walk around the garden?' With every eye in the room on us, we made our way outside, then sat on a garden seat, the furthest from the house. I don't remember our exact conversation. I think I breathlessly told him I had been to drama school and had just returned from Frinton. I do remember he listened attentively and before we went back to the house, he wished me every success with my career. Immediately after our return he left, and many reproachful glances came my way for having monopolised him. Nancy was full of glee and chuckled, 'Well darling, you certainly managed to cause a sensation.'

She must have reported this to Joseph, who referred to it the next day, saying, 'I hope you weren't drawing attention to yourself.' I always longed for him to pay me a compliment, but he never did.

Peter Streuli once more came to my rescue and offered me another acting/ASM job for the upcoming Pitlochry Festival Season. This excited me greatly. Pitlochry was a major festival, attracting good actors and distinguished directors. I was to have small parts in four of the six plays and work with stage management. Peter then asked if I would help with the day of auditions, which I was happy to do. What followed was an incident which was to change my life. The day of auditions arrived, and feeling rather important, I was armed with a clipboard and a list of those being auditioned. All was going smoothly, when in walked a tall man in a sheepskin coat, which he took off and threw down beside me saying, 'Look after that.'

He was about to go into the theatre when I stopped him, 'Excuse me, could you give me your name?'

He looked shocked but said abruptly, 'Toby Robertson.'

I glanced down my list and shook my head. 'I'm so sorry, your name's not on the list. But if you wait here, I will go and speak to one of the directors. They might be able to fit you in.'

He gave a roar of laughter and said, 'I *am* one of the directors!' And with that he strode into the theatre.

There was silence for a moment and then one of the waiting actors said, 'Don't you know Toby Robertson? He's the reason I'm here. He's a brilliant director, just done a great production of *The Lower Depths* at the RSC.' Others then joined in with similar praise, and my humiliation was complete.

I sat with lowered head the entire morning until the break

came for lunch. The directors emerged and Toby went to collect his coat. 'Coming?' he said. I shook my head, telling him lunch was just for the directors, but he insisted. At the restaurant Peter and another director sat talking over the morning's proceedings, while Toby devoted his entire attention to me, even asking what wine I would like. During our conversation we discovered we had a mutual love of Cornwall. He told me his mother rented a house on the South Coast where he'd go as often as possible, and I said we had a cottage in Port Isaac on the North Coast. I remember Toby laughed at this and said we would never be compatible. After this memorable first meeting I didn't see him again until he arrived in Pitlochry. By that time two of the season's six plays had already opened. Toby was the celebrity director and his productions, Pirandello's *Henry IV* and a specially commissioned historical epic, *Muir of Huntershill*, were anticipated with much excitement.'

Pitlochry must be one of the most romantic settings for a theatre, set among glorious countryside of mountains and

JM in Pitlochry (Toby's favourite photo of me), 1962

lochs, and often called the gateway to the Scottish Highlands. By the time Toby arrived, several weeks into the season, I had already fallen in love and embarked on my first affair. It therefore worried me little that Toby didn't seem to remember our lunch and paid me almost no attention. He also embarked on an affair with the leading lady, Lillias Walker, and took out most of the senior members of the company, of both sexes, always giving them lavish dinners. His social life held little interest for me, but what was fascinating was the brilliant way he worked. He worked without a plan, relying entirely on inspiration. His rehearsals were always exciting, if sometimes chaotic. He would change his mind a great deal, sending designers into a frenzy. The six plays, once all had opened, ran every day of the week, and the slogan was, 'Stay six days and see six plays!' This changeover every night put a great deal of strain on the stage management team. (Once I became a director, I always treated my stage managers with understanding. They have enormous responsibilities and are not always treated kindly or given the respect they deserve.) I was something of a disaster area as the ASM, especially in the music department, which back then was a primitive affair and all too easy to mix up the cues. On one occasion, during *The Hasty Heart*, which was meant to open in the jungle with a squark of native birds, I accidentally hit the previous cue, which was Charlie Kunz playing 'The White Cliffs of Dover.' On another occasion, the Duke of Athol was in the audience and for some reason we were instructed to play the National Anthem in his honour. This was not on tape but on a record, and I carelessly put on the wrong side. There was the long drum roll, then everyone stood up and out came 'Life on the Ocean Wave'. After this, I wasn't allowed any further music duties.

Toby had great success with the Pirandello and received rave reviews. His other production was less successful, but this was hardly his fault. It was an unwieldy piece, being a historical epic about an 18th-century Scottish reformer and revolutionary, Thomas Muir. The story was episodic, and the play had countless scenes, moving from elegant Edinburgh to the hulks where prisoners waited for transportation to Botany Bay, then on to Mexico, Havana and finally France where the unfortunate Muir died. The whole company was involved, some of us playing many parts. I remember I had six roles and five wigs! Toby brought all his brilliant inventiveness to the piece, particularly in the first half of the play, but ran out of time and the second act was under-rehearsed and a bit of a muddle. In the first act, during a scene in an Edinburgh Garden with Muir entertaining the grand ladies, Toby decided the ladies should be occupied doing archery, not easy in eighteenth-century costume. The management weren't happy about this request, considering it dangerous, and causing a good deal of extra expense, but we rather enjoyed it and became quite competitive. My prowess caused some envy and, to teach me a lesson, one night my bow was strung back to front, causing me to lose all control and my arrow to shoot through the Cyc, narrowly missing one of the stagehands. It also left a large hole, and I was made to pay for the repair, although the company did chip in.

In another scene, set in a tavern, Toby had me dancing on the table singing 'The Mingulay Boat Song'. It was while rehearsing this scene that Toby turned to Peter Streuli and said, 'I'm going to marry that girl.' Peter only told me this years later. It came as something of a surprise, as Toby never gave any indication of even noticing me at the time. He later told me he had noticed me, particularly in a very large sun hat sitting on the lawn, and that had decided him. The hat had caused some mirth within the company. For a joke I had written an ad in *The Times*: 'Girl with large hat wishes to be taken to Ascot!' I received many replies, some rather dubious, others downright filthy, but it gave us much amusement as I read them out each night.

After the first night of the epic, with his directing duties done, Toby left, but the season continued until September. My affair, wonderful as it had been, came to an end; the man in question had another job to go to and I returned to London. There were no regrets and we always remained great friends. Back in Hampstead, to my surprise, a postcard was waiting for me, of a Caravaggio, and sent from Venice. It was from Toby, and it read, 'All the young men in this painting look like you. Come and dine with me next week. Toby R.' And with that, my life took off in yet another direction.

Chapter Five

ENGAGEMENT, WEDDING AND HONEYMOON

MY LIFE NOW moved from the drab 'fifties and into the swinging 'sixties. But sadly, this new liberation had little effect on me. I seemed destined to be trapped in an old-fashioned world of marriage and children, and it all came about with great speed. Toby literally blew into my life like a whirlwind and took it over. He was a huge personality, charming and amusing, but, as I was soon to learn, also feckless and totally irresponsible. It wasn't in his nature to be organised, and when it came to money, he was hopeless. If he had money, he spent it; if he didn't have money, he still spent it. He always lived extravagantly. Everyone he encountered, including my father, presumed he had a large private income, which he didn't, but he lived as if he did. I was taken to wonderful restaurants, and he introduced me to delicious wines and gourmet delights.

Never once did he bore me. He could talk on every subject, and I never wanted the evenings with him to end. One of his first actions was to insist I move from living with my parents in Hampstead to a room he rented out in his elegant Cornwall Gardens house, where he had a lease on the first two floors. It was strange that my mother, having always been so over-protective, raised no objection to this plan. From the outset she seemed to trust Toby, partly because he was a good deal older and therefore in her eyes more responsible, and partly because she understood it to be a purely financial arrangement. Typically, Toby threw a large party to celebrate my moving in, and as always with his parties, many fascinating people were invited. As he was fourteen years older than me, most of his friends were established in their professions and had already made a name for themselves. There was Julian More, writer of *Grab Me a Gondola*, the English version of *Irma la Douce*, *Expresso Bongo,* and later *Songbook*. Julian had been at Stowe and Cambridge with Toby and he and his journalist wife Sheila were among his inner circle of great friends. Others included Natasha Parry, wife of Peter Brook, Eleanor Fazan (Fiz), the composer Monty Norman, Prunella Scales, David Korda, Richard Marquand and the TV scriptwriter Michael Ashe.

Soon after I moved into Cornwall Gardens, Toby and Michael Ashe went to Greece to seek locations for a proposed TV series. Michael was even more feckless than Toby. They over-ran their time, and over-spent their allowance, and the powers at ATV were not happy, constantly trying to recall them, but Michael and Toby disappeared, had a wild time and were gone six weeks. On his return, Toby took me to Yorkshire to stay with his younger sister, Toppet. She was named Teresa, but like me had taken on another name. Until now she'd been the most important person in Toby's life. Their childhood had many similarities to mine, with parents being mainly absent, and the two children parcelled around between grandparents and friends. Their father, David Robertson, hailed from a wealthy Scotch Whisky family who had sold out their business to Cutty Sark. However, David quickly squandered his fortune on four wives and a beautiful yacht, Sea Pie. He had trained as an architect but given up, embarking on a naval career, retiring early to live a carefree life with no responsibilities. He had great charm and spoke with a slight stutter, apparently brought about by forcing him to write with his right hand at an early age. He had divorced his first wife, playwright Felicity Douglas, when Toby was only six and after that saw little of his children. Felicity, who'd had a couple of West End successes with her plays, was like the character Judith Bliss in Noël Coward's *Hay Fever*, amusing but often dramatically hysterical, with swift changes of mood. She could also be dangerous, mixing people's emotions to create family scenes. By the time I met her, she had remarried, to Basil Dawson, known as B, who was a successful script writer and a steadying influence on his volatile wife. He often stepped in to take the heat out of situations which Felicity created, particularly with her daughter.

Toppet was small, lovely to look at, artistic and with a sweet personality. She had married Nigel Forbes Adam, the youngest son of a landowner family, who lived on the large family estate between Selby and York. Although the third son, Nigel, was due to inherit the estate when his father, Colin Forbes Adam, retired. This was because Nigel's older brother Desmond was tragically killed in a car crash, and the next brother, Timothy, went into the Church and gave up all claims to the estate. Toppet had trained as an actress but had given up acting when she married. When I first met her, she had just given birth to her fourth son, and with four small boys to look after had little time to mourn the loss of her career. We drove up to Yorkshire in Toby's sports car, a Sprite, which I privately considered too small a car for so large a man. On this occasion, although November, Toby insisted on driving with the roof down. It was a long journey and by the time we arrived I was completely frozen, windswept, and quite unable to speak until I'd thawed out.

Toppet and Nigel were warmly welcoming, but even so, the visit was quite an ordeal. The Forbes Adams were a large family. At the head were Colin and Irene, a rather grand couple with royal connections. Nigel's sister Virginia was married to the writer Hugo Charteris, and they had four children. Desmond, the eldest son, had married Viv, daughter of Oswald Mosely and Cynthia Curzon, and they had had three children, the youngest being born posthumously after the fatal car crash. (They were actually driving to Yorkshire for the christening of Toppet and Nigel's eldest son Charlie when the accident happened.) Timothy, the second son, was married to another actress, and they had four girls. So, it was a large clan for me to grapple with.

On the second day Toby and I went for a walk, and he casually said it might be a good idea if we got married. It wasn't a dramatic, or even romantic proposal, and I just gave a vague reply indicating it was something to think about. The following day he drove me into York and in one of the antique shops in the Shambles, he bought me the most beautiful antique ring, a green tourmaline surrounded by chip diamonds. In what I afterwards considered a devious ploy, Toby had told Toppet his plan to buy me a ring, which he thought might encourage me to accept his proposal. We were due to have drinks with Colin and Irene at Skipwith Hall, but as we arrived, the assembled family raised glasses of champagne to toast the newly engaged couple. I was in shock and felt I'd been ambushed.

On the return journey I told Toby I really wasn't at all sure about getting engaged and he agreed to give me more time. Despite my obvious misgivings, he went ahead and asked Joseph's permission to marry me. My parents greeted the news of the proposed engagement with delight, and some relief. Joseph liked the fact Toby was well-known, and mistakenly thought he was comfortably off and could provide for me without any further help from him. Ma, having been greatly alarmed by the Enrique incident, felt Toby would be a steadying influence and said she could see he was devoted to me. Devoted? This was not much comfort. 'But I'm not sure I'm in love with him,' I continued to wail. No advice was forthcoming from anyone else. Gabriel was in Canada.

Christopher would have been no help, unable to deal with his own marital problems. The man from my first affair said I couldn't marry Toby because he was gay, which I dismissed as ridiculous and merely coming from jealousy. Ben just became upset. Sonya didn't relieve my worries either, telling me friendship was the best basis for marriage. I continued to dither for two months, until Joseph finally lost his temper and put the announcement of our engagement in *The Times* and told me that was that.

The wedding was set for June, only four months away, and my mother went into overdrive. Rather feebly, I let myself be taken over and went along with it all. A great friend of my grandfather, a wonderful woman called Kitty Gladstone, granddaughter of William, made a large financial contribution, and the scene was set for a grand wedding. Joseph looked on the whole event as wonderful publicity for St Mary le Bow, and engagement photographs in the *Evening Standard* were quickly arranged, with me standing by Bow Bells tower. By this time the rebuilding of the entire church had been completed, and my parents had moved into the 'Rector's Lodgings' consisting of two floors inside the church, complete with a lift for my mother to take her up to the top. Once my engagement had been announced, Ma insisted on my returning to live with them, saying it wasn't appropriate for me to continue living in the same house as the man I was about to marry. I thought this old-fashioned, but it seemed simplest not to argue. My move back to live in St Mary le Bow led to some amusing situations when taxi drivers dropped me off in Cheapside late at night. They presumed I must have given them the wrong address and were even more surprised when I produced a huge key to open the heavy portcullis doors to enter the Church.

The next four months were both odd and exhausting. Ma insisted on shopping for a full-blown trousseau, including extravagant bed linen of Egyptian cotton, and a wardrobe of beautiful clothes. And there were dinner parties and receptions where I was introduced to Toby's endless relations, all very complicated, everyone seeming to have countless marriages and a great many stepchildren. Joseph insisted on a lavish engagement party, mainly for all his friends, inevitably including Joan and Nancy Spain, plus all his new city connections. However, I was delighted to see Athene Seyler, the great character actress, and her husband, Nicholas 'Beau' Hannen. I had met Athene many times over the years, and one of the treats of my childhood was when I was taken to tea in her delightful house in Chelsea Manor Street, crammed full of theatrical memorabilia, where she would regale me with stories about her long career. One of the funniest was when she told me about a mistake with her billing at a theatre in Liverpool which read 'And A Tiny Sailor'. By the time of our wedding, Athene was well into her sixties. She and Beau were such a romantic couple. They had fallen in love in 1922, but Beau was already married, and his wife refused to give him a divorce. This did not deter Athene. They moved in together and lived unmarried until Beau's wife finally died.

Joseph then married them forty years later. It was the first wedding in the newly restored St Mary le Bow, which Athene declared should now be renamed St Mary le Beau and Athene. She said she didn't sleep a wink the night before the wedding in case she died in a state of sin. But all went well, and she lived to become an 'honest woman'. She was awarded a CBE for her great services to acting but was informed she couldn't be made a Dame because she'd lived so long with a man she wasn't married to. How ridiculous is that?

The wedding invitations went out, Toby gave in his list and Joseph took the opportunity to invite all his friends. I think I only mentioned one or two of my own, but despite this there were two hundred guests. We'd decided to have our present list at the General Trading Company, and the presents started to pour in. A designer dress was organised and there were countless fittings. I went through the whole process in a state of limbo. I still expressed my doubts, but Toby dismissed them, calling me an 'agony beetle' and assuring me it was all going to be wonderful. At this time, he was preoccupied with a new production, aptly named *The Provok'd Wife*, with the brilliant Eileen Atkins in the lead. It was to open at the Georgian Theatre in Richmond, Yorkshire, and I joined him for the first night. He was also in the throes of forming his own theatre company, Prospect, which was to take over our lives for the next fifteen years.

The day of the wedding was grey, overcast, and cold for June. But that was the least of the problems. I was greeted with two further pieces of bad news. Ma had completely lost her voice and one of the pages had developed mumps. The hairdresser arrived and although I wanted my hair loose, she had been instructed to sweep it up into a bouffant style which I disliked. My designer dress was high-waisted and made of very heavy slub silk; privately, I thought made me look like a roll of parchment. The head-dress had the same slub silk roses, which held in place an extremely long train of tulle. Once ready, I went into the living room to say it was time. My mother, bridesmaids and pages had gone on ahead. Joseph, Anthony – who was giving me away because Joseph was marrying us – and Edward Carpenter, Dean of Westminster, were all gathered round the television watching the Lord's Test Match and seemed reluctant to leave it. Not one of them made any comment on how I looked.

As we reached the lobby, it was full of cameramen, who'd again been organised by Joseph for maximum publicity. I remember little of the service. I walked up the aisle to a very fast version of Handel's 'The Entrance of the Queen of Sheba', and this turned out to be a series of jerks as one of the pages kept stepping on the long train of tulle behind me.

At least three clergy were there to marry us, which seemed excessive; two of them were in scarlet cassocks, one belonging to my royal chaplain uncle and the other to Edward as Dean of Westminster. There was one amusing moment when my father intoned, 'Will you, Teresa Jane, take this man, Sholto David Maurice, to be your lawful wedded husband?' Toby had never told me his full name, and it made us seem like total strangers.

At last, we walked back down the aisle to the loud strains of Widor and once more I was greeted by cameras as we went outside to the cars waiting to take us to the Grocer's

Our wedding, 1963

Hall for the reception. The line-up, which I hadn't wanted, seemed to take forever, and most of the guests I just didn't recognise. The speeches went on far too long, especially Joseph's, who for once wasn't witty, but rather pedestrian and over-sentimental. I could see Ma getting agitated, but she couldn't stop him because she had no voice. Telegrams were read out from the great and good, including Sir John Gielgud and John Schlesinger. At some point I was told to go and change. I could hear Toby having a riotous party with all his male friends in the next-door room and suddenly felt very daunted by this future on which I had embarked. Was I to be an outsider and out of my depth? Too late now. I donned my going-away outfit, which was bright pink silk with a large black hat donned with a pink rose. Looking back, it was all very over the top. Toby joined me and we walked down the long staircase, being showered with rose petals, through the crowd below, then out of the door to the waiting car. And with that, it was all over.

JM on honeymoon, South of France

Toby on honeymoon, South of France

Our honeymoon was spent in Lord Glenconner's beautiful farmhouse near Antibes. It was totally secluded except for a discreet couple who looked after us, producing the most wonderful meals and then disappearing. We lazed by the pool or explored Antibes and nearby villages and it was all quite wonderful. But this small slice of heaven was cut short. Toby received news *The Provok'd Wife* was transferring to the West End, and he needed to return at once. It was an indication of how our future life was to be: first nights would take precedence over everything else. We arrived back in Cornwall Gardens to begin our married life in earnest.

Chapter Six

AND THEN WE WERE SIX

IT SOON BECAME apparent that Toby was ill-prepared for married life. He'd led a bachelor existence for so long – he was now thirty-five – he found it difficult to change his habits, and for some time he didn't. His childhood, spent mainly with old-fashioned grandparents, furnished him with many similarly old-fashioned ideas. Among these was the conviction the woman's place was in the home bringing up children. He also believed boys needed a good education and girls less so. This led to many arguments later. His financial affairs had always been chaotic, and he now found it difficult to organise the household finances to include me. It was some time before he agreed to a joint bank account, which caused endless problems with him away so much. Matters weren't helped by the fact I was also unprepared for married life, with little idea of how to run a house, order groceries, budget the accounts, let alone organise a dinner party. Toby always demanded the full three courses at these, and early on presented me with a brace of pheasant and expected me to produce a meal for eight, with all the trimmings. The fact I managed it with some success was something of a triumph, although afterwards Toby mentioned I had failed to provide breadcrumbs, apparently an absolute must for roast pheasant.

A couple of months after the wedding, I became ill with another bout of tonsillitis. It was so severe the doctor informed me my tonsils should be removed immediately. With typical extravagance, Toby booked a room in a private nursing home in St John's Wood, run by nuns. Removal of tonsils in an adult can be extremely painful. On the second night I was in such pain the surgeon prescribed pethidine. It had an instant effect. I just remember a wonderful feeling of floating happiness. What I don't remember is what occurred next. Apparently, I left the room clad only in a very transparent negligee and proceeded to walk into the men's geriatric ward, where I made my way, like Florence Nightingale, passing by each bed and bidding the aged occupants goodnight. I can only imagine the effect this had. Next morning the nuns tried, without success, to hide their giggles, and the surgeon told me severely there would be no more pethidine for me. My recovery was unexpectedly slow, and Toby became concerned at my sickness and apathy, until a few weeks later pregnancy was diagnosed. I continued to suffer from dreadful morning sickness, but thankfully after three months the condition gradually improved. Toby was frantically busy with new productions and television work and hardly around for the entire pregnancy. Once over the morning sickness, I went back to life as normal and didn't go on special diets, attend antenatal classes, or have an exercise regime. Gabriel, pregnant at the same time, was the opposite, reading endless books on the subject and following all the advice offered by the then-fashionable Dr Spock. I was never very good at taking advice.

With a child on the way, plus a dog, Toby now made the decision to leave Cornwall Gardens. We moved to a Regency terrace house in Wimbledon village, near the Common, with a small garden. Toby left the entire re-decoration of the house to me, and interior design became my new passion.

The first of our children, Sebastian James Lambert, afterwards always known as Bash, was born on 15 May 1964.

He was a wonderfully placid baby, who, up to the age of one, rather resembled Winston Churchill. Toby was up in Scotland for the birth, once more directing in Pitlochry, but sent ecstatic telegrams, overjoyed to have a son. I made a quick recovery and soon after this decided to visit Gabriel in Canada. Her first child, Vicky, had been born three months after Bash, and this seemed a good moment to meet up again. It was a long journey for a six-month-old baby, but he was well-behaved throughout. A kind of hammock was rigged up on the plane and miraculously Bash slept the whole way. I was so excited at seeing Gabriel again, I left him in the trolley by the baggage carousel, and it wasn't until Gabriel said, 'I'm longing for Vicky to meet Bash,' I remembered where I'd left him. I returned to find Bash smiling and gurgling at an admiring audience. So much for responsible motherhood.

Bash had been ten days late. The next baby was even later. We'd gone to stay with Toppet and Nigel in Yorkshire while Toby was directing a play at the Georgian Theatre, Richmond, and it had been arranged for me to go into a nursing home near York. The first night came and went and the baby was now three weeks overdue, which would certainly not be allowed now. Toby reluctantly had to leave me for theatre work in London. A few days after his departure, Francesca Kate Tomlin, Fran, was born, on 4 October 1965, St Francis Day. I now moved into a world of sleepless nights and au pairs. We were lucky with the first au pair, Henny Wordsworth, who was taking a year out before starting training as a nurse. Henny was not only a lovely person who quickly became a friend, but also quite brilliant with small children. Bash, no longer placid, was what our cleaning lady called 'a handful' and Fran, unlike her brother, cried almost continually during the first six months, so life was understandably fraught.

Toby at this time was detached from these family problems. Prospect Theatre was steadily building a reputation as an outstanding touring company, and he was hardly at home. He also took on directing television plays, which paid better and gave us a little more financial stability. I appeared in two of these plays. In one of them I played a nun, the habit disguising the fact I was six months pregnant. Athene Seyler, who was the Mother Superior, joked she looked more pregnant than I did. However, it was after appearing in these plays I decided my acting career, such as it had been, was over. It was too difficult to combine with bringing up small children, virtually on my own. This decision left me restless, longing for something creative to do. It was then Toby threw out the idea I should start to write biographical dramas, combining my love of theatre with my love of biography. Without realising it, he had found me my Valerie Hobson 'gimmick', and for the next thirty years these biographical dramas dominated my professional life.

Our third child, Sasha Corinna Jane, arrived on 6 February 1967 and was the most punctual of all the children. The promptness of her arrival may have been down to the fact a few days before she was due, I had developed a bad case of mumps, which was not only painful but meant with the swelling in my throat and in my belly, I now resembled a large pear. When I went into labour, none of the male medical staff would come near me because of the mumps, so I was put into a side room in Queen Charlotte's, attended by a wonderful midwife who stayed with me until Sash arrived. Despite my high temperature it was the easiest and calmest of all the births. Toby was unusually at home for this one but not with me. While I was in the throes, he paced around the kitchen, knocking back brandies, with poor Henny trying to calm him.

Once again, with the fast-growing family, we made the decision to move to a larger house and Toby found one in the most unusual way. While looking for TV locations, he visited a house in Spencer Park on Wandsworth Common. The large Victorian houses around Spencer Park were a hidden gem. Not only did some of them look out onto the Common, but they also had large walled gardens which led into five acres of private park, with rose gardens and a tennis court. The old couple in the house Toby was looking at informed him they longed to downsize and would be happy to sell. Toby, ever impulsive, put in an offer on the spot. I only saw the house after it had been purchased and was immediately daunted by the amount of work required. The place needed complete renovation. With three children under three, it seemed like the proverbial mountain to climb. Toby again gave me complete freedom to do what I liked, and once more I immersed myself in wallpapers and paint. The plumbing and electrics were as Edwardian as the décor and it took the workmen months to complete, but we finally moved in. The week that followed was freezing cold, and this nearly proved fatal. The gas central heating was turned on for the first time, but the outlet for the fumes had frozen over and we very nearly died from carbon monoxide poisoning. The fact we didn't was mainly due to Sash. She was in a cot in our room, and we were awoken by her making weird choking noises. Toby went to check on the other children and both were obviously woozy. He laid them out on our bed and called for an ambulance. The ambulance men immediately realised what was wrong and the boiler was turned off. Our bedroom had come off lightly because Toby always insisted on the window being wide open whatever the weather. By the time we were on our way to the hospital the children had recovered, Bash declaring he could hear bells, as we were blue-lighted to A & E. We had been lucky. A few months after this, I had a miscarriage, so there was a larger gap of two and a half years.

Joshua David Nathaniel arrived in 1969. Josh was the largest of the babies, almost ten pounds. He arrived too fast, and I had a haemorrhage. I was sternly told I should have no more pregnancies. I was in no state to make a decision, so it was made for me, and I had my tubes tied. Our family was now complete. We were six, plus a dog and an au pair. We'd also acquired three houses. Not only did we have Spencer Park, but my mother had given me the Windlass, her cottage in Port Isaac. The third house came about before Josh was born, through a reunion with Enrique Arias, who, true to his word, had started an artistic colony in the primitive Moorish village of Mojacar, near Alicante in Southern Spain. I introduced Enrique to Toby, who became excited with the idea of Mojacar, and on impulse agreed to buy a plot and have a house built. I think he even managed to persuade Ma to lend him half the money. Taking on the building of a new house in a foreign country seemed like madness to me, but Toby was determined. He travelled out to Spain with a suitcase full of property pesetas, which he nearly mislaid when changing trains, and met up with a builder with the wonderful name of Juan Garcia Flores, and the work began. Upon completion, Toby declared he would take three months away from the Prospect Company, while he worked on an adaptation of *A Room with a View* for a production when he returned.

We now decamped to Spain. I imagine it was a bit like the Durrells arriving on Corfu. Sash was only six weeks old, and I thought too young to travel, but Toby overruled any arguments against his plan. We loaded up the car, a large one by now, with Toby, me, the three children, and Henny.

Because of the mumps, I hadn't been able to feed Sash, so we took with us a large supply of Carnation Milk, plus bottles and a steriliser. The journey began with the car ferry to Bilboa, and then we embarked on the long, hot journey across Spain and down to Murcia. Mojacar was still a work in progress, with few buildings and only one shop. The village was perched high up on top of a very steep hill rising from the coast and all the supplies were brought up by donkeys. (It is now a popular tourist spot, with a main road, bars and hotels.) Enrique occupied the Castillo at the top, with the luxury of a swimming pool. Our house had no luxuries and consisted of three basic bedrooms, a large living room where the cooking was also done, a bathroom and a sun terrace. My mother flew out, ostensibly to help with Sash as she thought I would be frail after the birth and the mumps. It was kind of her, but I was fine and knew it would not take her long to point out the primitive conditions. As if to prove her point, when it became known I wasn't breast-feeding, an aged crone arrived from the village to offer her services as a wet nurse. When this was explained to me, I reacted with horror and Toby politely declined her offer.

Despite these initial problems, I remember this as a very happy time. We ate simply, with plenty of fresh fish and vegetables, although Ma had a running argument with Toby about peeling the tomatoes and was nervous about germs generally. Wine was cheap and in plentiful supply and so was the local brandy, which Toby would slosh into the coffee. The views from the terrace were spectacular, looking out across the plains and far below to the sea. In the daytime, we often played tracks from the Beatles and when I hear 'Good Day Sunshine', it immediately takes me back to this time. Somewhat in contrast, Ma started a tradition of putting on the Allegri *Miserere* every evening, and as the sun set, the sound of the choirboy hitting that top C would echo across the valley towards the mountains, in a moment of pure magic.

Unexpectedly, we had some social life as well. We made friends with another English family, the Allens, who had three children, the youngest, David, a bit younger than Bash. Pat Allen was a Concorde pilot, and his wife Penny, an art collector and a painter herself. They also had a house, but some distance from the village and involving a long hot walk. Occasionally we would be invited up to the Castillo. Enrique introduced us to his wife, Mary, an American, who was strangely awkward and plain, an unexpected choice for the fastidious Enrique. They made an odd couple, with little show of affection. Enrique treated Mary in a detached way, often hardly hiding his irritation. There was also a small daughter, I think Mary's, who they referred to as 'Pig'. I like most children, but poor Pig had little to recommend her, being obese, always whining and demanding continual attention. Enrique showed absolutely no interest in the child and often asked for her removal. These visits were awkward, and I felt uncomfortable. Enrique openly flirted with me, paying continual compliments. In the end I gave up going to the Castillo except on the odd occasion when Toby could be persuaded to come with me.

We had only been in Spain a month when I developed a fever. Toby insisted on calling in the local doctor, who proceeded to prescribe large doses of laxatives. Our builder Juan told me this was the cure the doctor had for everything. I certainly made a quick recovery, but by this time Ma was adamant it was not a healthy place for such a young baby, and I was reluctantly persuaded to let her take Sasha, still only ten weeks, back to England to be looked after by Toby's Aunt Prue, sister of Felicity. Prue had a large house in Surrey, where her daughter and grandchildren lived and said she would be happy to look after Sash until our return. We had a hair-raising drive to the airport with bad traffic in Madrid and very nearly missed the plane. I felt anxious about the stress this journey would put on Ma and was upset at being parted from Sash, but at the time there seemed to be no other solution. Making decisions as a parent is always a fraught business. Very few parents emerge unscathed by the experience, which is a mildly comforting thought. Children always vow not to make the same mistakes as their parents, but it is never straightforward. Circumstances occur that make compromises inevitable, and these compromises nearly always turn out to be unsatisfactory, and sometimes disastrous. You can only look back with a sigh, and say you did your best at the time.

Despite the upheavals and all the travelling around, I think our four children had a happy childhood, at least until they reached their teenage years, when all our lives became more turbulent and unsettled.

After the Spanish adventure we returned to the Spencer Park house, but our lives were soon turned upside down again. John Schlesinger, the brilliant film director and friend of Toby's, asked if he could use our house as a location for his next film, *Sunday Bloody Sunday*. He also wanted to have our children in the film, but I adamantly turned down this request. The house I gave a reluctant yes, but not the children. Toby was delighted by this idea, as a large amount of structural work would be done on the house which we could never have afforded. The kitchen now moved from the lower ground floor and became part of a huge L-shaped room with all the walls on the ground floor being knocked through. The downside of the filming was that it took much longer than we'd originally been told, and we were out of the house for six months. During school time we camped with Felicity and B in their flat. Three small children (Josh not yet born), plus an adult (Toby was away for most of this time), meant that we were extremely cramped, and a great deal of temperament flew around. I was relieved when we could escape to Cornwall for the holidays. John wrote to Toby, 'Lovely house, terrible film.' He was wrong about that. It won five BAFTAs and four Oscars, including best director and best film. We were finally allowed back, but a good deal of re-organisation and re-decoration was now needed. The lower ground floor became a self-contained flat which was to prove very useful. In the kitchen area of the

L-shaped room, we put a long refectory table with pews on either side, so we could seat up to twenty people. The whole space proved ideal for family living and the entertaining and large parties which were to follow.

Spencer Park turned out to be a perfect place for us to live. The children would arrive back from school and immediately go out into the garden and park. It was perfectly safe, and they had five acres in which to roam. This occasionally proved a problem when parents arrived to collect their children and it would take a while to locate them. Toby advised me to have a bottle of sherry on hand to keep the parents happy until their offspring could be found.

Other families now started to move into the houses around Spencer Park, happily with children the same age as ours. We were in number 5. The Allens moved into number

JM at Spencer Park

8. Max Hastings and his wife Elizabeth Beresford took over number 3, after the previous owner, the actor James Fox, had left London for Hollywood. One night Elizabeth visited us, hugely excited about an idea she'd had for a children's book, which was to be about furry animals with peculiar names, wandering around Wimbledon Common collecting litter. After she left, I remember remarking to Toby I didn't think that idea had much future. How wrong I was. The Wombles, both the book and television series, were a huge success. A year later, Elizabeth turned up on the doorstep with a giant Womble for the children, and soon after, she left Spencer Park to become a tax exile in the Channel Islands.

On the other side of the park were the Alexander family with their three children. Michael was a high-flier in the Foreign Office and later picked up several ambassadorial posts and a knighthood. Our greatest friends were the Patricks at number 2. Victor Patrick was a journalist and a wonderfully Rabelaisian character. He and Toby shared a great love of wine. One weekend, Victor organised a bottling session and a huge barrel arrived in his garage. The bottling took a whole day, all the families took part, and many glasses of wine were consumed. Few adults were left standing by the end. Victor's wife Beth was quite lovely, with a warm and calm personality, a doting mother, a great cook and always welcoming. Our two families spent endless time in her kitchen being fed wonderful meals, which were charmingly never on time. There were four Patrick children, three boys and a daughter, Anna, who became the special friend of Sash. With many of the children at the same schools we would share the school run, a task which could sometimes prove stressful. Often, I had six children crammed into my Mini-Moke. They all loved the Mini-Moke. It really wasn't a safe vehicle with so many and would never be allowed now. There were no seat belts and the kids all just clung onto the bars at the side. On one occasion a giant moth appeared, and the children started leaping about trying to bat it away from me. I had a horror of large flapping things like bats, birds, and yes, large moths. At one point the moth banged into me, causing me to swerve and bring the Moke to a swift halt. A passing policemen stopped by the car. I politely unzipped the side and he put his head in. The children were all shouting, trying to explain about the moth, at which point the creature made its escape. I apologised and the poor policeman seemed to be rendered speechless. He finally told me to drive on more carefully, zipped the side back and made a quick exit.

Another nearby neighbour was Timothy West and his wife Prunella Scales, who had moved into a house on Wandsworth Common Northside, just at the end of our road. They had two children – Sam, the same age as Fran, and Joe, the same age as Josh – and the children often spent time with us when Tim and Pru were both working. One Christmas morning, Toby had taken the children for a walk in Richmond Park, leaving me to enjoy a bubble bath before the main activities of the day began. Suddenly, a small face peered round the bathroom door. It was Joe, then about five. He said in his Eeyore voice, 'Hello,' and went on to explain everyone at his house was sleeping so he'd decided to visit us. My long soak abruptly ended, I sent Joe downstairs while I dressed, then rang Tim and Pru, who weren't the least worried and said that they were quite happy for us to keep him with us, as they hadn't yet surfaced. He remained in our house until lunchtime, when we were due at the Patricks and Toby delivered him back.

Life in Spencer Park was great for adults and children alike, with endless social events, games of tennis, dinner parties, lunches in the gardens, and a spectacular annual bonfire night party. As Toby said, 'It was a perfect rondeau of delights.' One evening, there was a dinner party at the Allens, and among the guests was the director of the distinguished American publishing house, William Morrow & Company. Inevitably, the discussion revolved around books and authors. Somehow, I must have made an impression, because a few days later I was offered the job of editorial scout. Although the job was to scout out new English authors and manuscripts for the American market, it was felt I should visit Morrow's in New York first and meet the team. The job was daunting. I'd never worked in publishing, but I decided it was an exciting opportunity I couldn't turn down and set off for New York. Everyone at Morrow's was kind and welcoming. I was introduced to all the editors, and one of them, Joni Evans, was assigned to work closely with me after my return to England. I was also entertained nightly with dinners. It was at one of these a dramatic incident occurred.

During the meal, my hostess left the table to take a call and returned ashen-faced. She explained she'd just received news Martin Luther King had been assassinated and for my own safety was ordering a car to take me back to my apartment in Kipps Bay Plaza, by the United Nations Building, the other end of Manhattan. She knew that after this event the black population would be out on the streets and extremely angry. The long drive took me through Harlem and for this reason she had thoughtfully organised a black driver. It was just as well. By the time we reached Harlem, the news of the assassination was out, and the streets were thronged with an angry mob who banged on the taxi windows. I cowered in the back of the cab, trying to remain as hidden as possible. I think the fact I had a black driver saved me that night and I will always be grateful for her prompt action.

My time with Morrow's was brief. We parted six months later, mainly because I had become pregnant again and with three small children as well, I just couldn't give the job the time it required, but I was also aware, despite Joni's help, I wasn't really cut out for this type of work. Looking back, I don't think I was particularly good at the job, but I did meet some interesting writers and publishers. Soon after this, another of Penny Allen's connections offered me a project. Her cousin Philip Adeane had a girlfriend who was a photographer, and they wanted to organise an article about Mojacar, using her pictures, but they needed someone to write the text. Philip asked if I would be interested, explaining it was all to be done in a three-day turnaround and on a shoestring budget and therefore no fee, just expenses. Even so, I was keen to go and Toby, busy with rehearsals, rather reluctantly agreed. As I remember, the whole project was totally disorganised, but somehow, we managed to finish in the three days and prepared to return home. At this juncture, Philip and his girlfriend decided to extend their stay in Spain. They dropped me at the airport, Philip assuring me my ticket had been arranged and left at the airline desk. It wasn't. I was stranded, without enough money to pay for another ticket and I quickly gave way to despair. Toby was about to go on tour, and I knew he would be furious if he had to delay. Panic set in, and I sat sobbing on my suitcase. At that moment a tall, elegant man, unmistakeably English, stopped and asked me if I needed help. I poured out my story, assuring him my husband would be meeting me at the airport and would repay him at once, if he could just get me on the plane. Without more ado, he purchased a ticket. To my alarm, I noticed it was first class. I stuttered I only needed economy. He smiled, informing me economy was full, but I only need repay him for the economy fare. As we chatted on the plane, I found out he was the managing director of Elliot Shoes. I told him, quite truthfully, his shoe shop in the King's Road was one of my favourite haunts. I will always be grateful for his rescue act, although the whole incident did seem like something out of a Nancy Mitford novel.

These occasional projects did relieve the tedium of

domestic life when I was on my own in Spencer Park. Being with the children I loved, but it was the general minutiae of running the house I found stiflingly boring. Holidays and half terms were generally spent in Port Isaac, where I was happiest. Toby was not often with us for these, and the long journeys were stressful, especially if the car broke down, which ours frequently did. Managing four young children and the animals – we now had two dogs and a cat – without, in those days, a mobile to get help, often turned into a nerve-racking situation, but somehow, we always eventually made it. Port Isaac then was not the fashionable tourist spot it is today. The trendy North Cornwall places were then Rock, Trebetherick, and Polzeath a few miles away. Port Isaac was still a small fishing village, and there were few second homes. One of these was owned by my great friend Mike Thomas, now married to Jane. They had two children, Emily and Archie, who quickly became part of the gang. Our cottage, a short walk from the beach, was opposite the home of Harold Brown, a fisherman, his wife Joanna, and their three children, Julian, John and Jeremy (who later became part of the famous sea shanty singing group Fisherman's Friends). Harold had an uncle, Nibbs, a retired fisherman and wicked old reprobate, who stood on the Platt all day. Once, when I walked past him, he said with a twinkle, 'Fancy a bit of moonlight bathing tonight?' There was really no answer to this.

We had no television in the cottage, but we did have a gramophone and each evening after bath time and hair washing, a long process removing the seaweed, sand, and general debris they had acquired during the day, we would sit round the fire listening to music, stories, and poetry on our many LPs. During the day, it felt safe to let the children roam around without adult supervision.

Immediately after breakfast they left for the beach, kitted out with life jackets and the firm instruction they were not allowed more than two pairs of wet jeans a day. Bash, the eldest, was told to return and tell me if there was any sort of trouble or crisis. Once, he returned in the evening to tell me there had been a crisis, but, as he proudly informed me, he had coped. His description sounded alarming. Josh, who seemed to have no fear, was in his very small rubber dinghy happily paddling around the bay, when someone playing ducks and drakes on the shoreline had punctured his dinghy with a sharp stone and it quickly sank. Josh in his life jacket flapped around in the water, completely unworried, shouting out 'Jaws!' Bash told me he was preparing to go in to bring him back to shore, but Harold on his boat had seen him and fished him out with an oar. This all sounds like a shocking lack of parental responsibility and of course wouldn't be countenanced today, but looking back, I am glad they had this freedom without adults hovering over them, something no longer experienced by the young. My children's daily disappearance to the beach also meant I could spend time writing, and Bash stuck a notice on the door which read 'Do not disturb. Jenius at work' and this seemed to have an effect, because I was generally left in peace. The great event of the week was when the St Breward Brass Band came for a concert on the Platt. This would finish with the band walking up to the top of the village and back, playing 'The Floral Dance', with everyone dancing along behind. On this occasion the children were allowed to buy fish and chips. Bash always managed to wangle far too much money out of me, and only later did I find out he was feeding half the children in the village.

On a few occasions, Toby and I would be away together when I joined him on various theatre tours. Felicity and B would act *in loco parentis* during these times, and we always had various au pairs and kind friends who helped. During the early Spencer Park years Toby was absent so much that Sash, then aged four, found him coming through the front door and inquired sternly, 'Who are you?' But when Toby was around, the household pace became more frenetic. There were many summer parties when Toby would invite the whole theatre company back to have Sunday lunch. This meant there were usually around sixty people to feed, and we developed a formula. The day before, I would roast up to a dozen chickens and Toby would organise French bread and selections of cheeses. On the actual day, he would go off early to Covent Garden to get fresh salad and fruit, and then all the food would be laid out on our long refectory table. Guests just helped themselves and then wandered out into the garden and park. Some played tennis and the resulting efforts of the inebriated players were hilarious. If the weather was hot, Toby would put the wine in a tin bath piled up as a pyramid with a cold-water hose running over the bottles.

These parties became famous, but even so, I had a slight sense of unease. It was certainly an idyll, but inevitably, the strain of living at such a frantic pace took its toll, and the cracks were beginning to show. There were also problems in my relationship with Toby, which sadly we never had the time to sort out. This lack of discussion had a profound effect on the future of our marriage.

Chapter Seven

A MANIC DECADE OF ACTIVITY

BY THE END of the 'sixties Toby had achieved another West End transfer with *The Beggar's Opera*. It was a major success, starting at the Edinburgh Festival and then brought into London. After the theatre season finished, it was televised, and a recording was made. The children knew all the songs by heart and would sing them endlessly on long car journeys. The lead was played by the wonderful Jan Waters, one of the few actresses who combined acting skills with a superb singing voice. Toby used her in many productions, and she became one of my greatest friends. This production was the start of a decade of successful productions for Toby. There was no let-up in the pace, and inevitably it affected his health. He had a major operation for a twisted gut, and this was followed by bouts of pneumonia. He was not an easy patient. There was one winter when everybody seemed to be ill except me, but this was unusual. Thankfully, in general the children were healthy, and I only had to concentrate on keeping Toby going.

The 'seventies took off with speed. The Edinburgh Festival became an annual summer event, with Prospect productions the main contributor. The success of *The Beggar's Opera* was quickly followed by others, and the greatest of these was the joint productions of *Edward II* and *Richard II*, with Ian McKellen brilliantly playing both roles. Not for the first time, Toby found himself in trouble. There were those in Edinburgh, including a couple of councillors, who objected to the homosexual kiss between Edward and his favourite, Gaveston, and their complaints were made loud and clear both on TV and in the newspapers. However, their objections were drowned out by the huge success of the two productions. Receiving rave reviews, the shows quickly transferred to London, first to the Mermaid Theatre and then to the Piccadilly Theatre for a sell-out season. The clamour for seats was so great Toby and I were constantly being rung by celebrities, even Hollywood film stars, to beg for house seats. Amid all this success, Toby was having another bout of pneumonia, and they even had oxygen standing by in the theatre while he was rehearsing. After the first night we were booked into the Piccadilly Hotel opposite the theatre. I was told this hotel had rather a dubious reputation and as we were going up in the lift, we saw a large notice saying, 'Gang bang tonight in Room 217!' This

JM in Paris

was our room! As Toby coughed his way through the door he said grimly, 'Fat chance!'

One of the perks for me during these years was joining Toby for productions abroad. In 1971, I went out to Rome for Ian McKellen's *Hamlet*. I admire Ian hugely as an actor, but I think he would be the first to admit this Hamlet wasn't his greatest performance. Luckily, it didn't seem to matter, as the Italian audience received the production with rapture and the ovation at the end was both ecstatic and long. Unlike some leading actors, Ian is superb at taking curtain calls, bowing to every section of the audience. The more he bowed, the more they clapped and cheered, so we left the theatre feeling it had gone well. Toby continued to feel glum about the production, but we were given generous hospitality, which he greatly enjoyed. Raf Vallone invited us to supper, and he took me into the kitchen to give me a lesson in cooking pasta. We finished the meal with large quantities of Aqua Vita, which is maybe why Raf told me I reminded him of Anna Magnani. A few days later, the whole company was invited out to lunch at Franco Zeffirelli's villa, which turned out to be a very Bacchanalian affair, and consequently the performance that night was somewhat ragged.

It was during these years Toby started to put on my biographical plays. One of the great assets for me was being able to pick leading actors from the Prospect Company to play the roles. The first of these shows was based on the life of Lord Byron, with the poet played by Derek Jacobi. This started a formula for these chamber works, which worked well, using two to four players, always with a musician or musicians, period costumes and a simple set. Because the material was drawn from letters, diaries, and poems, it made sense for the actors to use scripts, disguised as journals. This also meant these productions needed minimal rehearsal and were ideal for single performances, special occasions, charity events and theatre festivals. Toby would let me know he wanted a new chamber entertainment, and I would choose the subject and set about it. One of the earliest of these was *The Grand Tour*, an account of those 18th and 19th English travellers who went around Europe discovering the cultural wonders. It wasn't just aristocrats who made the tour but poets and writers as well, so I had a wealth of material to choose from, including the diaries and journals of Byron, Shelley, Keats, Edward Gibbon, Boswell, Johnson, Lady Mary Wortley Montague, and many others. I was presented with a wonderful cast of four: Derek Jacobi, Timothy West, Julian Glover and Isla Blair, another actress with a superb singing voice. Between them, they played all the roles, switching characters with ease. There were piano solos and singing as well. It turned out to be a huge success and received a rave review from Harold Hobson, no less, in *The Sunday Times*: 'a selection of travellers' tales put together with consummate dramatic sensibility by Jane McCulloch and superlatively directed by Toby Robertson.'

Derek Jacobi and Timothy West in The Grand Tour, *1973 (photo: Chris Davies)*

The actors received equally impressive comments, especially Derek. When he delivered Byron's final poem, 'So we'll go no more a-roving so late into the night.' Harold Hobson called it 'a moment of genius.'

The Edinburgh Festival years were quite wonderful, if demanding, for both of us. For most of the 'seventies, Toby and Prospect were responsible for the main drama contribution, with two plays, plus one of my chamber pieces. The family would be installed in a large house, and we would decamp for the duration. Toby usually went on ahead, and I would make the drive from Cornwall to Edinburgh, making a break halfway to spend a night with Toppet and Nigel at Skipwith. These were long drives, and with four children, an au pair and three animals in the car, it often proved an ordeal, and a great relief when we finally made it. Toby always managed to find wonderful houses to rent. One of them had a croquet lawn, and the children would take on members of the company at the game. Added to this, there were endless parties and Festival receptions. The productions overall were a success. Toby used the music of the brilliant Carl Davis and sets and costumes by the talented Robin Archer, and he built up a company of terrific actors. They were heady days.

Back in London the pace didn't slacken either, both in our work and social life. One of the most extraordinary events of my life, came from meeting Lord and Lady Adeane, relations of Penny Allen. Michael Adeane was Private Secretary to the Queen. He and his wife Helen were quite charming and, following our first introduction, we saw a great deal of them. When the Duke of Edinburgh went away on a long tour, Michael tried to arrange evenings which would amuse the Queen. One of these was to see a play at the RSC, who were performing at the Aldwych Theatre. The production chosen was *London Assurance*, a nineteenth-century comedy. Michael and Helen decided to make up a supper party for this occasion, and because we were a thespian couple, invited us to join them. This was a daunting invitation. There were only to be six of us, as PM Edward Heath was also invited. We were told to arrive at St James's Palace at six for cocktails. I asked Helen what I should wear and was told a cocktail dress would be fine. As my entire wardrobe was either jeans, or exotic dresses from Biba for first nights, I didn't exactly own a cocktail dress, so I borrowed one from a friend. Toby insisted on my wearing a set of Givenchy jewellery he had previously given me. They were earrings and a matching necklace in green and yellow glass with enamel leaves and flowers. Striking and beautiful, it was extremely heavy, and I almost immediately regretted it. It was a cold night, so I found a wool wrap for when we travelled to the theatre.

The first part of the evening with drinks passed off smoothly enough. The Queen asked Toby if the play was long. I'm not sure she was entirely looking forward to it. He assured her it wasn't long, adding encouragingly there were plenty of references to foxhunting. When we were told it was time to leave, the Queen and Helen were handed their fur coats, and I was given my rather inadequate wool shawl. The females of the party were shown to one car; the men travelled in the other. The Queen, noticing my lack of a fur coat, put a rug over my knees and firmly tucked me in. I had to pinch myself this was the Queen of England looking after me. 'Such a concrete jungle,' she remarked as we sped through London. On arriving at the theatre, I found to my horror, we were sitting in the middle of the stalls and not in a box, as I had hoped. There was clapping as we walked in, and I saw one or two people I knew, but did not dare make contact. I was sat on one side of the Queen, Edward Heath on the other. We did not move in the interval but sat making polite and stilted conversation. I can't remember if I enjoyed the play, I just know I was relieved when it was over and we left the theatre, once more to applause.

Back at St James's Palace, we were shown to the dining room. I think it was then the enormity of the occasion hit me. It may have been that, plus the heaviness of my jewellery, or even the rather disgusting brown Windsor soup, but I suddenly started to feel faint and knew I needed to leave the room. But how? Should I go out backwards? I muttered, 'Excuse me, Ma'am,' and then proceeded, in a series of pirouettes, towards the door, where I was helped outside by the butler. I sat on the stairs, wondering what to do next. The Adeanes' son Edward came up from below and asked me if I was alright. I told him I'd felt a bit unwell. He was sympathetic and said it was probably the soup and told me the next two courses would be better. So, I bravely returned. The Queen acknowledged my return with a nod, and I survived the rest of the meal. Helen then gave the signal for the ladies to retire, and I followed her and the Queen into the drawing room, where a tray was laid out for coffee. Helen went to pour and noticed that something was missing from the tray and, to my alarm, excused herself and left the room. I was left alone with the Queen of England. There then followed the most extraordinary conversation.

She gave me a sympathetic smile and asked, 'Are you feeling better, old thing?'

'Yes, Ma'am, thank you Ma'am.' I felt an explanation was needed here and a sudden inspiration came to me. The following week, I had booked Toby and I to go on a cheap bargain cruise, so I added, 'I think it may have been the jabs Ma'am, for our holiday. We are going on a cruise next week.'

The Queen looked interested. 'Oh,' she said, 'whose yacht?' I had no answer to this, and she must have seen my embarrassment and quickly asked, 'Where in London do you live?'

Another dilemma. I was only too aware that at that time Wandsworth wasn't a fashionable or well-known part of London, so I said, 'Putney, Ma'am.'

There was a long pause and then she said, 'Oh yes. We pass there on our way to Windsor.'

There was another pause and then she added, 'I understand you have children. What ages are they?'

I was on safer ground here, and I quickly reeled off their ages. She smiled and said, 'Your two older children are the same age as Andrew and Edward. You must bring them over for tea sometime.'

To my relief, Helen now returned, soon followed by the men. Edward Heath made his apologies and said he had to get back to the House, and the five of us were left to our coffee. It was now quite late, after eleven. The Queen, sitting on the sofa, suddenly tucked her feet under her skirt and proceeded to tell what I would term 'touring stories', many of them very funny, especially when it came to Prince Philip's reactions to foreign receptions and unexpected rituals. A man came in to say the car was waiting to take the Queen back to Buckingham Palace, but she waved him away. I don't know whether it was my earlier behaviour which had made her more relaxed, but she was certainly enjoying herself. When she finally left, Michael returned to the room, and both he and Helen expressed their astonishment, saying they hadn't seen the Queen enjoy herself so much for a long time.

There was a postscript to this story. The following day, Bash, aged seven, announced at school lunch, 'My mother went to dinner with the Queen last night.'

Miss Whitehead, the formidable headmistress of Hurlingham School, looked at him and said severely, 'Now Sebastian, we don't tell lies, do we?' He came home very indignant. I often think of that memorable night and how kind the Queen had been to me. She saw I was nervous and did her utmost to make me feel at ease. A wonderful and great lady.

Another incident happened at this time, and it was at one of the Awards Shows we attended.

This was at the Evening Standard Awards being held at lunchtime in the Savoy Theatre. Toby, who was in rehearsal, agreed to meet me at the entrance. I was in my Mini-Moke, and knew I was running late, so when a flunkey in the car park took one look at the Moke and told me there was no room for me to park, I was filled with panic. At that moment, a white Rolls Royce drew up beside me, and I saw the occupant was Richard Burton, who was obviously destined for the same event. I said to the car park attendant, 'I'm with him,' meaning I was also going to the Awards. Richard had got out of his car, and the attendant said suspiciously, 'Do you know this lady, sir?'

Richard looked at me and must have seen my desperate and pleading expression. To my great relief he nodded. 'Yes, I do,' he told the attendant. I was grudgingly allowed to park the Moke next to his Rolls. As we walked towards the foyer, I thanked him and explained I was the wife of Toby Robertson, whom he did know. The camera bulbs flashed, and Toby looked astonished, seeing me on the arm of Richard Burton.

'Your wife, I believe,' Richard said, as he delivered me. I again thanked him for saving me, and he said it was a pleasure. Richard Burton had been one of my great heroes since seeing him at Stratford as a child, so I was delighted to finally meet him in person, even in such odd circumstances.

The 'seventies progressed, with both of us working flat out. On the surface it must have looked perfect: lovely houses, four beautiful children and an amazingly extravagant lifestyle, but all this covered a mass of problems we were just too busy to deal with. The storm clouds were gathering, and it was inevitable the problems would eventually come to a head. They finally did, during one of the Prospect tours to Russia, then the USSR. The actual crunch moment arrived, unbelievably, in the middle of Red Square, Moscow.

JM with Fran and Sasha

Chapter Eight
RUSSIA AND THE AFTERMATH

THE TRIP TO Russia seemed doomed from the start. Even my flight out to Moscow was beset with problems. Toby was already there, having opened two of the plays, but I was set to join him for the first performance of *The Lunatic, the Lover and the Poet*, my play about Lord Byron. For some reason I didn't fly direct but was due to go on Finnair to Helsinki and the rest of the journey by Aeroflot.

When I arrived in Helsinki, to my great alarm I found all Aeroflot flights to Moscow had been cancelled until the following morning. This was long before mobiles. I had little money on me, not thinking I would need it, and this was also before credit cards. With the money I had, I rang the British Embassy, but being a Saturday, I was told there was nobody to speak to me. Apparently, the person I needed was on the tennis court. I was stranded and sat feeling miserable and abandoned.

One of the Finnair air hostesses must have noticed my dejected state and asked me what was wrong. I relayed what had happened and she offered help. Her pilot boyfriend had a room in Billet 4, just off the runway, and he wasn't using it that night, so at least I could have a bed. I thanked her, took directions, and set off for Billet 4. When I neared the appointed room, there was a party in full swing. I was invited to join and made very welcome. Unsurprisingly, I remember little about that night, except a large amount of vodka was consumed. The next morning, rather the worse for wear, I staggered back down the runway and boarded my flight for Moscow. Meanwhile, my disappearance was causing great alarm, with everyone trying to find me. The British Embassy kept sending people to Moscow airport in case I was on a different flight. Toby rang my parents to see if they knew anything or if I had contacted them. They had no news, and my father said laconically, 'It would appear Jane has disappeared into Finnair.' When I finally made my appearance there was a committee of officials relieved to see me. However, Toby was not so pleased and seemed to have no sympathy for my ordeal, merely pointing out that I had caused everyone a great deal of inconvenience, which I thought most unfair. There was little time for explanations as I had to get to the theatre in time for the first performance of the Byron play. I sat next to the British Ambassador and spent most of the evening in a daze, trying to keep awake. At the end, there was thunderous applause amid shouts of 'Arthur, Arthur!' I turned to the Ambassador and said, 'Who is Arthur?'

He smiled and said, 'That is you, my dear. They are shouting, "Author!" I think you had better get up on the stage and take a bow.' So, I did. And the cheering was immense, and a few gladioli were thrown at my feet. The whole thing seemed unreal. I remained on a high for at least a day. After that, I was brought down to earth in the strangest way, and I was finally forced to face the fact there was a real problem in our marriage.

Since the birth of Josh, our sex life had dwindled to being non-existent. I tried to put this down to Toby's constant bouts of ill-health and pressure of work. He always treated me with great affection, even pride, and showered me with presents, including jewellery, but this wasn't enough, and I felt unhappy and frustrated. I was also aware there was a certain amount of gossip about Toby in the company but tried to ignore it. However, in Moscow it was impossible to do this any longer.

We had just marched past Lenin's body, rather a macabre sight, except for the fact that someone pointed out he resembled Timothy West, and we had to stifle our mirth. These were the days of the Iron Curtain, and with the KGB always present, we had to be on our best behaviour. We emerged into Red Square, and at that point I was suddenly accosted by one of the leading actors, who angrily asked me if I realised Toby was having an affair with his boyfriend. He was shouting, and everyone could hear. Feeling hot and humiliated, I returned to the hotel. Toby hadn't been with us but had soon heard what had occurred. A prolonged and horrible row followed. I hate confrontation, but when I feel I have been wronged I fight my corner. A compromise was reached. We agreed to continue the tour and after that we would sit down and talk things through. Even so, I had to put up with pitying looks from the rest of the company. It was difficult for them to ignore the drama which was obviously taking place.

Putting my private life to one side, two interesting events occurred while we were in Moscow. The first was after a performance of Peter Shaffer's *The Royal Hunt of the Sun*. When the performance was over, I made my way backstage and noticed a small, stocky man standing at the stage door, who I thought I recognised. He introduced himself. To my amazement it was the great cellist Mstislav Rostropovich. He explained he was not allowed backstage, but would I please convey to the company his great admiration and tell them how much he had enjoyed the performance. It seemed totally ridiculous for a man of his stature not to be able to meet the actors, and typical of the USSR and their regime. I asked Rostropovich to wait, and then sped round the dressing rooms telling everybody what had happened. The company responded at once and rushed to the stage door, crowding round the great man. It was a joyous event, but one which landed Toby in trouble. It wasn't the last time he was hauled in by the authorities to express their displeasure.

For one of the performances Toby had invited the Panovs, two of their most famous ballet dancers. But they were under house arrest and were not allowed to attend. Instead, Toby, I, and some of the company went to visit them. These two beautiful dancers were in the smallest space, without anywhere to practise, and only a towel rail to use as a bar. They couldn't have been more welcoming, but it was a painful experience to witness their deprivation.

Despite Toby and the company having caused displeasure, Toby and I, plus Derek Jacobi and Jan Waters, were invited out to meet the Minister of Culture in her dacha. I will refer to her as Olga. She was a quite extraordinary woman, small, with a round face and short brassy coloured hair, almost orange at the roots. Her command of English was extremely good. On arrival, she took us for a walk in the woods, with tall white silver birches looking straight out of a Chekhov set. She proceeded to tell us about her life, full of tragic events. Apparently, her husband had been shot and her sister deported, and her daughter was in prison. This terrible tale continued until we returned to the dacha. Naturally we felt great sympathy for her. She now treated us to potato cakes and shots of vodka. At some point the subject of revolutions came up. She talked with pride of the 1917 Revolution in her country and scornfully remarked the English hadn't had an uprising since the Peasant's Revolt in 1381. She then made a toast, 'To Revolutions!' and we knocked back the vodka. Toby made a return toast and again the vodka shots were drunk. Every time someone made a toast, another vodka shot went down. Tongues were loosened; we felt we could talk quite freely and proceeded to be highly critical of the regime. Olga took it all in, nodding and listening. Her mood veered between the jocular and the melancholic, but when we finally left, we felt we had made a breakthrough in Anglo-Russian relations.

We couldn't have been more wrong. A few weeks later, after our return to England, we were invited to a reception at the Foreign Office, and I was regaling someone attached to the Embassy in Moscow, about our encounter with Olga, and how surprised we had been by her kind hospitality, and what a tragic life she'd had. He immediately started laughing. Not quite the reaction I was expecting. He then told me not only was Olga a Colonel in the KGB but responsible for most of the terrible things which had happened to her family. She was well known for being completely ruthless and had played us cleverly. I left the party thinking that Toby and I were probably now on some Russian blacklist.

The years that followed the Moscow revelations were difficult ones for me. Outwardly, life went on as before, but it was hard at the age of thirty to face a life of celibacy. Toby, now in his mid-forties, had finally decided the direction his sex life was to take. It wasn't that he didn't love me; he assured me he did, and I believed him. But now, with four children, he saw no need for our sex life to continue and, although feeling guilty, expected me to accept this. Looking back, I think he'd been in denial for years, but found it quite impossible to discuss the problem. Strange to think that homosexuality was still such a taboo subject at that time. This was before AIDS and people 'coming out'. For this reason, I realised Toby required it to remain secret and hidden.

My only remedy was to keep myself frenetically busy. This was not difficult. With the four children growing up fast, two houses to run – we no longer had the Spanish house, having lost it over a planning dispute which neither of us had had time to sort out – not to mention the entertaining, travel arrangements and constant demands from Toby,

I was run ragged. The little spare time I had, I spent writing. The Chamber pieces were now proving to be an asset to the company, and Toby was always demanding more. The leading actors also liked the chance to take on virtuosi roles. To add to the Byron and Grand Tour, I now embarked on a piece about the Reverend Sydney Smith, the great nineteenth-century wit and humanitarian, and Timothy West was perfect for the character. Although Sydney Smith was not famous or notorious, *The Smith of Smiths* proved very popular with audiences.

Toby, meanwhile, continued with a spate of highly successful productions. He directed *Ivanov* and *Pericles*, both with Derek Jacobi in the leading roles. I think Derek's Ivanov one of the most compelling stage performances I've ever seen. He was also wonderful as Pericles, but it was the actual production that caused the sensation. Toby was always far ahead of his time, and for this, one of the more difficult of Shakespeare's plays, he set a large part of it in a transvestite brothel, which made a powerful contrast to the saintly Pericles and his long-lost daughter, the pure and virginal Marina. Their reconciliation scene left not a dry eye, and the final chorus of 'New joy wait on you' produced nightly standing ovations and encores. Carl Davis's score throughout was masterly and it is not surprising after Edinburgh, *Pericles* came into London for a sell-out run. Once again, the Edinburgh councillors objected to the production, but Harold Hobson gave it a terrific review, admitting although he didn't much care for transvestite productions, Toby Robertson had overcome his objections with the masterly staging and moving performances.

There was a funny moment during one of the final rehearsals for *Pericles*. We sometimes took the children into rehearsals and at this one Josh, aged about six, was watching. He sat quite absorbed until the long final scene between Pericles and Marina. At this point in the play, the old King needs convincing that Marina is the daughter he thought he'd lost, and the questioning goes on for some time. As the scene continued, Josh became restless, and at Derek's final demand for proof, he lost all patience and loudly burst out, 'He must know her by now!' The actors collapsed with laughter, and the rehearsal ended abruptly.

The British Council now used Prospect as their main touring company, and productions were sent all over the world. *Much Ado About Nothing* with Julian Glover and Sylvia Syms went to South America, but the tours were mainly in Europe. I sometimes joined the company for these. Another *Hamlet*, with Derek Jacobi as the prince, was due to be performed in the courtyard of Elsinore. It was a royal event with the King and Queen of Denmark in attendance. During the afternoon, the storm clouds gathered. With great efficiency, the audience had been provided with plastic macs to wear in the event of rain. The play started and just as Horatio mentioned an eclipse producing dark and fearful events, the heavens opened. Nobody could hear the rest of the scene because of the noise of the audience putting on their plastic macs. By the time the rainwater reached the electric cables, it became too dangerous to continue. The actors were taken from the stage and the performance cancelled. It was performed the following day, but without the grand audience.

Another memorable tour went first to Vienna and then a drive across the Czech border to Bratislava. The contrast was marked. In Vienna we'd enjoyed the open café society. In Bratislava we were firmly back behind the Iron Curtain and secret police were everywhere. We went to visit my mother's great friend Piroshka and her husband George, a distinguished doctor. They had survived the second world war by hiding in the mountains, but just as their lives were getting back to normal, tragedy struck in 1968 when the Prague Spring was crushed by a Soviet-led invasion. Piroshka was nervous and warned us to be discreet, telling us she was being watched by the secret police. Later, when Toby and I went shopping, I happened to be wearing a long leather coat, with fur around the hem and collar and a fur hat. I suppose I must have looked Russian, because some children shouted angrily at me. They threw cans at us and then ran off. It was a show of hatred which was quite disturbing. You could feel this anger everywhere and the power of these feelings was in evidence one evening when we attended a concert. The programme finished with Smetana's *Ma Vlast*, their most patriotic piece of music. As it ended, the whole audience rose to their feet with a massive slow handclap which sounded sinister and menacing and I suddenly became aware the stalls were surrounded by police. The British Council representative ushered us quickly out in case of trouble.

I reported to Ma that Piroshka seemed sad and depressed. My mother had already helped their son leave the country and go to Canada to study medicine. She'd also helped Piroshka's uncle to settle in London, but despite her best endeavours, Piroshka and George refused to leave. They didn't live to see the return to normality, but a couple of years after our visit, they decided they could bear it no longer and took strychnine. Their joint suicide was a terrible shock, but I had witnessed their despair. I'm still filled with sadness when I remember them. It was one of those 'if only' moments. If only they had hung on just a few more years.

In contrast, one of the happiest touring experiences was to Dubrovnik, where we stayed at the Hotel Argentina and spent our days diving off the rocks, sunbathing, drinking cocktails, or exploring the magnificent old town. Toby and Jan Waters spent many happy hours in the Oyster Bar. The plays were being staged in the Revelin Fortress, which required climbing steep steps to reach it. It was a dramatic setting. Toby decided, for the end of *Pericles*, to ask Jan to climb to the very top of the tower to start the powerful anthem 'New joy wait on you.' It was an amazing moment and extremely brave of Jan. If she had missed her footing, it was a long drop down to the sea.

Amid these successes, there were some productions that were not so well received, and less than favourable reviews always plunged Toby into a deep depression. When reviews are great, they make little impression apart from quiet satisfaction, but when the criticism is harsh, it remains with you and can cause endless hurt. There were some critics who became the enemy, especially when the attacks became personal. I sometimes wondered whether reviewers knew what damage they wrought, not just personally but to the whole production. A bad review could make the difference between success and failure, and this had a drastic effect on the box office. For a company like Prospect, operating on tight budgets, the reviews became all important. I dreaded the day after a first night. Toby would sit and read all the papers, ignoring the good reviews and going into rages over the bad ones. This ordeal then had to be faced all over again with the Sunday papers. One huge disappointment during these successful years was his production of *King Lear*, with Timothy West. The audience seemed to like it, but the next day one or two critics went for the jugular and Toby was hit very hard by this.

In 1974, I embarked on my most ambitious project yet, the adaptation for a stage musical of *The Pilgrim's Progress* with a score by Carl Davis. Toby gave his full approval and, unlike my other work, it involved the entire company. I now found I had an aptitude for writing lyrics and loved putting them together using words from the book. Working so closely with a composer was something new to me, but Carl made it both easy and enjoyable. It amused us both that a very Jewish composer should be writing a score for such a very Christian and Puritan book. Putting the Christian aspect to one side, this was a story that had everything necessary for great drama. How could you fail to be moved by a man who gives up everything for his beliefs, struggling against great odds to reach his goal? The ordeals the hero, Christian, must overcome include the Slough of Despond, the fight with the monster Apollyon, the imprisonment by Giant Despair and the nightmare journey through Vanity Fair. When he finally succeeds, it's impossible not to feel relief, uplift, and joy. I witnessed the audience experiencing this at the premiere of the show at the Yvonne Arnaud Theatre in Guildford. A young Brian Cox played Christian and although his singing voice wasn't the greatest, his acting

Brian Cox in The Pilgrim's Progress, *1974*

was superb, and he really made you believe in the hardship and struggle. Despite the success in Guildford, we all agreed there were areas of the show which needed work before it opened at the Edinburgh Festival the following year.

A huge crisis now loomed and one that I had not anticipated. For the first time I was in total disagreement with Toby about the direction the show should take, and this filled me with alarm. He insisted on modernising and changing it to a rock musical. I strongly felt this would diminish the power of the story and it was imperative we remained true to its Bunyan roots. Toby disagreed. I think he saw the potential of the show as a commercial success following the latest trend in musicals like *Godspell*. Consequently, he dismissed my worries and overrode my opinions. He even advertised it as 'A Musical Trip', which gave it drug overtones leaving me feeling very uneasy. A completely new

Pilgrim's Progress

team was now brought in, recasting the show with singers rather than good actors who could sing. Costumes were also redesigned, and I disliked many of the changes, especially Apollyon's. At Guildford he had worn a huge pair of wings which were dramatically menacing. The new costume lost the wings and was just hideous, with a set of udders down the front, meaningless and just ugly. Apollyon should have looked magnificent, in contrast to the drably dressed Puritan, to make their fight more intense. But mine was a small voice, and Toby, at his most obstinate, refused to listen. This was a shock and, more than anything else, it led me to lose further faith in our relationship. He was crushing my artistic abilities, refusing to listen or compromise in any way. Carl was also unhappy, saying he was quite unable to adapt his music to the rock score now demanded. As a solution, he told Toby he knew of a brilliant young musician who could adapt his music, and Toby readily agreed to bring him onto the team. And this, ironically, is how I met Donald Fraser, and my life took yet another direction.

Chapter Nine
A MOMENTOUS MEETING

MY FIRST ENCOUNTER with Donald Fraser was one of those rare moments that I imagine only happens once in a lifetime, if that. Feeling depressed and apprehensive, I'd arrived early for the first day of rehearsals for the new version of *Pilgrim*, and without much enthusiasm was taken over to meet the latest addition to the team, the 'rock composer', Donald Fraser. We shook hands and it was at this moment something extraordinary happened. I can only say it was like being hit by a thunderbolt. I could hardly breathe. It may sound the stuff of romantic novels, but my heart was definitely beating faster. But it was more than that, a kind of recognition, as if I'd always known him. For a moment nobody spoke. The stage manager then annoyingly introduced me as the wife of the director and Don looked puzzled. I hastily added I was actually here because I was the writer, and he complimented me on my lyrics. After this brief exchange, rehearsals began, and I was left wondering if I'd imagined the whole thing. I later asked Don what he'd made of our first encounter, and he replied he just saw a beautiful woman who looked incredibly sad.

There were many new cast members, which I wasn't happy with. Brian Cox had been replaced by Paul Jones, who although a pop star, did not have the character needed to play Christian. It was all wrong. Paul, with his boyish looks and gentle persona, would never have survived the huge challenges Christian had to endure. With Brian Cox there'd always been the doubt he would make it to the Celestial City. Now all this tension was lost. Other cast changes were similarly wrong. Peter Straker and Paul Nicholas, both brilliant as rock singers, were wrong for the characters they were playing. The music was now loud and brash, undoubtedly rock, but losing all the subtlety and beauty of Carl's original score. It was not Don's fault. He had done what was asked of him, almost too brilliantly, but my unhappiness with the production increased. Added to this, as rehearsals progressed, I found it difficult to keep my feelings hidden. Don and I had few moments alone together but were both aware something had happened between us which was difficult to control.

The show went on tour before opening in Edinburgh. The audiences loved it, especially the young, who literally went wild, but I still felt uneasy about this new version. Throughout the tour Toby continued to change his mind about various aspects of the production, such as the costumes and the staging, while Carl and I were even asked to rewrite a couple of numbers. The company became increasingly exhausted by all this extra work. A whole set of costumes was thrown out and replaced by something we all felt less good. Scenes were cut and new lines put in with no reference to me. Toby, always ruthless with the pen, now put a line through whole sections and rewrote them himself. By the time we reached Edinburgh I was not only exasperated, but angry. Gabriel, who was staying with her two children for the summer, did not help. She'd always adored Toby and immediately took his side. One evening, after I'd protested about Toby's latest change, she infuriated me by saying, 'Honestly Jane, you need to remember, he *is* the director.' Neither of them understood this whole enterprise had been my idea, my adaptation, and my lyrics, and I had every right to be heard. When I tried to explain this, she said scornfully, 'It is basically Bunyan,' which ignored the expertise needed for the adaptation and the months of work writing the lyrics. I knew there was huge anticipation for this production from audiences and critics alike. It had been given massive publicity. Sick with apprehension, I attended the first night in Edinburgh feeling it was doomed to be a flop. I was right. All the main critics slammed it as a travesty of a great work and any hope of it transferring to West End were blown away. It had a brief season at the Round House and then died a quick death. This was a terrible blow. I'd had such hopes of success, both personal and commercial, and I still think of it as a great opportunity missed. If only we'd stuck to the original version. Carl felt this as well. He ceased to be the company music director, and I never worked with him again. He went on to great success with his hit TV and film scores, as well as conducting all the major orchestras. We remained friends, but I know the show left him bruised. *Pilgrim* was also a financial disaster, which Prospect could ill afford, but Toby quickly moved on to his next production, putting all these problems behind him.

Back in London, I tried to pick up my life, but it wasn't easy and hardly the best time to have fallen passionately in love. I'd so desperately wanted my marriage to work, and for five years I'd tried to live with the problems, but after *Pilgrim* it became almost impossible. Toby for his part simply refused to notice what was happening. Don's first impression had been right. I was miserable and could see no way out. It occurred to me Don might provide me with some sort of solution. But how could we possibly make it work? For the moment I had no answers. It was difficult for Don as well. He was in the process of finally extricating himself from a relationship with the actress Annabel Leventon, a relationship which he assured me was totally over. I never at any point asked him to leave Annabel, in fact I hardly knew her. Annabel later made an untrue and hurtful attack on me in her book about the *Rock Follies* trial. I know she was bitter, but her break-up with Don was happening before I even met him, and I was in no way responsible.

The *Rock Follies* trial dominated Don's life for two years. Some years previously he had taken his idea for a TV series about his band Rock Bottom, to Verity Lambert at Thames Television. She then stole his idea and turned it into her own series, *Rock Follies*. Don and the three Rock Bottom girls took the brave step of then suing Thames Television. They were lucky enough to obtain the services of a brilliant young lawyer, Keith Schilling, who at the time of this trial was at the start of his highly successful career. It was a difficult case, involving intellectual property, and was given little chance of winning, a sort of 'David and Goliath' contest. Against all the odds, after two years of high drama in court, they won and were awarded substantial damages. Despite their victory, the series *Rock Follies* became popular and even given a BAFTA for best series, shameful in the year of *I, Claudius*. Don never really recovered from this setback, although the proceeds allowed him to buy his own house, Elgar's studio in Sussex. It didn't take me long to realise Don had an exceptional and versatile musical talent, being at home with every kind of musical genre, from classical to pop. There had been no music in his background, his parents seemed rather bewildered by it, but by the age of seventeen Don had won a scholarship to the Royal College of Music, studying composition with Nadia Boulanger and conducting with Sir Adrian Boult. He went on to win all three composition prizes. I wasn't the only one to recognise his talent. Toby appointed him his Music Director, taking over from Carl.

In 1977, Prospect took up residence at the Old Vic, turning it into the Old Vic Company. Although this was an exciting move, it put enormous pressure on the small team which ran the company. Despite these drawbacks, the first year's productions were an outstanding success, with leading actors including Eileen Atkins, Derek Jacobi, Timothy West, and Dorothy Tutin. *Saint Joan* with Eileen, and *Hamlet* with Derek were shows that gained great reviews and full houses. *Antony and Cleopatra* had the wonderful Dorothy Tutin in the lead, but the casting of Antony was a rare mistake. For some reason Toby had asked Alec McCowan to play this, the most macho of all Shakespeare's heroes. I believe the decision was in slight desperation when other actors had turned it down, and they ran out of time. Alec was a wonderful actor, but woefully miscast as Anthony, and consequently the production had mixed reviews. The right casting can certainly make or break the success of a show. The next play, Dryden's *All for Love*, required two small children to play the daughters of Caesar. It took place during the summer holidays, so Sasha and Josh were put in the roles. Josh, aged six, had long hair, the fashion for small boys at the time, and in costume could easily pass for a girl. At first, he flatly refused to play a girl but was persuaded by the promise of payment. In fact, he looked wonderful, they both did, in the superb costumes designed by Nico Georgiades. I was standing in the wings on the first night before they went on, when Josh lifted his skirt and to my horror, I saw he was wearing his Chelsea football socks. We removed them fast, just in time for him to make his entrance. At the curtain call, he refused to curtsy, and Toby gave up the fight on this one. They had little to do and no lines, so it wasn't an ordeal, and they were both delighted to receive their pay packets.

At the end of rehearsals, when the company repaired to the bar, Josh hauled himself up on the bar stool and said to the barman, 'Avocado and Coke, please.' I hurriedly explained he'd heard someone ask for a Bacardi and Coke and thought he'd do the same. He was allowed the Coke. The show ended at the Edinburgh Festival and after that the children went back to school. When asked about their holiday reading, Sasha's teacher was startled when she said, '*All for Love* by John Dryden.'

Sash and Josh in All for Love *at the Old Vic (photo: Chris Davies)*

The last of the plays in the first season was the brainchild of Don. One of his great friends was the poet Christopher Logue and Don had the idea to adapt, as a stage drama, *War Music*, Logue's long poem based on Homer's *Iliad*. This whole concept was far ahead of its time, but Toby threw himself into the production, and the young company were equally enthusiastic. There was exciting choreography by Bill Louther and the bronzed bodies crossed the stage with spectacular rhythmic movements, their Greek helmets and shields designed by the sculptor Peter Eugene Ball. Most dramatic of all was the staging. Don's score, which went through the entire show, relied a great deal on percussion, and it was decided the musicians would be set in a huge cage mounted above the actors, a technical feat. This was a showcase for Don's star percussionist, Gary Kettel, especially his dazzling performance on the kettle drums. Timothy West was cast as Narrator, using Logue's words to take the audience through the Trojan Wars. Unusually, Tim gave a disappointingly lacklustre performance, but maybe this was just in contrast to the huge energy shown by the other performers. The show, with its modern music, always loud and sometimes jarring, and the rather obscure wording of the Logue poem, received a mixed reception. Many found it spectacular, while others found it a step too far. Overall, the notices were disappointing. When *War Music* went on tour to Europe it had greater success, particularly in Turkey where the audience treated it like a rock concert. Toby should have learned a lesson from the first season. The company just didn't have the money for huge extravagance. Regrettably, this was something he ignored. Don was now working flat out producing scores for all the productions. This necessitated him being at Spencer Park a great deal, and I found this a mixed blessing. I loved him being there, but Toby tended to monopolise him. We'd kept our affair hidden, but this was proving increasingly difficult. For now, we remained in a kind of limbo, seeing each other when we could.

During Prospect's second year at the Vic, I was commissioned to write another musical, and I chose the subject of Buster Keaton. I had always been fascinated by both his work and his life. The children loved his films too, having been taken to see them at the Academy Cinema in Oxford Street for their annual season. Buster Keaton now became the subject of this new musical, not a large affair like *Pilgrim*, but a two-hander. It was the first time I'd worked with Don on an original work. We had few disagreements and seemed entirely on the same wavelength, although he was a hard taskmaster and would continually ask for further work on the lyrics, but in general working with him was exhilarating and a joy. Once finished, we had the problem of casting. The actress not only had to sing well but be able to play all the women in Buster's life. Jan Waters seemed the obvious choice and, although she'd just had a baby, she bravely agreed to take it on.

Buster was more difficult to cast and a huge undertaking for any actor. I covered most of Buster's life, starting with the early years, then on to his journey to Hollywood and the great silent films. By the age of thirty he'd become the most successful star in Hollywood with his own studios. After this meteoric rise came his downfall with the arrival of the Talkies. Two failed marriages followed, and he was soon an alcoholic. At fifty he was sad and lonely, denied his brilliant talent for making films. Then a young actress of

Donald Fraser and Max Wall rehearsing Buster *(photo: Chris Davies)*

nineteen asked for his help in learning to play bridge and promptly fell in love with him. Against all his objections at the gap in their ages, they were married and remained happily so until his death. He started to find work again, and then his films were rediscovered. Towards the end of his life, the Venice Film Festival gave him a standing ovation, acknowledging the great genius that he was.

This extraordinary and dramatic story would present any actor with a monumental challenge. Who on earth could possibly play him? Then Toby had the brilliant idea of asking Max Wall, who was himself a legend. Max found great parallels in Buster's life with his own, and to our surprise agreed to take it on. Toby insisted on directing *Buster*. This was a mistake, not only because I had lost confidence in working with Toby, but also because he was directing two other major productions at the time. More worryingly, he and Max didn't hit it off. I think this was mainly due to Toby having so little time to give us, and Max felt neglected and under-rehearsed. Max was also intuitive and a keen observer of life. Once, when Toby absentmindedly kissed me on the top of my head as he was leaving, Max said in his unmistakeable tones, 'Significant that. Death of a marriage to be kissed on the head.' I laughed at the time, but his words had a horrible truth. Although Max could be cantankerous, Don and I both loved the man and worked well with him. I also admired his sheer professionalism. He was in his early seventies but still gave it his full physical and mental energies.

Buster was given a late-night slot at the Edinburgh Lyceum Theatre. It wasn't ideal, but the audiences loved it, visibly moved by the story, and of course fascinated to see Max Wall's performance. Max was typical of so many comedians, outwardly cheerful and funny, but inwardly depressed and sad. I will never forget him singing the very last number in the show. The way he performed it was truly heartbreaking.

> *Little funny man, Such a funny man*
> *Gotta make them laugh.*
> *I wanna cry*
> *Gotta make them live*
> *Why can't I?*
> *Put on a face*
> *It isn't mine,*
> *I must try to be a funny man*
> *Try so hard to be a funny man*
> *One more time…*

After Edinburgh it was decided to give the show a limited season at the Old Vic. Again, it was packed out and the reviews were good, but when the short season ended, so also did *Buster*. I think Max was very disappointed and I felt sad for him, but not altogether surprised. The company's energies were now fully taken up with the next season. They also couldn't take the financial risk of a transfer. There were already ominous mutterings from the Arts Council about the over-spending and mounting debts, putting the company's grant in jeopardy. The administrator and board tried to warn Toby about the crisis, but he was as cavalier with the company's finances as he was with his own. All his energies were concentrated on the artistic side of the work, and he proceeded with an even more ambitious season. Over-worked and over-stretched, we now hardly saw him, and he and I led our separate lives.

Meanwhile, my parents were causing me some concern. On the plus side, Joseph had made a great success of his time at St Mary le Bow. When the church was rebuilt, he had instructed there should be two pulpits, one either side of the nave. He had quickly recognised that because the City emptied at weekends, there was little point in holding Sunday services. In any case, St Paul's was at the top of Cheapside and provided all the services required. Instead, Joseph devised his 'Tuesday dialogues', and the two pulpits came into their own. During the lunch hour, someone famous would debate with him. The idea caught on, and the church would be packed with city workers. The dialogues covered a wide range of topics, depending on the celebrity. Over the ten years Joseph managed to debate with every well-known personality of the day, from all walks of life. Politicians, actors, musicians, philosophers, journalists – the list of dialoguers read like *Who's Who*, and among many others included Margaret Thatcher, Laurence Olivier, Yehudi Menuhin, Margaret Drabble, Judi Dench, Professor A J Ayer and Peter Cook. I was lucky enough to meet many of them. After finishing the dialogues, the celebrities were invited to lunch in the penthouse. Joseph was in his element, and it all appeared to be a great success, but he was now drinking heavily and fast becoming an alcoholic. From the moment the lunch started so did his drinking, and this would carry on long after the guests had departed. My mother found it increasingly stressful, especially as her health was not good. By the time she was sixty her heart had finally begun to give out. She was given open heart surgery, one of the first to have this done, to replace her damaged valves. By sheer will she made a remarkable recovery, but Joseph's drinking problem put an extra strain on her. Worse, he was in denial. If she criticised him, he would just turn to Sonya. I went over to help when I could, but there was little I could do in this situation, and Ma's stories of his drinking were increasingly harrowing.

My writing work continued as busy as ever. At the end of the second Vic season, an exciting offer was made to put three of my shows, the Byron, the Sydney Smith, and the Grand Tour, under one umbrella, *The English Eccentrics*, and to tour them, first to the Hong Kong Festival and then across Australia. Although this went under the name of 'The Old Vic Company' it had an independent producer, Michael Redington, who also came with us. The company consisted of myself, the four actors – Julian Glover, Isla Blair, Timothy West and Derek Jacobi – and three musicians (Don on keyboard, plus a horn player, Robin, and a guitarist, Alan). The sets were simple, in the main just furniture. A lot depended on the staging, particularly the lighting, and it was a great experience for me to work in so many different theatres, with challenges in each.

We flew to Hong Kong first. The landing at the old airport made the nervous fliers amongst us terrified, as we seemed to swoop down between buildings. Isla and I had thrown off our shoes and owing to the pressure in the cabin, our feet had swollen horribly. When we landed, we were quite unable to get our shoes back on. There was press awaiting us and rather embarrassingly we had to hobble off the plane barefoot.

I found Hong Kong incredibly exciting, noisy, bustling and like no place I'd ever seen. Derek was not so happy. On the way to the hotel, he'd seen a dog peeing on a box of oysters and vowed not to eat anything remotely exotic. Isla one night found a rat in her dressing room and did her make-up standing on the chair. Other than that, all went well. We were staying at the luxurious Hilton. John le Mesurier and his wife Joan had taken a penthouse suite on the top floor while he was performing in a season of plays. John was a great lover of music and he and Don became instant friends and drinking companions, and we were nightly asked up to their suite for drinks after the shows.

Wonderful publicity was organised by the festival's head of PR, Gillian Newson, and the shows were sold out. Gilli became a great friend to us all and has remained so ever since. Thanks to her, I was given a series of interviews and one headline read 'For Theatre read McCulloch'! I had originally thought my job was merely to stage the shows, but because I had devised and written all three, I was the person continually interviewed, which I really wasn't expecting. I think the actors were rather shocked by this as well. As with Gabriel and the Bunyan, they didn't consider these biographical shows original works, disregarding the expertise needed to put them together. At times I found this hurtful, but as the actors were also great friends, I tried to ignore it.

Hong Kong involved us in a good deal of socialising. One evening we were invited out and proudly presented with the delicacy of 100-year-old eggs. I'm afraid on this occasion we didn't behave well. The yolks were thick and oozed out a horrid shade of green and smelled terrible. Someone remarked it was like diesel oil, and Isla, often given to fits of helpless laughter, started us off. Each added remark increased our mirth and soon we were out of control. I think we finally pulled ourselves together and managed to thank our hosts politely.

Our next stop was Perth, Australia. Again, the shows were well received. The weather was beautiful and on our day off we were taken to the Perth races. Meanwhile, back in England they were enduring 'the winter of discontent' and as we basked in the sun and drank cocktails, I did have some feelings of guilt. From Perth we went to Adelaide and on our day off an excursion was arranged, this time to a winery in the beautiful Barossa Valley. A great deal of tasting was done, and it was a rather frail bunch who were delivered back to our hotels. In Adelaide, I and the musicians had been put in a different hotel from the actors. One night I was awoken by Alan, the guitarist, banging on my door shouting, 'Fire!' He had returned late and found the corridor on our floor full of smoke. We reassembled in the lobby waiting for new instructions as the fire brigade trampled through. At this moment I was told there was a telephone call for me. It was Toby. The poor man had been trying to get through to me for days and now he finally had, I had to say, 'I'm sorry Toby, I can't talk now, our hotel is on fire!' It turned out to be minor, but I was quite relieved to move on to Melbourne a day later.

Here we were staying in the Windsor Hotel, an amazing period piece, with a lift so grand and large, you could have had a party in it. Melbourne was the first venue where there was a real challenge with the staging. We were due to perform at the Dallas Brooks concert hall, a cavernous 2,000-seater, daunting for any theatre performance – and our chamber pieces were as far from a rock concert as they

PR picture taken on tour of Australia

could possibly be. I decided to rely on the lighting and reduced the performing space to a small area. This, combined with the amazing diction of the four actors, meant it somehow worked. Michael Redington was now worried the box office didn't look too good for Sydney, so I was flown up for the day to do publicity shots and interviews. It was an ordeal, especially for a nervous flier, but the photographs were the most glamorous ever taken of me and I did back-to-back interviews. This ploy appeared to work and, combined with the great reviews, we once again had good houses. The tour finished in Canberra, which was a less exciting venue than the others and a bit of an anti-climax.

The tour had been a wonderful experience, and successful, but it did have its downside. This was due to increasing problems with Don, which perhaps I should have anticipated. Don was not a professional actor nor an orchestral musician. He was a composer and as such was totally unused to performing the same work night after night. He had none of the discipline needed. The result was that boredom set in, and his answer to this was to drink. There were days when he took himself off to bars in the morning and didn't reappear until the evening performance, by which time he was obviously drunk. The actors became understandably nervous as Don's keyboard playing would be erratic and unreliable. I did my best to remonstrate with him, but he was angry and resentful and thought I was making a fuss about nothing. One particularly bad night, Robin, the horn player, and I poured black coffee down him and he just about managed the performance, but it was obvious the situation couldn't continue. I was in despair, knowing the actors were about to refuse to go on stage with Don in this state. Thankfully, Robin took him aside, reprimanding him severely and making him promise to behave for the rest of the tour. Luckily, this worked. Don respected Robin and after this kept his drinking mostly under control. What left me worried was the fact he wouldn't admit he'd been drinking or was drunk. It was a situation that was to become worse in the years that followed, where getting drunk with the boys was almost a badge of honour. I sometimes asked myself why I was destined to be surrounded by alcoholics.

After Sydney, the tour finished in Canberra, and on the long journey home came the realisation that reality had to be faced. The last eight weeks had been a break from any decision and, despite his drinking, my love for Don had not lessened. As we landed in London, I was brought down to earth with a bump. It was wonderful to be reunited with the children, but I realised the problems with Toby now ran too deep to be ignored. It was the worst possible moment for this to be faced. Toby was in a deep crisis at the Old Vic. The Art's Council, alarmed by the company's huge debts, had withdrawn their funding. Also, the third season hadn't been the same success as the previous two. The choice of plays was too obscure, and consequently they lost money. The only play which did well was *The Government Inspector* with a superb performance from Ian Richardson, but this wasn't enough to save the season.

Toby continued to bury his head in the sand and refused to listen to any warnings. There had been so much wastage and extravagance, especially on costumes. Nico Georgiadis was used to designing at the Royal Opera House with the most expensive fabrics and handmade leather boots. His designs alone far exceeded the company's budget. With mounting debts and no Arts Council funding, Toby was told by the Board that a final crisis had been reached. He was due to take *Hamlet* on an extended and prestigious tour of China, and he went ahead, vowing to deal with the financial situation on his return. What followed caused a great scandal, which left many in the theatre world deeply unhappy. While Toby and the Company were enjoying great success in China, Timothy West, in Toby's absence, did a deal with the Arts Council, agreeing to hand over all financial control of the company to them, on the condition that he immediately took over as Artistic Director. Toby arrived back from China to find he'd lost not only his job but also the company which he'd created and over the last fifteen years had made into such a success. The situation was made worse by the fact Tim had been one of his greatest friends. Toby had launched Tim's career by giving him leading roles and he felt this betrayal deeply. Tim's action sent shock waves through the artistic world as the news spread. Sir Alexander Gibson, the conductor, put down his baton at the start of rehearsals with Scottish Opera and said, 'Gentlemen, we will now have a minute's silence for the death of the English Theatre.' Tim's tenure at the Old Vic was short-lived, starting with Peter O'Toole's disastrous *Macbeth*, and ending after only a year. With the departure from the Old Vic, the Prospect Theatre Company also ceased to exist. To be absolutely fair, Prospect's tenure of the Vic would probably have ended anyway, as the financial crisis was beyond repair. But the way it was done left a great deal of bad feeling and Toby with a lot of bitterness.

Life with Toby now became increasingly difficult and his behaviour unpredictable. He was in shock, and it was heart-breaking to witness his suffering. Those closest to him feared he was having a nervous breakdown. He also had to come to terms with his relationship with me. Until now, he'd ignored our disintegrating marriage. Now he no longer could, and when it became apparent how far things had gone, he turned all his pent-up fury, bitterness, and anger on me. Deep down I understood, but life with him became almost impossible. The Old Vic debâcle had also left us in a perilous financial position. Toby had never organised a pension and was temporarily with no work. Reluctantly, the decision was made to sell Spencer Park. The children, already unsettled by us, were further upset by having to leave the home they loved so much. We found a smaller, Georgian terrace house in the Brixton Road. It had a pretty garden, which led to a driveway and parking. It also had the benefit of being near Stockwell Tube Station, but none of this made up for losing the Spencer Park house. Out of the proceeds of the sale, I was given enough to replace the earlier loss of the Windlass, which I'd sold to pay school fees, with another cottage in Port Isaac.

1981 was my *annus horribilis*. Toby, unable to bear remaining in England, took himself off to the States to work there. I was left to cope singlehandedly with the huge task of packing up Spencer Park and the re-decoration of the new house, while the children scattered for the summer holidays. I found it difficult to keep their spirits up when they returned in the Autumn. To add to my general misery, my poor mother had a stroke. Joseph had retired from St Mary le Bow the previous year and they'd moved to a flat in Belsize Park. Neither were happy there; my father missed the dialogues and was drinking heavily, and for once my mother's optimism deserted her. The stroke was a severe one and, unable to return home, she went into a nursing home run by nuns in southwest London. It was a difficult place to get to even for me, and I had a car. Joseph had to rely on Sonya to drive him over for his weekly visits. It became obvious Ma felt isolated and her condition deteriorated. An offer came from Gabriel and Philip to look after her in their house in Montreal, where the ground floor was easily adaptable for her needs. With some difficulty she was flown out and appeared to settle in well, but the parting was devastating for Joseph, who was lonely and miserable. The Belsize Park flat was sold, and Sonya found him another, near her in Lupus Street in Pimlico. Joseph made two visits to Ma during her year in Montreal, and according to Gabriel they had a sweet time together. Also, he and Gabriel at last had a kind of reconciliation. I also went out for a visit. Despite her frailty, Ma seemed content and greatly enjoyed the company of her grandchildren, but I sadly knew, as I left, it would be the last time I'd see her. I was right. In 1982 she had a further stroke and lay in a coma for ten days. None of us wanted to make the decision to turn off the machines but knew we couldn't put it off much longer. Then, on the eleventh day, she quietly slipped away.

Gabriel organised the funeral in Montreal and then Edward Carpenter arranged a later Memorial Service for her in the choir of Westminster Abbey. It was a beautiful occasion, although Joseph, broken by her death, took no part in the service. Edward gave the eulogy, which was a remarkable tribute. I will never forget his reading of the Byron poem, 'She walks in beauty like the night.' It was a fitting end. The more I think of Ma, the more I realise what a truly great woman she was, with a lifetime of public service, despite all her health problems. She and Joseph had a passionate and often tormented love, but without her he was lost, a lonely man, racked by guilt, finding increasing consolation in the bottle. Sonya remained loyal until he died and went over daily to see to his needs. He'd never had a relationship with his grandchildren, but Fran would sometimes accompany me on visits, but it was a thankless task. He remained wrapped in self-pity, occasionally blurting out that none of us could hold a candle to Ma. Mostly we were sent out to replenish his supplies of whisky. His last years were a sad ending for a brilliant man who'd achieved so much in his life but now remained angry and bitter at what might have been.

At the end of 1982, Toby and I finally divorced. I took nothing: no alimony, no settlement, only the proviso that Toby would support the children. Looking back, it was an unwise gesture, but I was desperate for things to be as simple and amicable as possible. I was also aware that when Toby left the Old Vic there was little money left and what there was, was needed for the children. The split was final. The Atlantic was now between us. Most of our friends and relations started to shun me, which I found both sad and shocking. In John le Carré's language, I was 'out in the cold'. I had to face it. My familiar world had gone forever, and I now had to find a new existence.

Fran and Sash

Chapter Ten
THE WILDERNESS YEARS

AT FORTY-TWO I embarked on a new phase in my life and one, as I soon found out, which needed endless compromises. I divided my time between the family home in London and Don's house in Sussex. This balance was not always easy, and I often had the feeling I was failing in both. Don had remarkably stuck by me during the seven difficult years while I'd dithered, trying to make a final decision. I lived in terror he would give up on me, but he never did. It can't have been easy. Our relationship had relied on a few snatched moments. Even now after the long wait, it wasn't as if he had me to himself, which is what he wanted, because there were four children calling for my attention and a household to run. The three older children had left, or were about to leave school, and Josh was away during term time at Stowe. The needs of the children were therefore less, but they still wanted me around and I certainly wanted to spend time with them. It was just finding the time for everything and everyone that became the problem.

I found it unfair Don was blamed for causing the break-up of the marriage, but inevitably people take sides in a situation like this. I never publicly explained the main reason for the break-up because I knew it would harm Toby's reputation if he was known to be gay. In 1982 homosexuality was still a taboo subject, and it became worse with the emergence of AIDS later in the decade. I sometimes wonder what would have happened if Toby hadn't been gay. Would I have fallen in love with Don? I suppose I might have done, but maybe not left the marriage. However, there is no point in speculating; life is what it is, and you just have to make the best of whatever is thrown at you. My one constant regret is that Toby and I didn't sit down with the children and explain the whole situation to them, but Toby refused to do this, and I was unable to tell the children the truth. In later years no explanation was needed, because by then his partner was a man. But when it happened, the children, particularly Josh, the youngest, blamed me for the break-up, and so did most of our friends and relations, including Gabriel and, sadly, the Yorkshire relatives. Some people shunned me publicly, and consequently I avoided all previous contacts. It's to the children's great credit they maintained a great relationship with us both. I can only say I did the best I could to see the children into adulthood. I did this almost singlehandedly because Toby, now in exile in the States, left their upbringing to me. As with all teenagers, they had their problems, but I am very proud of the way they overcame the setbacks and emerged as such outstanding adults.

Isolated as we were, Don and I became even closer, and our creative work increased as new projects arrived. For a charity gala in Westminster Abbey, I was asked to put together a work that involved us both, combining words and music. I decided to use the life of Elgar, delivered in conversation between the composer and his wife Alice, with each section of his life illustrated by a piece of his music. Anthony Quayle played Elgar and Jean Marsh his wife. The music was performed by the English Chamber Orchestra with Don conducting. It was a prestigious event and the Queen Mother attended. Wonderful Edward Carpenter, the Dean, was enormously helpful throughout. At one point I asked Edward if I might have Elgar making his first entrance riding up the nave of the Abbey on his beloved bicycle.

Edward, having consulted the Chapter, agreed to this, but on the night, one of the vergers who hadn't been informed, tried to stop him and it was only after a long conversation that Tony Quayle finally managed to assure him that he had permission, and the performance proceeded. It was a freezing night in February, and Edward's wife Lilian had kindly put hot water bottles in the pulpit for the soprano Teresa Cahill who was up there to perform two of Elgar's songs. These bottles were forgotten about after the concert, and Edward found himself squelching on them when delivering his sermon the following Sunday. Despite the cold the performance, with its combination of wonderful acting and superb playing of the orchestra, proved to be a moving experience.

Afterwards, there was a reception in the Jerusalem Chamber. We'd been informed the Queen Mother would only have one martini and then depart. Not a bit of it. She was enjoying herself and told us of her experience meeting the elderly Elgar after he'd written the *Nursery Suite* for the two princesses. Only after her third martini did she reluctantly leave. Meanwhile, Tony Quayle expressed his admiration for this formula of words and music and made a momentous suggestion: 'Why don't you continue with your work under one umbrella and call yourself the English Chamber Theatre?' It was a great idea and actually changed my career. For the next fifteen years I put together over thirty entertainments and dramas, some more demanding than others, but always involving words and music and the English Chamber Theatre came into being.

The first president of ECT was Dame Peggy Ashcroft, who was delighted with the concept of these portable and accessible shows, declaring they were in the spirit of Lilian Baylis. On Peggy's death a few years later, Judi Dench, also now a Dame, took over the Presidency. Judi was always supportive, even appearing in a couple of shows herself.

One of these was in Southwark Cathedral on Shakespeare's birthday and celebrating the Bard. On this occasion Michael Williams, Judi's husband and another wonderful actor, was in the cast. It amused me to see Michael giving Judi constant advice and occasional criticism, which she always accepted gracefully and without argument.

The last chamber piece we had performed at the Old Vic was *The Trial of Queen Caroline*, about the disastrous marriage between the Prince of Wales ('Prinny'), later George IV, and Caroline of Brunswick. George loathed Caroline and to be rid of her, put her on trial. This trial became notorious and a major scandal. Inevitably, with such a complicated story, it needed a larger cast. I had a brilliant one, including Prunella Scales, Barbara Leigh Hunt and Harold Innocent. Apart from Prinny and the Queen, there were two diarists, Creevey and Princess Lieven, the legal team of Lord Brougham and the Attorney General, and a narrator for the story, a ballad singer, where I used many of the original squibs and ballads of the time. This part was played and sung by the very talented Nickolas Grace. Don wrote a brilliant score and the show had been a great success. Now I had my own company, I decided to revive it, giving performances at many venues, including Greenwich and the Malvern Festival. ECT shows were now increasingly in demand throughout the country, not only at theatres but also at festivals and charity events, and I was adding to the repertoire all the time.

Although it was great to have total artistic freedom, ECT had no financial backing, and consequently I was always short of money. I took on other jobs to eke out the finances, one of which was creating a PR company, which I called Kestrel Publicity. This worked well for a while, especially when I was taken on by a music agency with many distinguished clients. The job started successfully enough when I managed to place an article about the soprano Teresa Cahill with a headline which read, 'Diva from the Docks!' But this success was short-lived. I soon found it hard to organise publicity for those who weren't a famous name, and brilliant as many of these musicians were, it was almost impossible to drum up interest in the press for an unknown string quartet, or American cellist, or obscure baritone. I also found my time over-stretched with the demands of ECT, where I was writing, casting and producing the shows. After a year, the PR experiment came to an end.

Just as I was beginning to wonder if I could continue with ECT without financial help, the British Council came to my rescue and the foreign tours began. These were exciting to do and happily far better paid. Over the next ten years, the

Harold Innocent as George IV in The Trial of Queen Caroline *(photo: Dominic Turner)*

British Council took our productions to Spain, Portugal, Cyprus, Greece, Turkey, Egypt, Jordan and Mexico. One of the first tours was with the Byron. It had a new cast, Timothy Dalton now playing the poet instead of Derek Jacobi. Tim may not have had Derek's vocal skills, but he was excitingly dramatic and more physically like Byron. After an extensive European tour, we flew to Mexico where we performed in Guanajuato and Mexico City. It was in the latter there was an interesting incident. We opened to a packed house and at the end there was great applause and shouts of 'Author!', so once more I was ushered onto the stage for the curtain call. I was wearing a long, white cheesecloth dress. We took our first bow and then the audience went wild, shouting and throwing their programmes in the air. Delighted with our success, we bowed twice more. It was then I noticed the British Council representative signalling frantically we should come off. As I walked into the wings, he took me aside and explained the back-lighting had shone through my cheesecloth dress, rendering me stark naked! I did not take any further curtain calls.

Exciting as these tours were, they could also be stressful. *The Grand Tour*, which we took on a long tour around the Middle East, was beset with crises. We had a cast of four – Jan Waters, Lee Montague, Jeremy Nicholas and Doug Fisher – plus our pianist Julia Hazleton, and me. We started in Cyprus, and the audiences were extremely enthusiastic. Buoyed with this success, we flew to Athens, and it was here the problems began. Each of the actors played many different characters, all equally important. At the first rehearsal, Lee was taken violently ill with a ruptured stomach ulcer and rushed to hospital. We urgently needed a replacement. After endless telephone calls with the British Council in London another actor, Trevor Martin, was flown out, arriving just in time for the performance. The tour seemed back on track. Our next stop was to be Salonica. The taxis arrived to take us to the airport, but Doug Fisher didn't appear. Jeremy Nicholas was despatched to fetch him, only to find Doug passed out cold, either from drink, drugs, or a combination of both. Somehow, Trevor and Jeremy managed to get him dressed and hauled out to the taxi, but he remained out of it, someone having to support him onto the plane. By the time we reached Salonica, he could walk but his speech was still slurring, and he made little sense. I called an emergency meeting with the remaining cast, and we all agreed Doug couldn't carry on with the tour. We knew in the countries we were going next, drug offences could have drastic consequences. I informed the British Council representative. It must have seemed to him like carelessness to have lost two actors out of a cast of four and I'm sure I was unfairly blamed.

There followed an unpleasant interview with Doug, where I told him we couldn't take the risk of taking him further. It is the only time I've ever had to sack an actor. Doug was angry, but thankfully the British Council now took over and he was put on a plane back to England. There was no way another replacement could be sent out, so I was faced with the daunting task of changing a script written for four actors to three. The remaining three were wonderful, all taking on extra roles, and somehow, we managed it. The rest of the tour went ahead as planned, but it was clear recent events had affected us all. There was one night in Salonika when it was very cold, and we were feeling exhausted and depressed. It was then Jeremy managed to revive our spirits by singing one of his silly songs about the Boy Scouts and this not only had us helpless with laughter but immediately restored morale. Only in Ankara, Turkey, did the British Council representative make it plain he thought we were a troublesome group. Otherwise, throughout Egypt and Jordan, we were shown nothing but kindness and sympathy, and the shows were very well received. In Amman we gave a workshop on 'Acting Shakespeare' to 500 schoolchildren. They were so excited and full of questions; I only wish we could have done more of these workshops. We were taken to the great sights, including Petra and the Pyramids. There was also shopping, and Jan Waters and I stocked up on some beautiful rugs, which I managed to squeeze into the costume bag. It had been a tour which for several reasons none of us would forget.

Their Finest Hour: *William Hootkins as Churchill (top); Bob Sherman as Roosevelt (bottom) (photos: Dominic Turner)*

I was now working flat out, writing, directing and producing the shows. Some of the new productions were my ideas, others were commissioned. One of the most rewarding of these was the adaptation of the Churchill and Roosevelt correspondence from 1939 to 1945, a monumental task. There were three large volumes of letters, luckily in public domain, so this meant I didn't have to bother with the copyright. I decided on a simple set consisting of two desks either side of the stage, a smart one for Roosevelt in the White House and a shabby and cluttered one for Churchill in the War Rooms. Telephones played a big part because I'd found transcripts of their actual calls. Roosevelt had a single, elegant phone, whereas Churchill had several old-fashioned Bakelite models in different colours. I also used Churchill's broadcasts and speeches in Parliament and Roosevelt's to Congress.

Don put together a terrific and atmospheric soundtrack, starting with evocative war sirens and ending with Dvořák's 'Going Home' from his Symphony No 9, as Churchill delivered his eulogy to Roosevelt. The show was in two parts, the first from the moment Churchill became the British War leader in 1940, up to the first success at El Alamein. The second part moved through the rest of the war until Roosevelt's death in 1945.

The opening performance was at Churchill's old school, Harrow, and although too long, it had the boys riveted. One boy asked me at the interval, 'Did we win the war?' Not surprising. The first half showed how near we were to defeat, with a long series of terrible disasters. Another interesting aspect of the play was how the relationship between the two great men changed. At the start, Roosevelt was offering what help he could to the beleaguered British, but after the States came into the war, he took a more commanding role, and the power shifted from the diminishing British Empire to the rise of America as a superpower. Despite this, Roosevelt and Churchill never fell out and their friendship and affection for each other held, even if towards the end there was a good deal of tension and disagreement. After the first performance I worked on the show, cutting and reshaping, before reviving it. Surprisingly, the part of Churchill now went to an American actor, William Hootkins, one of the most interesting men I've ever met. Knowledgeable on so many subjects, he even spoke fluent Chinese. Bill not only looked like Churchill but had studied his voice until the match was uncanny, so much so that at a performance in Hyde Park, Roosevelt's mansion, in front of a gathering of the Roosevelt and Churchill families, Winston Churchill, grandson and namesake of the great man, went up to Bill after the performance and said, 'Grandpapa!' The part of Roosevelt was played equally well by Bill's great friend Bob Sherman. Bob may not have had the build of Roosevelt, but once in costume, with the cigarette holder and pince-nez, he became the man, also managing a complete match to Roosevelt's voice.

We took *Their Finest Hour* to many venues as well as the prestige event at Hyde Park, including a wonderful week in Bermuda. There was a less wonderful time in LA where the producer turned out to be a crook and we were never paid. To make up for this, I arranged performances crossing the Atlantic on the QE2, both to New York and back. I loved touring with these two actors, always the greatest company, but who could sometimes behave outrageously. On the QE2 they went swimming in the pool, although forbidden, in very rough weather. A crew was sent to rescue them, and an unrepentant Bill was highly amused at having a land rescue when he was at sea. When we played in London, the show didn't have the audiences it deserved, mainly because neither of the actors were star names. It is something that has always irked me. No matter how brilliant the performances, it is rare the public will attend unless there is a star in the cast. Small audiences are particularly damaging to a company like ECT, dependent on good box office. The other disadvantage is inadequate publicity. When taking part in a festival, we had to rely on the venue, but again their budgets were often too small to make a difference. Frequently we would find our fliers hadn't even been distributed and, worse, no publicity had been organised at all. Despite these problems, ECT kept afloat, and Don and I found we had little spare time.

At some point I was invited to take part in a new project outside ECT. This was a show Toby had actually planned to do at the Old Vic but never had the chance, a musical which I'd named *The Cockney Show*. It was set in an East End pub run by the same family, covering two world wars and the years in between. Interwoven into the story were all the well-known Cockney and popular songs of the period, so a good deal of audience participation was anticipated. With the departure from the Old Vic, the project had been shelved, but suddenly, out of the blue a West End producer became interested, and plans were put in place for it to go ahead. The casting team were keen to have Georgia Brown play the leading role of the landlady, and I was despatched to Los Angeles to persuade her to take part. Georgia was instantly welcoming, and an immediate friendship was struck. One night during my visit, there was a party at Lauretta Feldman's, widow of Marty. The moment I entered her house I noticed the place was full of Buster Keaton memorabilia. Apparently, Marty had been an obsessive fan and a great collector. At some point, after several glasses of wine, I told some of the guests about the musical I'd written about Buster and then, unbelievably and no doubt fuelled by alcohol, I started to sing the beautiful number which describes the nineteen-year-old Eleanor Keaton's first meeting with Buster, now in his fifties. She'd asked him to teach her to play bridge, and the lyric began:

> *The cards are on the table, which one should I play,*
> *never knew that the game would go this way...*

It continued with her dithering until the final line, 'I know, I'll play my heart.' There then followed the chorus:

> *I never saw a man so beautiful, so sad.*
> *I never saw a man like him before.*
> *He's gentle, he's kind, wish he could read my mind,*
> *Then he'd know that he's the man I'm waiting for.*

A guitarist who was present at the party started playing chords behind my singing, so I hope the performance wasn't too embarrassing. In any case, as I finished the room burst into applause and then we went back to partying. A little later, Lauretta came over and told me there was someone who wanted to meet me. An elegant, elderly woman held out her hand and introduced herself. 'I am so pleased to meet you,' she said. 'I'm Eleanor Keaton.' My heart stopped. I started to bluster out some sort of apology, but she stopped me. 'I want to thank you. What you sang was so moving, and you had it just right. That was exactly how it happened.'

I wish I could remember the further conversation we had; sadly, I can't, but I hope I managed to convey to Eleanor my passion and admiration for her husband's work. Her approval of the lyric meant more to me than any rave review could ever have done.

The Cockney Show never made its way to the West End, but I did direct a production at the Guildford School of Acting some years later. The audience's enthusiastic reaction confirmed my view this musical could have been highly successful, but regretfully it was yet another work that joined the file of those which for some reason didn't make it.

Returning from LA, I took a break from my travels

abroad and settled back into life in England. ECT productions started again, time was spent with the children, and Don and I somehow fitted in a busy social life as well. In 1984, an invitation arrived from the great soprano Jessye Norman to join her for a Christmas Eve dinner at a large house she was renting, deep in the Kent countryside. So off we set, little knowing it was an event which would have such an unexpected outcome, resulting in a brilliant and exciting two years for us both.

The four children, 1989 (photo: Mark Douet)

Chapter Eleven
THE GREAT JESSYE NORMAN

MY FIRST MEETING with Jessye Norman happened in the most bizarre way, at the Edinburgh Festival in 1972, at a large reception given by Peter Diamond for all the artists taking part in that year's performances. Toby and I found ourselves among a throng of very distinguished guests. I was introduced to a formidable-looking man with a large beard, who I was told was a famous conductor. I noticed he had a cigar in his mouth which wasn't lit, so trying to be helpful I picked up the table lighter off the nearside table and flicked it on. To my alarm, a flame shot out and caught the side of the conductor's beard, which started to singe. With great presence of mind, I now threw my glass of champagne over him, which had the instant effect of putting out the fire.

A huge commotion followed, and people thronged round the man mopping his singed beard, so my profuse apologies were lost. It was then I heard the famous laughter. Looking across the room, I saw a large black woman, stunningly dressed, and seated on a sofa, who was laughing helplessly. She beckoned me across to sit beside her. Between her laughs she gasped out, 'Honey, I've had many arguments with conductors, but I've never first set fire to one and then drowned him.'

And that was how I met Jessye Norman, and we became instant friends. It wasn't always an easy friendship. Jessye was a highly complicated and volatile character and, as with so many of the people I've loved the most, she could be either wonderful, or terrible, with not much in between.

After Edinburgh we often saw each other socially. I also went and helped when her secretary fell off her horse and couldn't work for a couple of months. Jessye had a small mews house as her London base, and I would clock in daily. Jessye was a hard taskmaster and often sent me back to retype letters, but during this time I began to know her well and had the pleasure of meeting her friends, many of them stars of the music world. Jessye was also one of the few friends who maintained a good relationship with both Toby and me after the break-up. She was a great admirer of Toby's theatre work, and later he directed her in several operas in the States. She was always a bit wary of Don, finding him a little uncouth – her word – which I presumed to mean he was rough around the social edges. But she recognised his talent, admired his work and was happy to let him compose for her.

If Jessye was working in England for any length of time, she often took a large country house for entertaining her friends, and it was to one of these Don and I repaired one Christmas Eve for a party. She was a wonderful hostess, the conversation constantly interrupted by her famous peal of laughter. I remember at some point early in the evening, Don said, 'Write me the words of a carol and I will set it to music, and we will perform it for Jessye after dinner.'

Jessye was in the kitchen, and I went and asked her for pencil and paper. She provided me with a long piece of kitchen roll, found me a pen and I went to a quiet corner of the living room and tried to find inspiration. As I stared at the Christmas tree, the words came to me, and I wrote the first verse:

> *Green and silver, red and gold*
> *And a story born of old,*

Truth and love and hope abide,
This Christmastide...

I added two more verses with the same refrain and gave them to Don, who quickly composed the tune. We told the rest of the guests our idea, and as two of them were singers, there was no trouble in putting a performance together. After a long dinner, by which time it was late, Jessye lit all the candles in the room, and it was at this point we told her of the surprise. Her carol was then performed, and it was a magical, unforgettable moment; the candlelit room, the words, Don's beautiful music and above all Jessye's face, obviously greatly moved. There was a short silence at the end and then she burst into tears. She then insisted on singing it several times herself. As we left, she asked for the piece of kitchen roll on which I had written the words, saying she was going to have it framed. We drove home thinking the evening a great success and thought that the end of it. We couldn't have been more wrong.

The next day the telephone rang. It turned out Jessye was so thrilled with her carol she wanted to make a Christmas album based around it. Her record company then commissioned Don to compose a Christmas Symphony and we set about the fascinating task of putting a large selection of well-known carols into the format of a classical symphony. My church background was helpful in this. The first movement was based on Advent carols, starting with 'O come, O come Emmanuel' and ending with a tour de force arrangement of 'O Holy Night'. The second movement, the scherzo, included 'I saw three ships' and ended with my carol, to which I added three more verses. The third movement, slow and beautiful, contained a stunning version of 'Silent Night' and a beautiful 'In the bleak midwinter.' The last movement rounded off the Christmas story and included 'We Three Kings'. Don then decided to write an 'Amen' which demanded virtuoso singing from Jessye, with her voice souring above the choirs to an impossibly high note before gradually fading into silence. The whole symphony was a challenge for orchestra, choirs, and Jessye.

We flew to New York for the recording and met the chosen team. Bob de Cormier was the conductor, a tall and rangy man who had great energy and endless patience. He was also a perfectionist and very demanding, but his charm and gentle manner were an asset, especially when it came to Jessye. Don had written difficult solos for her throughout the symphony and a lesser voice might have failed. For this recording, the services of John McClure had been obtained. He'd worked on recordings with many great musicians and composers, including Stravinsky. (John went on to make the famous recording of *West Side Story* with Leonard Bernstein, which brutally showed the tensions that can emerge between soloists and conductors. Poor Jose Carreras bore the brunt of Lennie's temper and frustrations until he was on the point of collapse.) Jessye, despite the demands made on her, worked in a totally professional manner and there was only one scare when at the end of a day's recording, she declared she had a sore throat and there was a frantic search for a doctor late at night. To everyone's relief she appeared to quickly recover. Those recording days in New York were among the happiest, and most rewarding, I have ever spent. Everyone involved believed in the project and loved it. Bob and his wife Louise, John and Susan McClure, were already friends and colleagues. Don and I now joined them, and the six of us spent all our time together. The famous American Boychoir joined the adult choir, and the boys' rendering of my carol brought several to tears. The lead cellist, who was Jewish, said to me as it ended, 'If this is Christmas, I'm having some of it!' The album, recorded on the Philip's label, was finally finished and named *This Christmastide*.

The recording of my carol remains one of my proudest

achievements, and still brings in annual royalties. In the States it has become a standard, but for some reason has had less success in the UK. I am still hoping it will gradually catch on. When I went to a Christmas service at Jess's school (Josh's eldest daughter), I was delighted to see it was one of their chosen carols, so I remain hopeful.

To our amazement the repercussions from that dinner party continued. A year after the recording was released, we heard a film was to be made of the Christmas Symphony for video (later DVD) and TV, using the same team of Bob and John, but this time made in the UK. The six of us were once more reunited and if anything, this was an even more joyous time. The chosen venue was the stunning Ely Cathedral. We were filming in July, so it was odd to see the large Christmas tree and decorations. The invited audience were also required to wear winter clothes. Luckily, cathedrals are notoriously unheated, so nobody felt too hot during the recording. The Bournemouth Symphony Orchestra was now used, also the Ely choristers, but it was felt only right to fly over the American Boychoir as they had played such a large part in the New York recording. Bob, as always, kept calm and patient throughout proceedings, and as the last sounds faded away, the audience gave a standing ovation. During the speeches at the end, I was called up to take a bow for my carol which, after all, had started off the whole enterprise. It was a proud moment. Jessye gave superb performances, both in New York and at Ely and afterwards always insisted on the carol being called 'Jessye's Carol'.

I saw a great deal of Jessye in the following years, often visiting her in her large house in Westchester, NY. These visits were fun, with Jessye again relishing the role of hostess and at her happiest in the kitchen, especially with late breakfasts making her favourite pancakes. But her moods were mercurial, and could change in a minute, so there was always the slight feeling of treading on eggshells. On one occasion when staying in New York, Jessye summoned me to stay for a couple of days, and then her invitation must have slipped her mind, because my arrival coincided with a visiting male friend, and it was made very clear my visit was now inconvenient. Jessye, notoriously protective of her private life, sent one of her staff to tell me she couldn't see me until the following day. It was late afternoon and as her house was isolated, there was nowhere I could take myself until she was ready to receive me. I was then informed I could spend the night in one of the buildings on the estate. There were several of these: a gym, a studio, an office and the one I was shown into, which was obviously intended to be an overflow for guests but was in the process of being converted and unfinished.

There was little in the house, apart from a bed, thankfully made up, a bathroom with no towels and a kitchen with no food. However, when I opened the fridge, it was stuffed full of bottles of Bollinger. So, I opened one and that was all the sustenance I had until morning. The next morning, feeling hungry, cross, and slightly hungover, I vowed I would somehow make my way back to New York as quickly as possible. Then, to my surprise the telephone rang, and a voice told me to make my way over to the house to join Miss Norman for breakfast. I arrived, and there was no sign of any man; he must have left first thing. There was no apology either. Jessye greeted me warmly and carried on as if nothing had happened. We spent a happy day together and then she had her chauffeur drive me back to New York the following day. With anyone else this behaviour would have been baffling, and angry words exchanged, but with Jessye they never were. It was a roller coaster. One moment, she would be warm and generous; the next, obnoxious and cold.

This behaviour was amply borne out by our next project together. Jessye had ventured into being a producer, something she wasn't cut out for, and mistakes inevitably followed. Her first project was a hugely ambitious one, Duke Ellington's astonishing biblical work, *The Sacred Ellington*. The production was complicated, demanding, and expensive, involving a band of virtuoso jazz players, a string quartet, a concert pianist, a small choir, a specialised dancer, and Jessye herself. Having contracted her performers, Jessye booked the first performance at the London Barbican, but instead of the concert hall she had booked the theatre, which acoustically was totally unsuitable. Sound problems immediately arose. At this point Jessye rang me and asked me to come in and stage the project. It was obvious at once we were in the wrong venue. A meeting was called with the Barbican staff at the highest level. I asked if there was any possibility of changing to the concert hall, and was told a definite no, the hall was fully booked with concerts. Jessye then became her most haughty and demanding. At the end of a long and difficult meeting, it was agreed to put sounding boards round the back, making the theatre acoustically viable for her concert. This was extremely expensive, and the Barbican were not happy. I did what I could, but my powers were limited. Some suggestions I made were accepted, and I worked long hours with the lighting designer creating effects which greatly helped the production overall, but it was not enough. Jessye had not seen the performance as a single cohesive piece, which meant it was fragmented and episodic with no links. Her chosen dancer, also a friend, was not allowed to be criticised, although her sections were far too long and just didn't work. But there were stunning moments, particularly Jessye herself. The virtuoso trumpeter was also brilliant and had a solo which won him long applause. Despite this, the critics were unimpressed and there were less than good reviews. The Barbican, having made a substantial loss, had a major falling out with Jessye and after this she was never invited back.

The next venue was the Châtelet in Paris. Some of the same problems occurred, although here the acoustic was fine. Jessye had a habit of hiring and firing her assistants with regularity. In Paris she had two new girls, and they were charged with booking all the artists. What followed was a series of muddles and mistakes. The worst one was on the day of the dress rehearsal when it became apparent the string quartet had been double-booked and were not available for the evening performance. A frantic morning of telephoning finally produced a string quartet, but they could not be with us until 5 pm on the day of performance, which left us little time to rehearse them in. It was a frantic rush for all, leaving everyone ragged, but the show went ahead. One of the lighting effects I'd added, a sky full of stars, received an ovation which greatly pleased me. It was a better performance than at the Barbican, the dances were shortened, and it hung more effectively together. The Parisian audience was madly enthusiastic, and the applause went on for a long time. Jessye gave a dinner afterwards, in a fabulous apartment on the Quai Voltaire. I was one of a select few she invited, and she was generous in her particular thanks to me. I left Paris feeling it boded well for the last two performances of the tour. However, I made the mistake of mentioning to Jessye that before the next performance in Amsterdam, she should get her two assistants to double-check all their bookings, as they had failed to do in Paris. Jessye's response was instant. She had taken umbrage. I received an unpleasant email, saying in stark terms my services on the show were no longer required and my contract was terminated. She added that she always picked her excellent staff very carefully and they were of the highest quality, so I had absolutely no right to criticise them. Thankfully, I had other work to go to, because it could have been a financial blow (something Jessye would never have considered). I heard afterwards from Jessye's agent that the performance in Amsterdam had been disorganised and the lighting a disaster. For Jessye's first entrance at the top of a flight of stairs, she was only lit from the knees down. I'm sorry to admit this gave me quiet satisfaction. Her two assistants didn't last either, both being fired after the tour ended.

I didn't hear from Jessye for over a year. Then, out of the blue, came an email. No apology. She explained there was to be a performance of *The Sacred Ellington* in Epidaurus, Greece and she required me to stage it. Was I available? Luckily, I was. There was a lull in ECT work and the children were now of an age when they didn't need my constant attention. So, I nervously agreed. I flew to Athens where the whole company assembled, and I was given a warm welcome, many of the original cast telling me how much I'd been missed. This company had a smaller choir, a new dancer, and a different string quartet. One major asset was the appointment of an assistant producer, Bill Cronshaw, who was already a great friend and someone I had worked with before. Poor Bill became Jessye's dogsbody, and she brutally ran him ragged, but he did help her with the organisation of the show. I was also introduced to Claudia, the Greek producer. She and Jessye had similar temperaments and spent a lot of time screaming at each other. The main company were given accommodation at the nearby village and were taken by bus to rehearsals each day. Jessye had taken a private hotel, entirely for herself, but insisted Bill and I stayed in the luxurious splendour of the annexe. We occasionally shared a dinner with Jessye, but these dinners were an agony. Jessye's behaviour was at her worst. The poor woman who ran the five-star hotel provided superb cuisine which I thought fabulous, but Jessye continually complained, sending the food away. I was embarrassed by her behaviour. One night, Jessye stormed off to the kitchen to show this top chef the way things should be done. After four nights of this, I said as tactfully as I could, I thought it would be best if Jessye had the evenings to herself and Bill and I would make our own arrangements for supper. We found a perfect small, family-run taverna who were delighted to have our custom, and we spent many happy, and peaceful, evenings there.

Epidaurus, the great amphitheatre, is the most astonishing and spectacular wonder, a 12,000-seater, with a perfect acoustic. Standing on the circular sandy stage you could make a soft pinging noise and it would be heard right at the top of the arena. No need for mikes, but there were plenty of other logistical problems to sort out. Claudia was on hand, but her constant 'No problem, Jane' was not helpful. I would say as patiently as I could, 'But there *is* a problem, Claudia, and we need a solution.'

One of these was caused by the recent rainstorms (the locals shook their heads about the unusual weather, and maintained the gods were angry with the intrusion). This resulted in another difficulty. The Steinway was delivered, and the pianist started to play. As he continued, I saw, to my horror, that the piano was sinking fast into the wet sand. Claudia was again summoned and a solution finally found by putting wooden boards under the piano. These setbacks caused delays to rehearsals. The rain ominously fell on the day of performance. How could we cancel, with 12,000 people already on their way? Luckily, it stopped just in time for us to go ahead, and we were only delayed by half an hour. I had been provided with a lighting man called Demetrius, who resembled a Greek god but spoke little English. The lighting was primitive, basically consisting of two huge spotlights mounted on a bar built right at the top of the theatre. On the night of performance, I mounted the steps and positioned myself nervously on the narrow platform beside Demetrius. It was a long way up and difficult to keep my vertigo under control. I was given the signal to begin, and the house lights went down. Pitch darkness. This was the moment Jessye was meant to start her solo and for the lights to come up as she made her entrance. Nothing happened. Panic! How on earth was I to find a black woman, dressed in black, in all the blackness surrounding us? With many gestures, I told Demetrius to put the spots back up to full and take them round in a circular way, hoping I would find Jessye. The audience, thinking it was some sort of Son et Lumière, started to applaud. It was then I caught sight of her. She was bent over the car, in the car park behind the theatre, with the chauffeur bent behind her. It did not look good. Was she ill? I told Demetrius to make the lighting circuit once more and finally, to my huge relief, Jessye moved towards the stage and the show began.

Afterwards she explained the zip at the back of her dress had jammed, and the chauffeur needed to repair it before she could make her entrance. The early delay produced a comment from the laconic bass player. I had been wearing that long white, cheesecloth dress, and during the crisis waving my arms around, while giving instructions to Demetrius. He said, 'I looked up and thought I saw the Angel Gabriel flapping his wings.' I don't know if it was an angel, or the gods, but someone was smiling on us, because the show was a fantastic success. At the end, the audience of 12,000 simply went wild and shouted for more. Jessye did a couple of encores and then the trumpeter gave two encores of his solo. It was like a pop concert. I think if I hadn't put up the house lights, the audience wouldn't have let us go. Jessye was at her happiest. There was a great party afterwards which seemed to involve the whole town, and even Claudia was smiling.

After this, I didn't see Jessye for some years, mainly because I was working abroad, but in one of the gaps, she invited me to join her in Hamburg, where she was giving a concert. We flew first class, and I was amused to see Jessye had booked two front seats for herself and I was sitting in the row behind. She also touched none of the food or champagne on offer, whereas I wolfed the lot. Our hotel, of course, was a very grand one. Jessye never rose before mid-morning, especially on concert days, so I had time to explore.

On the second day I was bidden to meet her for lunch, and it was then an alarming incident occurred. The lift became stuck. I pressed the emergency bell and, after several minutes which seemed like hours, a disembodied voice spoke in German, asking, I presume, what the problem was. I tried to keep the panic out of my voice telling them I was English, and the lift was stuck between floors. I also mentioned I was the guest of Jessye Norman. That name produced instant results. I was now spoken to in English. There followed a great many bangs and clicks and finally it was explained I was being winched down. After what seemed an eternity, the lift arrived on the ground floor and the door opened to a reception committee. The manager stepped forward, profuse with apologies. I was so relieved to be on terra firma, I just said I had to hurry as I was late for my lunch with Miss Norman.

Jessye found the whole episode hilarious, which I thought a little insensitive – after all, it had been quite an ordeal – but we were treated to a free lunch, and a bottle of champagne was sent over to our table. The rest of our short stay was thankfully without incident. Her concert was superb, and she returned for three encores. The long queue outside her dressing room was kept waiting a good while before being allowed to see her. Despite obvious exhaustion, she took trouble with everyone, and I marvelled at her stamina. There was then a late reception and dinner, but at the coffee stage she asked me to make her excuses, and we escaped back to the hotel.

The following day she was difficult and irritable, and the return journey was made in silence. I understood. The trip, although a wonderful experience for me, made me realise what a strange and difficult life Jessye led, with all the extreme pressure of performances, the constant highs and lows, the endless travelling, the receptions, the meeting and greeting and then at the end, the loneliness. There is no doubt her career, particularly at the start, had been hampered by the fact she was black. She was always conscious of this, although at the same time proud of her heritage, especially her Cherokee Indian ancestry, which came from her grandmother. She was extraordinarily beautiful, tall like an Amazon, and uniquely striking. Her choice of wardrobe was also impeccable. She would sweep on stage like a force of nature, in amazing multi-coloured silk robes, dazzling the audience before she even started to sing. She'd told me how much segregation had affected her as a child growing up in Georgia. When she was about six, she became aware that black children were made to drink from a different water fountain to the white children. 'Why?' she asked her mother, 'The water is all the same colour.' The anger and bitterness she felt at this injustice never left her.

The last major work with Jessye was an oratorio which Don and I had written called *The People's Passion*. It was the story of Holy Week as told by the ordinary people involved, characters like the Donkey Minder, who provided the animal for Jesus to enter Jerusalem. Each of the seven days had a different story. Don and I originally created this work for one of his friends, who needed an event to raise money for their church roof. The performance by the amateur choir was charming, money was raised, and we were pleased to have helped. Sometime later, Don played a recording to Tim Woolford, the producer of the Christmas programme at Ely. Tim became excited and said if we could get Jessye to perform, he would take the idea to the BBC for an Easter project. Don had composed the most beautiful lament for Mary after the death of Jesus, and when Jessye heard it, she immediately agreed to take part. Her fee and costume took up a good deal of the budget, but despite this, a splendid cast was assembled, including Ron Moody as the Donkey Minder, Robert Hardy and Patricia Hodge as Pontius Pilate and his wife, the great Sir Tom Allen as the Centurion, and most surprising of all, Kevin Whately, who turned out to have a great baritone voice, playing the part of Judas. Added to this were the orchestra, John Scott the conductor, a small adult choir, the choristers of St Paul's, and the beautiful dancer, Jonathan Cope, who performed two dances as the spirit of Jesus.

This was a stressful production and less enjoyable than *Christmastide* had been. Don by this time had left to live in the States. We were horribly limited on time and the recording of the actors took far longer than the two great singers, Jessye and Tom Allen. Jessye was therefore given less time than she wanted, but we were up against the clock and only an hour's overtime was reluctantly allowed. The director, Tony Cash, did a great job in the circumstances, but I know we all felt it could have been better, with less of a rush. Jessye gave a dinner on the night it went out and then with a few friends we watched the recording. They were all appreciative and visibly moved and Jessye herself seemed delighted. One viewer wrote to the *Radio Times*, '*The People's Passion*, with the great Jessye Norman, was worth the annual licence fee on its own.' At the time I felt unsure it had really worked, but I saw a repeat a few years later in the States and found myself greatly moved. I wish it had been possible for it to have more exposure.

Jessye's last years were a sad tale of deteriorating health, when she became a recluse, but I look back on our long friendship as one of the most special in my life. It wasn't always easy, but endlessly rewarding and full of extraordinary experiences. I will never forget her, nor that unique voice, nor the many moments of creativity, fun and laughter I was lucky enough to share with this amazing woman.

Chapter Twelve
THE GREAT AND THE GOOD

OWING TO MY father having collected celebrities as others collect Toby Jugs, I had learned never to be overawed by someone's celebrity status, so when it came to working with famous people myself, I tried to treat them as I would anyone else and not allow their fame to overwhelm me or interfere with the work. When I occasionally told an anecdote involving one of these famous people, my children would groan and accuse me of name-dropping. I thought this unfair and would protest I wasn't telling the story just because they were famous, but because they were the subject of the anecdote. Anyway, work with them I did, and they cannot be left out of this memoir.

These surprising work opportunities usually arrived out of the blue. Owing to the long gaps between my English Chamber Theatre performances, I was happy to accept whatever freelance work was offered, to help with my ever-dwindling finances. One of these offers excited me from the outset, because it involved working with two of our greatest dancers, Margot Fonteyn and Robert Helpmann. I admitted at once I knew little about ballet, but the Australian producers assured me it was only my biographical writing skills that were needed. The format required was to trace the dancer's early careers, through WW2, ending with the start of the Royal Ballet Company. Margot and Bobby were to narrate the show, and each section would be illustrated by excerpts from the actual ballets they performed. To get complete accuracy, I needed to spend time with both dancers. My first trip was to meet Margot in Panama. I was relieved my friend Bill Cronshaw was the manager of this enterprise and to have his help and support, especially with all the travel arrangements. As a nervous flier, I was terrified when we bumped our way towards Panama in a violent storm, with both thunder and lightning. Bill was not helpful on this occasion, saying he wished he could replicate the amazing lighting effects of the storm in the theatre. Personally, I just wanted to survive.

The first meeting with Margot was with her husband Roberto Arias, who I found out was a distant cousin of Enrique Arias, my early seducer. This encounter wasn't entirely satisfactory. We met in a restaurant and Margot was shy and elusive, her time taken up with seeing to the needs of the invalid Roberto in his wheelchair. I told Bill he must try and make a time for me to see Margot on her own when I could have her undivided attention. He arranged this, and I now managed to break through her reserve. At the outset I told her my theatre work was usually about long-departed famous people, and my speciality was in writing death scenes. This made her laugh and she commented she couldn't help me on the first and hoped she wouldn't on the second. I added apologetically I knew little about the ballet world. She found this amusing; it somehow set her at her ease, and she began to talk about her early life.

Once prompted, the memories poured out. She was sharply observant, especially describing Lilian Baylis, Ninette de Valois and, of course, Bobby Helpmann. The most detailed and extraordinary of her accounts described the ballet company touring the Netherlands at the start of WW2. It was meant to boost morale for both countries, but unfortunately at the same time as the ballet company arrived in the Hague, the Germans entered Holland and were quickly advancing towards them. Guns could be heard in the distance. Propaganda leaflets were dropped demanding surrender, and a sniper bullet narrowly missed Bobby while he was sitting in a restaurant. After a hurried gala performance, they were told to leave everything behind and climb on a bus which would take them to Rotterdam and a boat back to England. At first only the women were going to be taken, but to Bobby's great relief, Ninette de Valois stood firm saying either they all went, or none of them. Wardrobe, sets, scores, and their own personal belongings were all left behind. Bobby and Freddie Ashton wore their entire wardrobes, in layers. The company were then told to lie on the floor of the bus in case of snipers, but having reached halfway, they were turned back. In the distance, they could see Rotterdam was on fire. After hours of driving, they were finally put on a minesweeper and arrived back somewhere on the East Coast of England, completely exhausted. Freddie was despatched to get help and reported back that, as it was Sunday, there would be a long delay getting transport to take them back to London. Despite having no costumes, lost scores and no sets, a show went on the next day.

Margot was extraordinary in her description, vivid and lively, no longer shy and reserved. She added one further interesting anecdote. After the Gala in the Hague, a small girl presented them with flowers. This girl grew up to be Audrey Hepburn, and her mother was a leader in the Dutch Resistance. On our last evening in Panama, Bill persuaded me to tell Margot and Roberto the story of my dinner with the Queen and my balletic exit in the middle of the meal. Margot laughed till the tears poured down her cheeks and when she met Toby later, she told him I was one of the most amusing people she'd ever met. Maybe I should have had a different career as a stand-up comedian.

Our next task was to meet up with Sir Robert Helpmann

(known to my children for having played the terrifying child-catcher in the film *Chitty, Chitty, Bang, Bang*.) He was staying in the most spectacular house on Diamond Head, Honolulu, so Bill and I flew to Hawaii for the next set of interviews. Bobby was the opposite to Margot and not shy in the least. His greatest joy was to make people laugh and this he certainly did. After a session with Bobby my ribs would be aching. It was one hilarious anecdote after another. A great deal of the same ground Margot had already given me was now covered, with some personal variations. Margot had told me little of her early years, but Bobby was happy to expand on his life in Australia and struggle to become a dancer before leaving for England. Again, he made it sound hilarious but there was an underlying bitterness and anger at the treatment he'd received for choosing a career in ballet and for being so noticeably gay. Bobby determinedly made no compromises and even pranced along Bondi Beach entirely clad in black leather and then was outraged when he was thrown into the surf. He left Australia soon after this incident.

Our stay in the Diamond Head house was full of surprises. The occupants included an aggressive female parrot, who lived in a large cage. It turned out this parrot only liked male company. I was the only female in the house, and she took an instant dislike to me. If I stood in front of the cage, she would give me a furious stare and squark loudly, 'Bugger off!' Apart from the menacing bird, my stay in Honolulu was fun. I returned to London to work on the script but found further interviews were needed. I again flew to Hawaii to see Bobby, but my second interview with Margot was in Houston where she was working. I became immediately worried by her appearance. She seemed drained and lacking in enthusiasm for this, or any other ballet project. She confided in me she longed to give up working, but for financial reasons she couldn't. Her great wish was to retire to look after her herd of cattle. It was hard to think of this frail woman dealing with such huge beasts, but they were her passion. My instincts told me she would pull out, and I was right. The production was ready for a first performance in Australia, when I received a call from the producers to tell me Margot would not be going ahead. She was too worried about the deteriorating health of Roberto to leave him. Bobby was hugely disappointed and expressed the hope she would be able to join him for the production later. I was sure this wouldn't happen. Roberto died and Margot retired to her farm and her cattle, almost becoming a recluse, until her own health deteriorated. Despite this work being filed as a shelved project, I will always be grateful for being given the chance to meet two such exceptional people.

The most popular of all the English Chamber Theatre productions was the Byron, and it was a performance of this play which led to my meeting a legendary woman. In 1983, I decided to adapt the original work from a four-hander to just two performers. Derek Jacobi continued to play the poet, while Isla Blair took on the formidable task of portraying all the women in Byron's life. She cleverly managed to be different in all the roles. A new and far more elaborate score was added, not only to provide atmosphere, but also setting many of the poems to music, making full use of Isla's beautiful singing voice. This time the score was recorded, so there were no live musicians involved on stage. This saved money and enabled the production to be moved around more easily. One amusing incident occurred while Don was composing the score. My daughter Fran, aged ten, took it upon herself to set the poem 'Could Love Forever, Run Like a River' to music. As she sat playing her composition on her guitar, Don was so taken with what she'd written that he decided to include her setting and arranged it as a duet for Derek and Isla. It was perfect and very touching. (Jessye Norman later chose this song as one of her 'Desert

Island Discs'.) The other change was that scripts were abandoned, and it was entirely learned. Finally, it was given a new title, *Mad, Bad, and Dangerous to Know*. With fabulous costumes from COSPROP (famous for collecting Oscars for their costumes for Merchant Ivory films), the production was ready to be launched. With its simple set of furniture using peacock chairs, and aided by atmospheric lighting, it was an immediate success and from the outset audiences loved it. There were performances all over England including at Stratford and the Barbican. Invitations then poured in from further afield and these had to be fitted

Isla Blair and Derek Jacobi in Mad, Bad and Dangerous to Know *(photo: Chris Davies)*

around the actor's busy schedules. It played for a week in Israel, and a season in Los Angeles at the Doolittle Theatre, but for me the most memorable performance was at the Morgan Library in New York. This was a Gala to raise money for the library's collection of original manuscripts. Among their already vast collection was a couple of the actual Byron poems we were using in the play. New York's rich and famous turned out for this lavish event and it was a very grand affair. Once again, the audience was enthusiastic, giving long applause at the end, after which we sat down to a grand dinner. I was at the top table, and it was something of a shock when I found myself sitting next to Jackie Kennedy Onassis. There followed one of the most amazing encounters of my life.

Once we fell into talking, Jackie and I didn't stop for the entire meal. She'd loved the show and wanted to know why and how I had put it together. I explained about the English Chamber Theatre, our biographical dramas, and how we worked on a shoestring. This she found difficult to understand when the work was of such obvious high quality. (I didn't think it was the moment to explain the huge problems I'd had, applying for a grant from the Arts Council, and then being rejected.) One of the other ECT plays I did mention was *Their Finest Hour*. She showed particular interest in this, especially when it came to Churchill's problems with Stalin. She laughed and said it sounded like Jack's problems with Khrushchev. Her voice was low and soft, but it still managed to convey excitement and interest. At the end of the evening, she asked for my telephone number. We were staying with Susan and John McClure, so I gave her theirs. The next day the phone rang in the apartment and Susan answered it. The voice on the other end said, 'This is Jackie Onassis. Is it possible to speak to Jane?' Susan was so shocked at hearing her name, she accidentally put the phone back and cut Jackie off. Thankfully, Jackie tried again, and told me she'd had a few ideas that could be of help, and could I meet her for lunch? I explained I was going to Vermont to spend a week with the McClures, so we arranged to meet the following week, at a Japanese restaurant. What followed was a highly embarrassing incident.

To return from Vermont in time for this lunch, I had to fly back to New York in a small plane. On the day I was due to travel, John warned Don that the weather report predicted bad storms and it was going to be a very bumpy flight. Don explained how nervous that would make me and they decided to put Valium in my coffee, to relieve the stress. As predicted, the flight was truly terrifying and the other two passengers, a young couple, spent the entire time saying goodbye to each other, which didn't help. I sat white-faced with knuckles clenched as the small plane seemed to be tossed around in the black sky. My adrenalin was running far too high for the Valium to work, but when we finally landed it wasn't just relief that swept over me. I started to feel decidedly odd, unable to focus on anything. It was then Don told me about the Valium, and now, far too late, the drugs were kicking in. I was horrified. I was about to meet the most famous woman in America, and I could hardly string two words together. I had never taken Valium, or any other drug, in my life. How was I to explain my weird behaviour to Jackie? I also panicked about coping with the menu, so Don advised me just to order California Rolls. Jackie greeted me warmly, but as the lunch progressed, I felt increasingly weird. I remember trying to manoeuvre the California Rolls onto my chopsticks without any success and I knew my speech was sounding blurred. Jackie finally asked me if I was unwell, and the explanation poured out. She was instantly sympathetic, quickly organising a car to take me back to the hotel. I kept apologising profusely, but she sweetly told me she totally understood, and I was to think no more about it. Once I'd slept off the effects of the drug, I turned my fury on Don for giving me the Valium without asking. He became extremely huffy and said they'd only been trying to help. In the end I had to admit, apart from my embarrassment, there was little harm done.

Jackie and I met up soon afterwards and as promised she was immediately helpful. First, she put me in touch with her brilliant attorney, Robert (Bob) Montgomery. He was the most famous of all show business lawyers and among his many illustrious clients were Andrew Lloyd Webber, Marilyn Monroe, Andy Warhol, and Mike Nichols. He was also Trustee of the Cole Porter Trust. I don't know what Jackie had said to him, but he never once charged me for all the work he did on my behalf, saving me thousands. He was kind and charming, but I quickly recognised his toughness and the reason for his great success. I quickly grew to love and trust him. The other way in which Jackie offered help was her own exciting idea. She now worked at Doubleday and suggested I put together a proposal for a biography of Jessye Norman. If the publishers liked the idea, we would work on it together. I immediately agreed and my first action was to approach Jessye to get her reaction. It turned out Jessye was in total awe of Jackie, being the nearest to Royalty America had, so when I told her of Jackie's proposal she was thrilled and agreed at once for the three of us to meet. We drove together to Jackie's Manhattan apartment, and it amused me to see the great Jessye Norman so nervous and completely overwhelmed by the occasion. Over tea Jessye seemed enthusiastic, and it was agreed I would put a proposal together. No official contract was drawn up at this point, but Jackie assured me if Doubleday went ahead, Bob would organise a good advance.

Over the next few months, I worked hard on the proposal. Jessye at the start was co-operative and helpful, especially about her childhood, also providing me with an enormous amount of material about her professional career.

However, it soon became abundantly clear nothing would be included about her private life. Jackie and I discussed this. We both felt that just a list of her concerts and recordings would not make for an interesting book and Doubleday would never go for it. With some foreboding I tackled Jessye, explaining if she didn't want to talk about her romantic relationships, we did at least need to know something of her personal life outside the concert hall and recording studio. Jessye became immediately hostile, and a long silence followed. Then out of the blue a formal letter

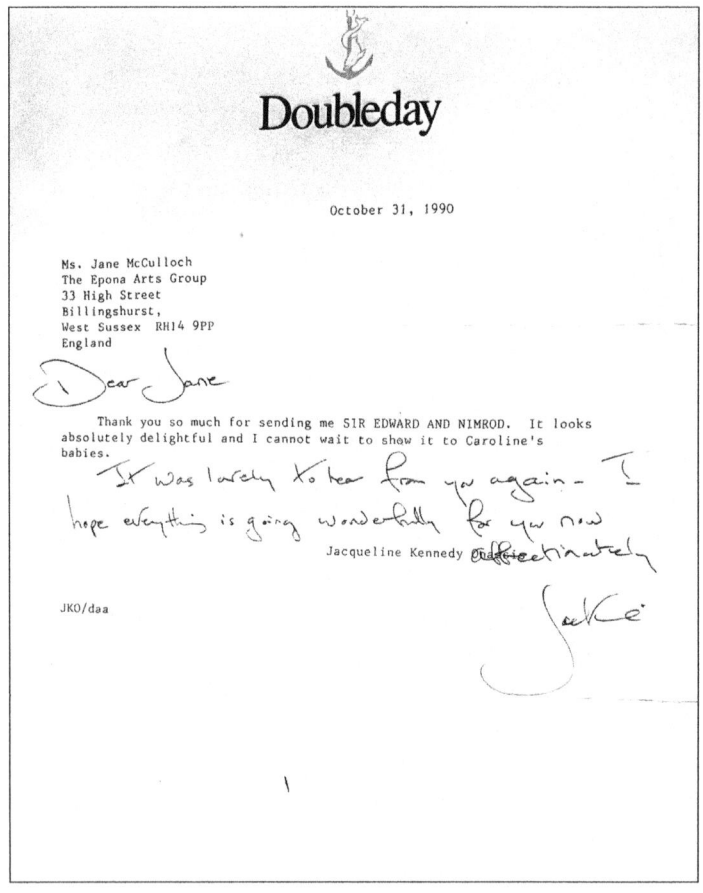

A letter from Jackie Kennedy Onassis

was sent to Jackie, telling her in the strongest terms that Jessye no longer wished to continue with this project. Jackie was upset, mainly I think on my behalf. Bob was also angry and said he took a dim view of Jessye's behaviour, but there was little any of us could do because Jessye was adamant.

Jackie and I remained in contact for the rest of her life. She always enquired about my latest projects and told me one of her favourites was the recording of *This Christmastide*, which she played in the car when taking her children to school. Her kindness and friendship I will always remember. As for the Jessye debâcle, I remained sanguine. I was becoming used to these major setbacks. Stars were unpredictable and no outcome was ever guaranteed. This opinion did not change on my next project, working with the film star Anthony Quinn.

Tony Quinn! About as difficult, touchy, and volatile as Jessye. Working with him was certainly stressful, although fascinating at the same time. After my initial nervousness, I grew quite fond of him. My commission was to write a one-man show about Picasso. Tony was also a painter, and his novel idea was to paint throughout the play and then sell his paintings to the audience at the end.

With my long list of biographical dramas, I was thought to be a suitable candidate for writing this project. Bob Montgomery managed to get a small advance from the producers, with the promise of a lucrative contract once the play went into production. It was mid-December when I first went to New York to meet Tony, and I had just finished working in the warm climate of Bermuda. I remember I was wearing a silk suit and landing at JFK was met by an icy blast. The plane had been delayed by snowstorms and, not wanting to be late for our first encounter, I took a taxi straight to the apartment he used as his office. He later explained this was somewhere he could work in peace without disturbance from his turbulent home life. I arrived on his doorstep shivering and blue with cold. On explaining the reason for my frozen appearance Tony said, 'I can't work with you in that state. Go to SAKS and buy yourself a coat. Put it on my account and then get back to me.' This I did, and purchased a full-length, military-style coat in charcoal grey, with double buttons down the front and a high collar. I loved it and lived in it every winter until years later when the moths got to it.

Working with Tony Quinn was a strange experience. He would pace up and down telling me excitedly what he wanted from the work. There were constant interruptions, usually to yell for his PA, a beautiful girl, and it was obvious to me there was a romantic involvement. I was right. She later became his final wife. Occasionally he'd answer a telephone call where he would rant at some poor soul on the other end who had obviously displeased him. One day his wife arrived. She was a small, dumpy woman with an angry expression and heavy Spanish accent. They immediately fell into a loud argument. She regarded me with great suspicion and some hostility. Tony told her I was English and was writing a play for him and would be returning to England soon. This seemed to satisfy her. After she left, Tony explained she behaved like that towards any good-looking 'broad' she found him with.

Another interruption occurred one morning when Bill Cosby was the visitor. He was then at the height of his fame and a major star. (He has since landed in prison.) Tony had summoned him, angry because at a birthday party for his wife the night before, Bill had given her a present worth twice as much as his own offering. There now proceeded an almighty row while they threw verbal grenades at each other. I sat in the corner of the room watching as if at a tennis match. Then, as suddenly as it had begun, it finished with a great bear hug. Bill Cosby, to my surprise, walked across the room, shook my hand, and said it was great to have met me. We hadn't even been introduced. Tony and I then carried on working as if nothing had happened.

After three weeks, I felt I had enough material to thrash out a first draft. Although he'd made me nervous with his constant mood swings, Tony always treated me with respect, although if I disagreed with him on some point, he would growl and say I was 'too goddam English'. His PA later told me he found me unnerving because my voice was so like the Queen of England's. Bob Montgomery took me out to dinner before I left New York and was highly amused at the account of my working relationship. (Tony Quinn had been very impressed Bob Montgomery was my lawyer, and I went up a notch in his estimation.) As Bob said goodbye he warned, 'Beware man who speaks with forked tongue.' He was right. The drafts went back and forth, with endless quibbles. Just as I was about to throw in the towel, an affectionate letter arrived, telling me I had the play just right and was particularly pleased I now seemed to understand Picasso's '*duende*'. He went on about the '*duende*' a great deal, telling me it was something he and Picasso shared. I understood this to mean the very black moods they both suffered from. But I think it also referred to a highly passionate and extreme nature, beset with heightened emotions. His '*duende*' moments were certainly a recurring event.

Writing a one-man show is a difficult undertaking at the best of times because there is no foil for the leading character, therefore no tension. For this reason, Derek Jacobi had never wanted the Byron to turn into a solo performance, and I agreed. Tony Quinn had no such qualms. I eventually found a way around this problem by letting Picasso have imaginary confrontations, not only with the wives and women in his life but also turning on the friends who didn't defend him. One Picasso anecdote I particularly liked was the painter being paid a visit by the Gestapo during the war. His paintings of Guernica were on display on the walls of his apartment. One of the Gestapo turned to him and said, 'Did you do this?' 'No,' Picasso replied. '*You* did.' Brilliant!

Once the play was finished, the next task was to find a director. I was summoned by the producers to meet a possible candidate, and it was something of a shock to find their chosen man was Toby. They started to introduce us when we both burst out laughing and Toby explained I was his ex-wife. I was asked if this would worry me, and my immediate answer was no. However, to be honest, it did worry me. It wasn't I doubted Toby's directing skills, but I was very aware of his over-use of the red pencil with new work. I had been a victim of it in the past. He would cut and rewrite at will with no respect to the author. This script for Tony Quinn had taken all my time and skill to get it accepted, I just couldn't risk Toby messing about with it.

My worst forebodings were quickly justified. Two weeks later Toby sent me his suggestions and they were even more radical than I feared. It would have meant a major rewrite and reshaping, and I was sure Tony would never accept these changes. I was saved from telling the producers of my worries because word came back to me saying Mr Quinn had insisted on choosing his own director. I had the definite impression he wanted an American to direct him. He'd had enough of the English with me. Toby later told me he'd found Tony very difficult and wouldn't have enjoyed working with him. In any event, the fates now took over. We were due to start rehearsals in Cleveland, the 'mistake on the lake' as Tony called it, when I received the news there would be a delay because Tony was unwell. It subsequently turned out he'd had a minor heart attack. To my great disappointment, the whole show was then cancelled. With only one performer who was irreplaceable there was no understudy, and it was therefore impossible to get insurance. Without the insurance it was too great a financial risk to go ahead. Letters of apology were sent, Tony sent me a signed copy of his autobiography and an affectionate letter expressing his regret, but it was a great blow. Once more my work was consigned to the file of shelved projects. This play would have been financially rewarding had it gone ahead. I began to feel I was destined never to make money. My father's words came winging back to me: 'Better to be born lucky than born rich!'

I cannot leave the subject of the great and the good without mentioning Jack Rudin.

Jack was nothing to do with show business. He was a billionaire, a real estate developer, owning a vast number of valuable properties in Manhattan and two skyscrapers, one on Park Avenue, the other on Broadway. I like to think he was the nicer version of Donald Trump. Whereas Trump's buildings were flashy and vulgar, Jack's were sleek in design and stylish. Jack was also a great philanthropist, and the Rudin Foundation supported many New York causes, ranging from cancer hospitals and the New York Marathon to Jazz at the Lincoln Centre. I first met him in England, when a TV producer we knew asked Don and me to join him for dinner, to meet an American he hoped would put money into his latest project. I was sat next to this large man with a strong New York twang, and without having been properly briefed, asked him what he did. He answered, 'I'm in real estate.'

'Oh,' I said, 'I think we call that an estate agent.'

My host was horrified by this, but Jack was greatly amused. It was the start of a long friendship and there was an immediate mutual attraction. The moment Don and I were in New York we were summoned to his favourite restaurant, and these dinners were a constant fixture during our stay. Jack was always enormously generous, although quick to inform me he never put money into 'showbiz'. One time he took me to Tiffany's and told me to choose myself something I liked. I became rather English. Nothing was priced, but I knew the jewellery on show would be enormously expensive. Apart from that, none of it was my sort of thing, so I asked Jack if we could go to the floor above, which had Tiffany gift items. Jack was highly amused and, I think, surprised. Most of the women friends he'd had since his wife died would most certainly have gone for the diamonds. I now found a silver fountain pen and happily accepted his gift.

One day, when we were walking in Central Park, Jack turned to me and said, 'How about you and me, kid?' It was a puzzling question. Did he mean mistress or wife? I was pretty sure it wasn't the latter. Even if I learned Yiddish, I was hardly the right choice for such a prominent member of New York Jewish society. My hesitation produced a roar of laughter from Jack who said, 'I know. It's that damned piano player!' I agreed Don was the obstacle to any relationship between us, and the subject was never raised again. To celebrate my 50th birthday, Jack threw a large party, taking over the Four Seasons Restaurant. Jessye was invited and to Jack's annoyance made her entrance rather late. In the middle of dinner, Jack did something rather embarrassing, asking the present company to give their opinion of me. It made me uneasy, and I had the feeling Jessye didn't like someone else being the centre of attention, but she was gracious and said I was a 'Renaissance Woman'. After this, the cake arrived: an exact replica of St Mary le Bow (Jack had been fascinated by the story of my father and the church's rebuilding). It was spectacular and a feat for any chef. The whole dinner was touching and generous, and Jack had given me a truly remarkable night. The other great action he took on my behalf was to use his influence with Cunard to suggest the English Chamber Theatre would make great entertainments for the QE2. This resulted in my making twelve crossings on that wonderful ship, with various entertainments, plus a cruise around the Mediterranean.

Some years after this, Jack finally took the plunge and married. He and Susan remained happily together until his death. The last time I saw him was after the first night of the Byron in the West End, when we took Jack and Susan to dinner at The Ivy afterwards. I had no reason to go back to New York after that and we lost touch, but the decade with Jack had been the greatest fun, a rare taste of the high life. I will always be grateful to him for that.

Chapter Thirteen
TOWARDS THE MILLENIUM

THE 'NINETIES BEGAN with the death of my father. It was very sudden, although his health had been deteriorating for some time, not helped by his alcoholic consumption. He was taken into hospital suffering violent nosebleeds. Naturally he was not allowed alcohol and the sudden deprivation caused too great a shock for his system. He died four days later. The obituaries were extraordinary: detailed and lengthy, and many with pictures of his more famous dialoguers, particularly Diana Rigg or Judi Dench. The headlines alone made interesting reading: 'Radical Spirit', 'Maverick Cleric' and so on. Bishop Richard Harries in his generous piece in the *Independent* wrote, 'Joseph McCulloch was consistently the best preacher I ever listened to. His sermons were both highly interesting and profound, the best of them a work of art.' But it was the saintly Edward Carpenter, Dean of Westminster, who most captured Joseph's elusive character and troubled genius. Under the headline 'I do now know... The maverick cleric who found sanctuary under the great bell of Bow', he wrote:

> Joseph's excess of talent left him frustrated, as he struggled to find expression and fulfilment and suffered from black moods and migraines. With his well-modulated voice, his ability to write evocative

and elegant English, there were almost too many outlets left open to him.

With his early published successes, he could have been a novelist. He could have made broadcasting his career. As a conversationalist he could be brilliant and witty and would have made an excellent lawyer or actor, but as it was, he became an Anglican Priest.

Edward then described his career in the Church, saying the one appointment he had wanted, the Dean of St Paul's, had

Joseph's book on his Dialogues in St Mary le Bow.

eluded him. He was too maverick for that. Edward finished by saying:

> His final appointment was to the bombed St Mary le Bow, the Cockney Church, which he not only had rebuilt and restored, but with the two pulpits he installed, his famous lunch-hour dialogues began and reigned supreme for ten years. After the death of his wife Betty – so beautiful, so intelligent, so natural and uninhibited – he retired from the city and for the last years of his life became a recluse.

It struck me, reading this obituary, how Edward had understood Joseph as very few did. I also liked the tribute to my mother, who I know Edward had deeply loved. The reading of the obituaries made me feel sad for my own failed relationship with Joseph. When I was a child, he was a remote figure and I had adored him unconditionally, but as I moved towards adulthood my adoration turned to anger at the way he treated Gabriel and Christopher, and of course my mother. I have never understood how cutting people out of your life should ever be necessary. It is a cruel and hateful action causing endless hurt and damage, but sadly many use it as a weapon of displeasure. It is what Joseph did to Gabriel and Christopher, for no better reason than they disagreed with him. He would then turn on my mother, who tried to support and protect her children. I know how torn she must have felt. My own relationship with Joseph became tenuous and difficult, especially when trying to support Ma. As he constantly said, 'If I am not number one in your life, I have no interest in you.' I always longed for some praise, but never had it, although others said he was proud of me. There was little I, or anyone, could do for him in the years after Ma died, when he cut a lonely character, only finding consolation in the bottle. His black moods and deep unhappiness were sad to witness. Looking back, I find it odd he was able to help so many outside the family circle, when his own close relationships failed so miserably. My mother told me he'd been sexually abused as a child by a local priest. This may have accounted for some of his behaviour in adult life, but I still find it hard to forget or forgive the major damage he'd caused to those closest to him.

As the 'nineties progressed, sadly my relationship with Don began to deteriorate. There were many reasons for this, mostly beyond our control. We were both still working as hard as ever, but no longer with each other, and often apart. Don had become a successful arranger, working in Los Angeles with Delos recordings. He also had a part-time job conducting a chamber orchestra in Chicago, which meant for a large part of the year he was away. I remained in Sussex, directing several plays at the Redgrave Theatre and at various drama schools, especially the Guildford School of Acting, which was conveniently close. I enjoyed working with students, although on occasions they could be difficult and sometimes surprisingly arrogant. I then received an invitation to direct a pantomime in Bermuda. This was something of a challenge, but two months in winter sunshine in Bermuda was too tempting to turn down. However, it did mean Don and I were hardly in the UK at the same time, and this was logistically difficult. Don had acquired two border collies, Sir Edward and Nimrod – Eddie and Nimby – and it was necessary for one of us to be around to look after them. This required difficult planning, and organising our diaries put a strain on us both.

Another reason life was becoming increasingly difficult was Don's financial problems. After the success of his *Rock Follies* case against Thames Television, Don unwisely pursued further litigation, chasing supposed lost royalties. This time his case failed and made a heavy loss. The huge legal costs meant he lost the Elgar Studio, which he had lovingly restored. It was a terrible blow and left him bitter and angry. Thankfully, the nearby cottage, Brinkwells, where Elgar and his wife Alice had lived during WW1, became vacant, and he was able to rent it. I loved Brinkwells. It was a charming, thatched cottage full of beams, quaint small rooms, and atmosphere. It was, after all, where Elgar had written his cello concerto. Best of all, it was set in a beautiful wild garden with an orchard and a field to one side where the dogs could be exercised. I turned an overgrown patch the size of a tennis court, into a vegetable garden, where I spent all my spare time.

Added to his financial problems, Don was unsettled, resentful of the English musical establishment, which he referred to as the 'Cambridge Mafia'. He felt an outsider, having the wrong roots, and was angry he was being ignored as a serious composer. The one concert of his original music received unenthusiastic reviews, and he again lost money. His frustration increased and so did his drinking. I started to dread every social gathering we attended. I'd watch in despair as his behaviour quickly became out of control as he swayed about, shouting and swearing. If I tried to persuade him to leave, he would angrily push me away and only drink more. Usually, he was repentant the following day. By way of apology, he would sit at the piano playing one of the romantic numbers from *Buster,* or compose some beautiful new melody, and hopelessly I would melt and forgive him.

At the start of the 'nineties another problem emerged, perhaps the most distressing of all. He suddenly developed a deep resentment of my family, which rapidly grew worse. In December 1990, Bash and Paulette had their wedding. It was in St Mary le Bow and was a wonderfully happy family occasion. Judi Dench, Bash's godmother, recited Shakespeare's Sonnet 116, 'Let me not to the marriage of true minds' and the music, arranged by Don for trumpet and organ, was superb. But in the days that followed, Don's mood darkened. He finally went on a drinking bender for two days and after returning declared he felt totally oppressed by my family 'baggage', could see no way out and would never be free of it.

As if to prove the point, the first grandchild, Oscar, arrived a few years later. I couldn't celebrate this happy event because Don's behaviour was now so unpredictable. I found myself permanently treading on eggshells, taking care not to mention anything to do with my family. The situation finally came to a head when Oscar was due to be christened. Don told me if I had any loyalty to him, I would not attend, adding it was now time for me to choose between my family and him. I was shocked, inevitably torn in two. I didn't want to lose him, but how could I possibly miss the christening? I went, but felt miserable and panicked throughout the entire ceremony. It was also a strain trying to keep up a normal front for the family. On my return, Don was gone. He was missing for three days and soon after this left for a season of conducting in Chicago. At least it was a breathing space. Having my loyalties so severely torn in two was having an adverse effect on my health. Some medication I was given caused me to put on weight, which I found depressing. Even Toby noticed. 'Darling! You used to be a Modigliani and now you are a Rubens!' I protested I wasn't that changed, but I was certainly no longer skinny. My migraines also became more frequent and debilitating.

Don and I somehow limped through the years that followed, and occasionally the good times returned. He sometimes surprised me with his romantic gestures, and one of these was an invitation to join him in Hawaii, where he was working on a new musical. It was to celebrate my 50th birthday – Hawaii Five-o! After his musical opened, the two of us explored the other Hawaiian Islands. It was to be the last truly happy time we spent together.

On our return to England, a strange invitation was

waiting for me. Toby, back from the States, was now Artistic Director of Theatr Clwyd in Wales. To my surprise, he asked me to direct a revival of the musical *Buster*. I was keen to work on it again, so I agreed. Ian Lavender and Jacqui Dankworth now took over the two roles. Ian made a remarkable Buster, and although very different from Max Wall, he caught many aspects of Buster's character that Max had missed. Don joined me in Clwyd as music director, but I found this an added strain, especially when he joined Toby for long drinking sessions. Toby also constantly interfered with my directing. I had become used to having complete artistic control and disliked his interference. Amazingly, despite all the stress, it was a successful production, and Toby told me later the Chairman of the Board had said it was his favourite production of the entire year.

It was to be the last time I worked with Don. Soon after this, he went back to Chicago for another long stint of conducting. Before he left, I took a short holiday in Tunisia. It had become a habit of mine to take off on solo trips abroad, for a week of writing in sunnier climes. I returned to look after the dogs and wait for Don's return from Chicago. And then, in July 1997, the bombshell dropped.

It shouldn't have come as a shock. I had known for some time the relationship was in trouble. The initial passion had lasted a long time, but in recent years it had faded. Don didn't hide his unhappiness with my family situation, and once he was drunk, he was often cruel and abusive, even in public. When living with an alcoholic, it is difficult not to drink as well. This I started to do, to the further detriment of my health. With hindsight, I should have left Don after Oscar's christening. But I didn't. I couldn't bear to. We'd had such an extraordinary life together. There had been so many wonderful things about it – the dogs, the music, the loving, the laughter, the friends, the cottage and the garden. At some point, Don had said jokingly I spent more time in my bloody garden than I did with him. After the arrival of a second grandchild, something in him snapped, and he made an astonishing demand: I must give up my family completely, cut myself off from everything in England and start a new life with him in Chicago. Shocked at the idea, I said I couldn't possibly do this, it was totally out of the question. With foolish optimism I just hoped things would improve and ignored the danger signals.

The end arrived suddenly, on a beautiful summer day, as I sat in the garden, feeling happy he was back and sipping coffee in a state of contentment. Then it happened. He told me bluntly he was leaving me. He had found someone in Chicago and would be setting up a new life with her and her child. I sat completely stunned and then, in a state of numbness, got in my car and returned to my flat in London.

Don had been so keen to proceed with his new life he hadn't bothered to work out the complications which would follow. Some of his actions were deeply hurtful. As soon as I left, he moved his new woman in. Having always scorned weddings and family life, he now proceeded with both. He arranged a wedding in the nearby village of Wisborough Green, where he and I had spent such happy times together and had so many mutual friends. This was desperately painful. He bizarrely spent his honeymoon in Disney World – anathema to me. It was bewildering, as if I'd never really known him at all. His American wife took an immediate dislike to Brinkwells, horrified at its primitive conditions, and soon after they departed for a suburb of Chicago.

I was left realising I'd hopelessly missed Don's inner longing for a family of his own. When I'd first met him at the age of 27, he was a free spirit, having thrown off all the shackles of his working-class, Essex roots, and declaring he had a horror of marriage and family. Now at 50, all that had changed. His departure for America also enabled him to reinvent himself as a composer of stature. He detached himself completely from all his English connections, and this left many of his close friends bewildered and hurt. In leaving for good he also left various problems behind, most of them financial. One of the many shocks that awaited me was to find there was nothing in my savings account. I had stupidly asked Don to open a dollar account for my savings, so that I wouldn't be tempted to touch it. Finding it empty, I was bewildered and asked what had happened to the money. Don replied truculently it had been spent on our living expenses, pointing out we'd had an extravagant lifestyle. That was true, but this had been mainly his choice which I went along with. He had never asked me about dipping into the dollar account, and I would never have agreed. Most of these savings had been from the sale of the Port Isaac house, some years earlier. Now I was left with a rented London flat and not much else. Don eventually paid me a small sum and told me there would be no more. He also left me to wind up dealings with the Brinkwells landlord and pay off other bills. I had lost partner, home, dogs, garden, a way of life, friends, and was virtually penniless.

GSA offered me another directing job. It was an obscure musical and turned out to be my only failed production at that school. I fell into despair. Thankfully, Bermuda asked me back for another pantomime, and although not my favourite format, two months in beautiful surroundings among the many friends I'd made, allowed me some recovery time. I returned to spend Christmas with the family. The children and Toby were kind and full of sympathy, but I was in a daze, unhinged almost to madness, and no good to man or beast.

The following years were unhappy and difficult. I was unsettled, tortured by not only missing Don physically, but also the life we'd shared, every aspect of which had now gone. The jealousy lingered on and stubbornly would not leave. Jealousy is a terrible thing. Shakespeare nailed it brilliantly in so many of his plays. It pervades every aspect of your being and forces you to behave completely out of character. In calmer moments, I was left to ponder and reflect on what had happened. I began to blame myself for my two failed relationships. I'd missed Toby's double life and Don's changing needs. However, I'm not sure, even if I had discussed these problems with them, there was much I could have done to save either situation. I tried to look for positives. For forty years my life had been divided between two extraordinary and gifted men. Difficult they may have been, but there had been joyous times with both. Toby had given me four amazing children and started me writing. Don, with his great musical gifts, had enabled me to have an extraordinary burst of creativity, setting up the English Chamber Theatre, and so many other fascinating projects. In many ways I'd been lucky, but I gradually came to realise there'd been one major drawback. I had spent my entire life trying to please them, to fit into their lives and do everything the way they wanted. I'd somehow lost my identity along the way. Often their demands forced me to act against my better judgement. Now I had the opportunity to change. It was time to live the way I wanted, make my own decisions and, for the first time in my adult life, become an independent woman.

Chapter Fourteen
LIFE AS A SINGLE WOMAN

MY FIRST ACTION, after the departure of Don, was to retreat to Cornwall and look for a cottage. With my remaining savings and generous help from the family, I managed to scrape together enough for a deposit. I found the perfect place in Trebarwith Strand, just up the coast from Port Isaac. This cottage was one of only a few straddling either side of the lane that plunged down to the dramatic beach and onto miles of golden sand, with steep cliffs on either side. In the middle of the beach, rising out of the Atlantic, was a huge rock, which the grandchildren named 'Puff the Magic Dragon Rock.' Cumbrae Cottage was only a short walk from the beach, set back from the lane, with a small driveway and parking space. It had been the coach-house to the main house, now no longer in existence. Looking small from the front, it was like Doctor Who's TARDIS, amazingly spacious inside. The whole place had been built in and around the rocks behind. All the rooms were quirky in some way. The main living room was held up by a huge beam which had been saved from a nineteenth century wreck and had the name and date of the ship carved into it. There was also a large open fire which burnt fiercely with a mixture of logs and coal. In another big living room, I installed a sofa bed for the overflow of visitors. This also turned into a good playroom for children, when the adults wanted some peace and quiet. There were three other bedrooms, a bathroom, and a shower room. A door from the top attic bedroom led out to steps and a steep climb to a high garden with fantastic views out to sea. The lower garden wrapped around the cottage and, like the building, urgently needed restoration. I immediately set about both, being greatly helped by Mark, a roofer by trade, but who miraculously could turn his hand to anything. Over the next five years, we restored and renovated not only the house and garden, but also built a studio by the steps that led up to the top. This studio was built into the rock and consequently the walls were oddly shaped. I put in a daybed, a desk for my computer and telephone, and moved in all my work files. It became a wonderful writing room.

Cumbrae proved the perfect place for my recovery. I would go for long, solitary walks across the deserted beach. Also, at this time I started writing poetry, and this proved very cathartic. Into the first volume I poured my most angry, critical, and bitter thoughts about the break-up. Three more slim volumes followed, all of them self-published. These verses proved surprisingly popular, although if Don had read the first volume, I doubt he would have enjoyed it. Several years later, Gyles Brandreth included 'The Old Lover', one of the lighter and racier poems, in his bestselling anthology. But my favourite was one that summed up the break-up.

THE GIVEAWAY

I do not know whether you knew
But before you went away
There was one thing you used to do
Which was a sure giveaway.
You would whistle.
Whenever you felt guilty, or had lied

You would whistle,
And by the time you had decided to go
You were whistling all the time.
I just thought you should know.

I included this poem in the English Chamber Theatre entertainment *Love and Marriage*. Isla Blair performed it quite brilliantly. As she finished, there was a sharp intake of breath from the audience, whether from shock or recognition I don't know, but it caused a definite frisson. After finishing the fourth volume I felt cured, and I haven't written another verse since. These verses were by no means all doom and gloom; some were observations about current events, and many were humorous. I wrote one about Edie, my very clever granddaughter:

EDIE

Edie, my eldest granddaughter
When she was five
Informed me she had written
Two books of poems already
And was working on the third.
This meant that by the time she reached my age
This child prodigy
Would have works filling several shelves
Of the London Library

I am happy to report her early brilliance did not fade. Edie went on to get a first in English at Newcastle and a distinction in her MA at London University.

Although I spent as much time as I could at the cottage, I did have to return to London for proper work. For two months every year until 2004, I continued to direct in Bermuda. No more pantomimes, but now plays of my choice. In five years, I directed Chekhov's *The Cherry Orchard* (my own English version), Rattigan's *The Deep Blue Sea*, Noël Coward's *Hay Fever* and *Present Laughter*, and most ambitiously of all, *Love's Labour's Lost*. This last was not the easiest of Shakespeare's comedies, especially with limited casting on the island, so I was pleased with the result. I always took enormous care with the music and costumes in these productions. I set the Shakespeare in 1913, just before WW1, which allowed an especially poignant moment at the end. As the four reconciled couples stood under the gazebo and the sunset faded, I had a poppy drop, indicating they might be happy now, but the men were destined to go to war, possibly to meet their deaths within the year.

I was proud of all the Bermuda productions, and of course, it was the most wonderful place in which to work. In addition to the major productions, I also mounted four English Chamber Theatre works for the Bermuda Festival. This took place in February, the only month with slightly dubious weather. These four were *Love and Marriage*, *If I Should Die* (Rupert Brooke), *Their Finest Hour*, and *Beethoven in Vienna*, with James Bolam brilliant as the composer. After the Beethoven performance, the cast and I were invited to Government House for a reception. It was during this, one of the guests came over and told me how much he had loved the play. He then issued an invitation: would I and the actors like to have a drink on his yacht? Yachts in Bermuda were plentiful, so I wasn't too surprised by this, and it sounded a pleasant way to round off the evening, so I accepted. Gathering up the two actors, we went outside to his car. I should have guessed he'd be a man of some importance, and this was soon confirmed. As we reached his large limo there was a flag flying on the front of it. A short drive took us to the quay, and in front of us was the Royal Yacht *Britannia*. There was a great deal of saluting as the Admiral walked us up the steep gangplank. We were first taken to his quarters, very splendid and grand, and he then asked if we'd like to take a tour of the ship. It proved fascinating, especially as the Admiral regaled us with endless anecdotes along the way. It was nearing midnight, but we were taken down to the engine room, where an immaculately dressed crew leapt to attention. I have never seen so much gleaming copper. The whole place was spotless. We returned to the Admiral's quarters and, as I looked at my watch, I realised we had moved into February 4th, my birthday. I announced this fact and the Admiral at once said we should celebrate with champagne, adding, '*She* won't miss it!'

So, my birthday that year started with the Queen's champagne. What followed was one of the most interesting few

James Bolam as Beethoven in Beethoven in Vienna *(photo: Dominic Turner)*

hours I've ever spent. The Admiral was a born raconteur. After discussing the play, he told us he had a particular love for Beethoven. When he was plunging through mountainous seas, he would either play the storm sequence from Beethoven's Sixth, or Wagner's 'Ride of the Valkyries', with the sound full on. After this he embarked on his adventures at sea, some of them very funny, and many stories about his time on the Royal Yacht. I finally, and reluctantly, said we had to leave as the actors had a performance later. We were about to make our precarious journey back down the gangplank when I turned to the Admiral and said, 'May I kiss you goodbye?'

He gave a roar of laughter and said, 'I'd be bloody cross if you didn't!'

Rear Admiral Sir Robert Woolard was one of the most remarkable men I ever met. It was only a short encounter, but certainly one I won't forget. He was passionately devoted to that ship, and I am sure he shared the Queen's great sadness when this beautiful yacht was later decommissioned.

After the Shakespeare, I didn't work in Bermuda again. Another offer of work came in and anyway, I didn't feel I could top *Love's Labour's Lost*. For a decade I'd been lucky to spend time on that beautiful island, I'd even experienced a hurricane, and I'd made many friends. But now pastures new beckoned. I was summoned to the island of Roanoke on the coast of North Carolina. This new adventure was arranged by an extraordinary, eccentric American woman by the name of lebame Houston. Her real name was Mabel but, loathing it, she spelled it backwards and insisted on it being lower-case. It is difficult to adequately describe lebame. She was, and is, a complete one-off, living on a diet of cigarettes, whisky, and hot dogs. Her great passion has always been Elizabeth I and all things Elizabethan. She's worked as a historian, dramatist, and archivist, living in

Manteo, where the first English settlers arrived on nearby Roanoke Island, perishing in 1587. lebame had seen one of my productions in England and suggested to the Board of the Lost Colony Theatre I should be invited to do a series of workshops with the company. These were a success, and the following year I was asked to direct the actual play of *The Lost Colony*. This traced the extraordinary story of how these colonists disappeared. The mystery remains unsolved: no trace of them has ever been found, and it's been a source of fascination ever since. In 1937, Paul Green wrote his outdoor drama, *The Lost Colony*, and it has been performed every year from May to August, since that date.

A special outdoor theatre was erected on the exact spot where the colonists landed, and it could not have been a more dramatic setting. Directing this play was a daunting task. The cast of well over a hundred was mainly drawn from the local community. There were also ten professional actors for the leading characters, a large group of trained dancers, a choir, and ten children. The casting sessions for the main roles took place two months before rehearsals were due to begin, at vast casting sessions. These were totally alien to me. Producers and casting directors from all over the States gathered in a chosen venue, to find performers for their repertory theatres and summer seasons. My first casting session was in Memphis, Tennessee. I never managed to visit Elvis' mansion Graceland, but did get to the iconic Beale Street, 'Home of the Blues'. Apart from that, I found the five days of castings an ordeal. The thousands of auditioning candidates were each allowed three minutes, and a buzzer would sound if they went over the allotted time. Impossible to find out if someone is suitable for a role or can even act in that time. I felt desperately sorry for them. At least we were allowed callbacks in the evening, but the producer, Carl Curnutte, would get impatient if I kept anyone too long. The whole process was exhausting, but somehow, we managed to find suitable actors. We then returned to Roanoke for the remainder of the castings.

Rehearsals started at the beginning of May, and it was a huge undertaking. The play was a creaky, old-fashioned vehicle, with many inaccuracies, particularly in the first half set in England, where Walter Raleigh begs the Queen for a ship and supplies for his expedition to the New World. I was told from the outset I was not to change a single word of the text, which was frustrating. The England as presented, with the pretty costumes and constant merry making, gave a chocolate box vision of life in Elizabethan England and was a long way from reality. The second part was on surer ground and gave a more accurate picture of the colonists' struggle against hunger and illness. The various groups of the production rehearsed in different areas. I endured the worst of it, being on the outdoor sandy stage where it became exceedingly hot, and I was horribly bitten by insects. The lucky choir and dancers were in air-conditioned rooms. At some point I suggested it would be good to have a star actress to play the part of Queen Elizabeth for the first week, and then had the brainwave of asking Lynn Redgrave. It was a joy to see Lynn again; we'd lost touch since Central, but as always with thespians, the years rolled away. William Ivey Long, the award-winning costume designer, set about creating an exact replica of the Queen's costume and the result was superb, although it took poor Lynn hours to struggle into the costume and have her elaborate make-up done and a wig fitted. It was logistically far more complicated than any production I had done previously. The fight scenes and the dances were all spectacular but had to be included seamlessly within the play. A new sound system had been fitted, but this could be horribly affected by the wind. New lighting equipment was badly needed but could not be afforded while I was there, so I had to make do with what we had, which was barely adequate.

Outdoor drama is always dependent on the elements and although storms constantly threatened, on opening night they thankfully stayed away. Lynn was superb. There was one amusing moment when she made her first entrance. I had her coming down the steps from the stage with her procession of courtiers and pages, and then walking across the front of the audience. One member of the audience in the second row became so excited he shouted out, 'Hi, Queen!' Lynn slowly turned on him with a chilling look of haughty contempt, pointed a menacing finger at him and then moved forward with the procession. The poor man shrank back into his seat. Apparently, he said later he thought he was going to be sent to the Tower.

My time in Roanoke, despite problems, was a truly wonderful experience. I stayed in a log cabin, right on the water, and this could be challenging. I battled with cockroaches and, early on, some freezing nights, when the gales blew in from the sea. The days were extremely hot and humid, and there was no air conditioning. One morning I went for my usual stroll by the water and saw what I thought was a large stick. And then it moved. It was a snake. I beat a hasty retreat, then rushed to the next-door house, which lodged some of the stage management. They immediately responded and I didn't watch as they despatched the poor snake, finally assuring me it was now dead.

As with Bermuda, there were endless parties. The producer, Carl Curnutte, was a particularly generous host and loved to throw impromptu gatherings. At the end of the season, he asked me back for the following year and I accepted. This time the castings were in Florida. Six of us made the journey from Manteo by road. I remember it as being hilarious, with much laughter, punctuated by constant stops at fast-food outlets. Rehearsals this time went more smoothly, but I missed Lynn being the celebrity guest performer. This year being the seventieth season, there was a glittering opening night with local celebrities, including veteran actor Andy Griffith, who made an over-long speech. Carl asked me to make a speech as well. He gave me no warning and I found it daunting to stand up in front of two thousand people. I also disliked the way the speeches held up the performance, but hope I managed to sound gracious, saying I was honoured to be the first English and first woman director allowed to tackle such an amazing and moving story. Moving it certainly was. The play ended with the starving colonists leaving their settlement to go in search of food. They marched up through the theatre in a long, bedraggled column, singing a hymn of hope. As the sound faded away, the lights faded to blackout, with only the sound of the howling wind. It was an unforgettable moment of pure theatre. I returned to Roanoke to see the play last year, 2023, sixteen years after I had last directed it.

The production has changed enormously. For a start, the director has been allowed to change the script. He's also put in huge visual effects and a film-like score which runs through the entire show. This certainly makes it more accessible to a modern-day audience, but I couldn't help feeling the storytelling had been lost, the acting rather neglected and the very young cast unable to deliver the full impact of those momentous events.

In the middle of all this, I somehow found time to visit Savannah, Georgia to direct a performance of *Othello* for their Shakespeare Festival. This presented me with a whole new set of challenges. It was performed in a large park and the sound system was hardly adequate. There was also the cold. The temperature plunged to freezing at night. Poor Desdemona in her flimsy nightdress turned blue and I was seriously worried she would be struck down with hypothermia. The casting had already been completed by the time I arrived, and the talents were mixed, but the leading actors playing Othello and Enobarbus were excellent, and I somehow managed to produce solid performances from the rest. Despite all these problems, the audiences didn't leave halfway through as I'd feared but remained rapt till the end. The producers were surprised and delighted by this success. I also found Savannah fascinating and unlike anywhere else I'd visited in the States.

On my return, I was offered another challenge, this time in London and again one that took me in a new direction. This was a chance to work in opera. It was to keep me fully absorbed for the next ten years.

Chapter Fifteen
CALMER WATERS

MOST OF MY adult life had been something of an emotional roller coaster, dominated by two long relationships, Toby and then Don. I now moved into calmer waters. Once I'd recovered from the break-up, I became surprisingly contented with living on my own. Being single had its advantages, perhaps rather selfish ones. Not having to consider anyone else when making decisions was a welcome relief.

My time was now divided between Cornwall and a small flat I rented in Putney, which became the base for my London work. It was on the ground floor of a house, built around 1900, which opened onto a large and beautiful

Family gathering with children and 10 grandchildren, 2002

garden. The house was run by the Soroptimists, a charity founded at the end of WW2 to provide homes for single professional women. Being in London gave me the chance to see my ever-expanding family. The last of my ten grandchildren was born in 2002.

On the occasions we were all gathered, we numbered twenty. However, my greatest joy was the renewal of my relationship with Toby. Although we now lived separately, we quickly reverted to where we'd begun all those years ago. I still found him the most perfect companion and when in London, we had lunches and dinners every week. He sometimes came to stay in Cornwall, and I took him to Venice for his seventy-fifth birthday. There were also many family times when we'd meet at one of the children's houses. Toby loved the company of his grandchildren, and it saddened me to reflect how much he'd missed of his own children's early years. He'd now retired from the theatre and most of his time was taken up with his great passion, painting, and on my sixtieth birthday he presented me with a beautiful small landscape of the Tuscan countryside, inscribed 'My darling J, For forty years, onnish and offish, but always with constant love and devotion, Toby.'

In 2005, the invitation came to direct *Cosi fan Tutte* for a newly formed company, Opera UK. Toby was an immediate support in this new venture. He'd directed many operas with such major stars as Pavarotti and Jessye Norman, so his advice was invaluable. I quickly found the process of directing an opera very different from directing a play. The duties of an opera director are divided, the music rehearsals taking up half the time. I was lucky to have Stephen Hose, whom I had worked with on several projects, as music director. At the start I found it frustrating not to have overall control, but I gradually fell into a rehearsal regime which suited us both. During the time Stephen took over, it was wonderful to sit back and just listen to the glorious music.

Opera UK had been started by a retired businessman, John Mullis, who had a passionate love of opera and musicals. He was married to a Puerto Rican singer, the exotic Scheherazade Pesante, and wanted to give her an opportunity to show off her powerful, but untrained, voice. He chose two operas to start, *Cosi* and *Tosca*, with Scheherazade singing the demanding role of Tosca herself. Every other singer was auditioned, and these auditions were an astonishing experience for me. Those auditioning had usually just recently left the music colleges and conservatoires and were hugely talented. In an over-crowded profession, most of them, despite their talent and potential, would find work opportunities scarce, many progressing no further than the back row of the chorus in one of the opera houses. Opera UK gave them perhaps their only chance to play leading roles. With so many to choose from, it often came down to the singers best matched, both musically and physically.

After the first two productions in smaller venues, John decided to take the Bloomsbury Theatre for his next two operas. Once again, he chose a role for Scheherazade in *Simon Boccanegra*, one of the more obscure Verdi operas, and if Tosca had been demanding, this was even more so and not surprisingly she struggled. I was happy to be directing the other choice, *The Merry Widow*, and it proved to be a wonderfully happy experience. I not only managed to pick a wonderful cast but also had a great creative team. The costumes were designed by the brilliant Michael O'Connor, who had just won the Academy Award Oscar for Best Costume Design for the film *The Duchess*. He has since become a great friend. Michael not only gave up his time but miraculously did the whole thing on our minimal budget. The result was it looked as rich and exotic as any opera house production. The other stroke of luck was to have Donna Berlin, a clever and inventive choreographer. Her can-can at the end brought the house down. I added in a role for seven-year-old Edie, who made a brief appearance in the opening party scene, being told to go to bed and refusing. It produced many 'ahhhs' from the audience, so I felt justified for this indulgence.

The Merry Widow has a lot of clumsy dialogue in between its charming music, so I set about writing a new English version. This proved successful, mainly because I cut down the dialogue to a minimum. Singers always find it difficult to switch from the singing voice to speaking. It is why Gilbert and Sullivan operettas can often prove so difficult. The audience's reaction on opening night convinced me this production had all the makings of a commercial success, but unfortunately, John, an amateur producer, had no knowledge of how to promote his productions or which West End producers to approach. He had generously financed the company, but sadly, because of his inexperience, large amounts of this money, which could have been used on marketing and promotion, were wasted. Just after *Widow* opened, I had to leave for my last production in Bermuda and was unable to help or advise. Despite the four weeks being a sell-out, with nightly standing ovations, the production ended after its run at the Bloomsbury. It is one of my lasting regrets that *The Merry Widow* didn't have a longer life.

On returning from my stint in Bermuda, John called me in for a meeting. To my delight he asked me to become the permanent Artistic Director of Opera UK and informed me he'd taken on an administrator as well, Eric S. (I am not saying his full name because of what occurred later.) John generously put both of us on retainers. (I only learned later Eric's was far larger than mine, as he'd told John he wouldn't work for less.) I knew little about Eric, but John said he'd had experience in every aspect of theatre production. All started well enough, and we embarked on the most ambitious production yet, *The Barber of Seville*. Eric was keen to design the set and I made the mistake of letting him. The finished design would have been excellent had we remained in one theatre, but after opening at the Bloomsbury, we were off on an eight-week tour around Ireland, and the logistics of packing up this heavy set each night became a nightmare. We were short staffed, having only one stage manager, Dan Norris. It took Eric and Dan over an hour each night to pack up the van. Dan was also put in charge of booking the accommodation and travel arrangements, and these did not always go to plan. The company, which included a string quartet, were often unhappy and complained about this. Somehow, despite all the difficulties, the tour was a success, particularly in the South where we visited many of the old theatres and opera houses which hadn't seen an opera in years. There were also tours set up in England, my favourite venue being the Buxton Opera House.

After *Barber*, we took a break from major operas and I put together an evening of opera 'hits', popular arias the audiences would know. I called it *A Night at the Opera*, and this proved enormously popular. We took the show to Dubai, where we were treated to first-class flights and first-class hotels. It was a luxury we were unused to, and the company quickly returned to normal when we arrived back at Luton and transferred to Ryanair, to embark on another tour around Ireland. With a smaller cast of six, no musicians, apart from Stephen on keyboards, and no set, this was a far easier operation. Scheherazade came with us on this Irish tour and with her big voice and personality she proved a great hit. The Irish loved her, and she nightly received huge cheers from the audience. We always ended the evening with Puccini's 'Nessun Dorma', and many times there were two or three encores, and always a standing ovation.

With the success of *A Night at the Opera*, we started to plan the next season, and this is when disaster struck.

Eric, as administrator, managed the company accounts, but from the outset it was agreed with the bank that all cheques would be signed with two signatures. At some point I needed to pay a bill, only for Eric to tell me there was not enough money in the account to cover it. I couldn't understand this. We should have had a substantial amount left from the previous tour. I asked to see the bank statements and Eric began to make excuses, saying they were not available because he was preparing the company annual return. Meanwhile, John received a letter from Companies House informing him of a fine for late filing of Opera UK accounts. He summoned Eric to a crisis meeting, and Eric's dealings unravelled. To put it bluntly, he had defrauded the company of thousands of pounds, paying all his personal bills including his mortgage with Opera UK cheques. It was a terrible blow and a shock. John and I had completely trusted him. Worse was to follow when we found he had managed this removal of funds by using only a single signature on the company cheques. John and I started a long dispute with the bank, who refused to recognise this was their fault. Eric went into denial and wouldn't discuss it. With no repayment in sight, we reluctantly went to the police.

It took nearly a year for me to sort out the exact sums Eric had removed from the UK account and prepare a case against him. Meanwhile we were unable to move forward with any productions while the case was pending and consequently were without income. The excellent police officer looking after the case finally summoned Eric to the police station, with his solicitor in tow, to answer the charges. After a momentary defiance, Eric had no answers and put up no defence, accepting the evidence against him. Threatened with a prison sentence if the case went to court, Eric's solicitor made an offer in settlement. It was two thirds of the amount taken, but we were informed this was probably the best we could hope for. The case might take months to make it to court and even then, a more successful outcome was not guaranteed. I think John and I were just relieved to see an end to the whole horrible business, but we were left feeling bitter about it, especially the bank's refusal of support.

We now had a dilemma about the future of Opera UK. We had no administrator and, with our reduced finances, could not afford one. John was devastated his beloved company might come to an end. He'd poured money into it, but after the Eric debâcle, he made it clear he could no longer afford to do so. With all the success we'd achieved it seemed a terrible waste. Always given to impulses, I now

Opera UK flier

made one of the riskiest decisions of my life. I told John I would take over both roles, administrator and artistic director. Financially, we would be limited to the money we earned from our performances, along with the few fundraising activities I had time to organise. I had to learn fast. Dealing with accountants, spreadsheets, Companies House, and VAT, on top of directing, casting, designing, lighting, artwork, advertising, and the logistics of organising and booking the tours was a mammoth task and madness to have undertaken, but I was determined to keep Opera UK going. I revived our successful production of *Cosi* and embarked on another major production, *La Traviata*.

Other smaller concerts were created, which helped finance the larger ones. Among the most popular of these was *Keep the Home Fires Burning*, a show built around the music and songs from WW1. These smaller shows were ideal for the beautiful Normansfield Theatre in South London, where we performed regularly. Against all the odds, Opera UK continued, and I was grateful to everyone involved for taking minimal fees. Even making every economy I could, I still found I had to dip into my savings to meet all the demands. Inevitably, the strain of all this began to tell, especially as I was now in my seventies. However, while the performances met with success and many young singers were given their chance to perform leading roles, I was determined to continue.

Added to the disaster of Eric and keeping Opera UK going, there was now another worry, and that was Toby's health. It was obvious to us all he was deteriorating, but he refused to make any adjustments to his lifestyle and continued to smoke and drink as much as ever. A lunch with Toby would be a four-hour event, always ending with brandies or grappa. One event which cheered him was a party given in his honour by the friends of the Old Vic, in memory of his time as Artistic Director. Kevin Spacey, then running the

Old Vic, made a very gracious speech, starting with, 'If I had one-tenth of this man's genius, I would count myself lucky!' Of course, it was over the top, but I was happy Toby's work was at last being recognised. It was only just in time. After a bout of pancreatitis, he was diagnosed with liver cancer. There followed four years of chemo, recovery, relapse, and more chemo. Throughout it all, he remained cheerful and stoical, still refusing to change his lifestyle. After each chemo session, as soon as he was well enough, he resumed his outings to restaurants, entertaining friends, smoking, and drinking.

Occasionally he would have a sudden decline. I was in North Carolina in the middle of rehearsals with *The Lost Colony* company when I received a call from the children advising my return, as Toby was in intensive care. I made the difficult journey, helped by a great friend, Cindy McEnery, who kindly drove me from Roanoke Island to Raleigh Airport. I arrived at Heathrow, going straight to the hospital, only to find Toby no longer in intensive care. When I walked into his room, he greeted me cheerfully, but with some surprise, 'Darling! What are you doing here? I thought you were in North Carolina!' I explained I'd been told he was at death's door, and he seemed rather indignant about this. I returned to the States that evening, again collected by Cindy, and was not at my best for rehearsals the following day.

However, this setback meant Toby was not strong enough to manage his Camberwell Grove flat, which was on the first floor. A more suitable ground floor flat was found for him in Stamford Brook Road, just round the corner from Sasha. While he convalesced in Denville Hall, I undertook the move and the re-decorating of his new flat, which proved a totally exhausting process. Toby had always lived in theatrical splendour, but also in chaos and disorganisation. I found unpaid bills and correspondence from years back among the piles of books and papers which littered the rooms. Although unhappy at downsizing, he grudgingly agreed the new flat was more manageable, and there was the bonus of a small garden on which he soon worked his magic. His time was now spent painting, gardening, and socialising. Despite his health problems, he seemed very content, but somewhat to our alarm insisted on driving, his small car resembling a dodgem, completely battered. How he was never breathalysed we will never know.

One summer, when he was sufficiently recovered from a bout of chemo, Toby and I gave a joint party, to the delight of all our friends. Many remarked it reminded them of the famous Spencer Park parties. My lunches and suppers with Toby also continued unabated, and I wrote a verse about one magical evening which seemed to sum them all up.

DINNER WITH SDMR
(Sholto David Maurice Robertson)

A few snatches of Rochester
Read in Gielgudian tones
Then throwing into the risotto
A stock, made from old bones
And all washed down with a wine Maroc
Accompanied by a Fielding sonata
Or some other obscure Baroque.
And always, that very faint
Gentle aroma, of turpentine and paint.
There is the touch of the White Knight
As many topics tossed and gored
Discussed and mauled
Into the night.
There is lightness, there is dark,
But always that unique energy and spark.
Advice on slugs and other garden woes

Advice on scripts when in the throes.
So, the evening wears happily on
In chipped but theatrical setting.
Warm glow of candles and of fire
Mellow the soul.
'Try these broad beans in peppers
And goat's cheese wrapped in vine leaves.
Another bottle?'
'Why not?' you sigh,
The night is young for you and I.

It was inevitable this pace of life couldn't last for ever. To those closest to him it was a miracle he lasted as long as he did. I was at a wedding in Oxford when I was told he'd had a stroke. Unable to move, or speak, his cognition damaged beyond repair, his face still lit up whenever I entered the ward, and he would cry out, 'Janey!' One day he added to this by suddenly saying, 'Whimsical.' It was the only other word I heard him say. It was terrible to watch someone who'd been such a great communicator reduced to this state. There was no improvement over the next two months, and Fran finally gained permission to move him from the stroke unit to Denville Hall where, to his delight, he was given a great welcome. But that great heart could take no more and finally gave out. Two days later, on 4 July 2013, Toby slipped peacefully into a permanent sleep.

News of his death caused an immediate outpouring of affection and love. The coverage in both English and Scottish newspapers was extraordinary, many of the long obituaries carrying pictures from his most famous productions. His funeral was one I hope he would have liked, with favourite readings and hymns, and contributions from Eileen Atkins, Julian Glover, myself and Bash. His coffin left the church to the strains of 'The Mingulay Boat Song', the song he'd heard me sing on the Pitlochry stage, and which afterwards he'd sung to the children. His ashes were scattered in the Fowey estuary in South Cornwall, a place he'd so greatly loved. A few months later we held a party in celebration of his life. Bash made a brilliant speech full of hilarious anecdotes, and there were many other contributions, including the thirteen-year-old Evie (Bash's eldest daughter) in her beautifully pure voice singing 'O Mio Babbino Caro' ('Oh my beloved father'), which reduced many to tears.

His departure left a mammoth gap in our lives. We talk of him often and toast him every year on the anniversary of his death, and all the memories remain as strong as ever. I think I feel the loss even more than the children and grandchildren. In Byron's words, Toby had been 'My guide, philosopher and friend'. During all the ups and downs of our relationship, our love had been deep and constant, and in the last fifteen years of his life, this attachment had grown even stronger. I miss the conversations, the long lunches and suppers, our shared love of music, books, paintings, and

Toby on the houseboat, 2010

so much more. Quite simply, I miss him. It is strange and something I can't quite fathom. Although Don had been my great passion, I now no longer think of him at all. It is Toby who remains constantly with me.

After losing Toby, I again poured myself into work, filling the void he'd left behind. There were new works for Opera UK, and I revived some of the English Chamber Theatre shows as well, especially the three 'correspondence' plays: *Their Finest Hour*, *Chekhov's Leading Lady* – with Barbara Jefford brilliant as Chekhov's wife Olga – and finally the dramatised letters of Nancy Mitford and Evelyn Waugh, *Dearest Nancy, Darling Evelyn*, with Fenella Fielding quite wonderful as Nancy. Fenella already had a huge following, which ensured every performance was sold out, and we had a successful season at the Jermyn Street Theatre. An invitation for the same show came from Desmond Guinness, nephew of Nancy, to tour Irish castles while raising money for his Irish Georgian Society.

That first meeting with Desmond was unforgettable. I was summoned to his London house in the King's Road Chelsea, ostensibly to organise the tour. My first impression was of an extremely attractive man, with startling bright blue eyes and a shock of white hair. My second impression was that he was obviously drunk. His famous Mitford blue eyes were bloodshot, he was visibly swaying, and there was a rather sinister trail of blood running down his forehead. I also noted his otherwise immaculate beige linen suit had grass stains down one side. He admitted at once he was a trifle tiddled, explaining a 'Lady B' had poured wine down him at lunch, then chased him round Strawberry Hill where he'd slipped on a bank by the Thames trying to escape her seductive advances. This explained the grass stains. He added, sadly, that while she fancied him, she was a raddled old hag, and he didn't fancy her at all. Throughout this explanation he was trying to find a bottle and bottle opener, but failing to do so, suggested we should go straight out. He then panicked because he couldn't get the pockets in his new jacket open – they were sewn up – so I managed to find a kitchen knife and sliced them open for him. He stuffed a wad of notes into one of the pockets and we set off for Thierry's, opposite his house.

Crossing the King's Road was most alarming, with Desmond waving his arms and lurching at the traffic. Miraculously, we arrived at the restaurant without injury and from the moment we were seated he not only wickedly flirted with me, but also the waitress. It appeared she was quite used to him, patiently waiting for his order. He didn't appear to be too fussed about food, but I couldn't stop him ordering Campari sodas, a bottle of claret and eventually Irish coffees. He remained cheerfully drunk throughout the meal, told me a lot of outrageous stories, some of them several times, but was utterly charming and very funny. Finally, he called for the bill, shouting at the waitress, 'Just give me a ballpark figure, I don't want any of your nonsense.' He fished in his pocket and threw the wad of notes on the table. The waitress calmly took them away and brought back his change, which without a glance he returned to his pocket.

We then made the return journey, equally precariously, across the King's Road. He kept saying he would see me to my car in case I got raped, but I assured him this wasn't necessary, found his keys in the other pocket, opened the door and practically threw him inside. His parting words were that he looked forward to seeing me in Ireland. I asked if there was anything I could bring for his wife Penny and he roared with laughter and said, 'Just a new face!' And with that, he staggered off up the stairs.

I wasn't sure I would hear from him again, but a week later I received a long email with a detailed list of the castles we were to visit and suggested dates. The hospitality was to be given free, by the owners of the castles, but Desmond agreed a generous fee for us and all travel expenses. Any profit he made from the shows was to go to his Georgian Society and the restoration of the buildings.

The Irish tour of *Dearest Nancy, Darling Evelyn* was one of the most unusual and extraordinary I ever undertook. There were only four of us: Fenella, playing Nancy, Nigel Anthony as Evelyn, John Rowe as the narrator and myself. The set, basically two desks and three chairs, was to be provided at each venue. Desmond had sent our requirements to all the castles, but as they were not theatres, I just hoped they would be prepared in advance. We flew to Dublin and picked up the hire car. Our first destination was to Grey Abbey, just outside Belfast, and our hosts were Bill and Daphne Mongomery. They couldn't have been kinder. On this occasion the performance was not in the Abbey but the Linenhall Library, Belfast.

On our first morning at Grey Abbey, I set out to explore the grounds with John, and crossing a field found myself in danger of being mown down by a herd of angry bullocks. John bravely diverted them, and we made a hasty retreat onto safer ground. I am eternally grateful to John for saving me! The show went well, and the following day we left Grey Abbey, making our way to the next venue, Black Hall Drogheda, where again we were given generous hospitality. This performance was in the local church. The acoustic was not ideal, but the audience gave it appreciative applause. Our next venue was Desmond's beautiful Leixlip Castle, where he greeted me like an old friend. I'd been worried how Fenella, now in her seventies, would deal with this punishing schedule, but so far, she was holding up well. Desmond and his wife Penny were wonderful hosts putting everyone at ease. I was shown to the main guest room, with a fabulous four-poster bed. I loved this castle, almost as much as I loved Desmond. The main staircase was a spectacular sight, with large tapestries hanging on the walls. It was grand, but at the same time comfortable and relaxing. Desmond took great delight in showing us around the grounds with the Gothic outbuildings, including a small theatre, but this was not the venue for the show. Desmond had arranged a huge gala event in the Long Gallery at Castletown, which was a fantastic setting. The whole evening, performed in front of the great and good from around Dublin, went wonderfully well. We were on a high as we left Leixlip the next day.

The drive to Huntington Castle was a long one, and Fenella now began to show signs of fatigue. Our hosts, David and Moira Durdin-Robertson, couldn't have been kinder, but the accommodation was less adequate than previously experienced, and the plumbing definitely on the primitive side. Fenella wasn't happy. Our performance was to be in the quaint small theatre, an outbuilding of the castle. It had a gallery, and to my alarm I was told this wasn't strong, as only two slim pillars supported the entire structure. Because the performance had sold out, every available space was needed, so the person on the door was advised to only let the thinnest people go up to the gallery! While I was trying to organise some adequate lighting, I was sent a message that Fenella had experienced a meltdown and declared she wasn't up to doing the performance. The main problem seems to have been that in her small room she had lost one of her false eyelashes and refused to go on without them. Poor Nigel was despatched to sort this out. Somehow, he managed to calm her and to my relief, and at the very last minute, she appeared. She gave a wonderful performance; they all did.

At the reception afterwards the compliments flowed, and Fenella's spirits seemed quite restored. The next morning, we explored the castle and made some astonishing finds. In the crypt we came upon 'The Temple of Isis', an extraordinary series of rooms decked in rich fabrics, with altars and golden images. Apparently, this temple was the centre for the worshippers of Isis. Great Aunt Olivia Durdin-Robertson was the head of this cult. Stranger still was an exotic pagoda in the grounds, again with lavish décor. It was all rather a shock, because Huntington Castle on the outside gave no indication of anything so eccentric. If Huntington had been a surprise, we were quite unprepared for what was to happen next, as we set out for Charleville Castle, Tullamore, Co. Offaly. Desmond had told me about the Long Gallery in the castle, with its spectacular ceiling, which was one of the finest examples of Gothic architecture in Ireland. This may have been so, but as we drove through deep forests, finally reaching the dark castle, a feeling of foreboding swept through me.

At first, we could get no answer from the creaking bell pull, but then the large doors swung open, and a very aged caretaker told us crossly we were early. He then led us up the great stone staircase and into the famous Long Room. There was a small, raised platform at one end, otherwise the huge room was empty. He informed us the seating would be coming in later and we could choose the set furniture we needed from a box room next door. I rootled around and managed to find suitable desks and chairs, but then asked about the lighting. He pointed to a chandelier halfway down the hall and said otherwise there would be candles, adding two huge log fires would also be lit. I patiently explained that the actors would need adequate lighting on the stage area, and he grudgingly went off to find some lamps. He returned with two standing lamps, one for each side of the platform. It wasn't brilliant but the actors agreed it would suffice. Fenella was looking tired, so I enquired about our rooms. The old man explained Charleville wasn't normally lived in, but he'd done his best. He proudly added people came from all over the world to stay in the haunted room, telling us it was the most haunted room in the whole of

Ireland; at times during the night it shook so violently it was like a jumbo jet landing. When asked why it was haunted, he said darkly that terrible things had taken place in the castle over the centuries and there was a dungeon full of torture instruments. He now informed us one person could stay in the haunted room and the other three could be in turret rooms at the top of the castle, which were up a precarious staircase. At this, Fenella, white-faced, stated she flatly refused to stay in a castle which was haunted. I could see no alternative but to find her other accommodation, although it wasn't in the budget. Nigel said he would stay with Fenella, but John generously agreed to take one of the turret rooms and I decided to brave the haunted room.

I then despatched the actors to find a hotel, leaving me to get the Long Room ready. I asked if there was any more help available, and the old caretaker introduced me to Patrick, explaining he was retarded, with the mind of a child, but very willing. He was a sweet young man. I nicknamed him 'Smike', and he quickly became my devoted companion, working tirelessly, bringing in huge logs the size of small trees, and soon the great fires were blazing. Chairs were set up in the centre of the room, and around them were placed sofas and armchairs. The finishing touch was the candles. I have never seen so many; they were on all the windowsills down the long room, and on the two great mantlepieces as well. When they were lit the effect was spectacular. To my great surprise, that evening performance was the best yet, and the audience simply loved it.

Afterwards, the caretaker told us he'd made supper, but Nigel and Fenella decided to go straight back to their inn. John and I were shown into a baronial hall with a great banqueting table and another roaring fire. We sat either end, like the lord and lady of the manor, and were given delicious chilli con carne with hunks of Irish bread. The old man put bottles of red wine on the table and declared he would be locking up and going home but would return in the morning to give us breakfast. We heard the big keys turning in the rusty locks and were now alone in that huge, haunted castle. I think John knew I was reluctant to go to the haunted room. He even suggested tying a piece of string on his doorhandle in the turret and then running it down the stairs to tie it onto my door handle, so if I was worried in the night, I could tug on it. Kind but impractical. For a start, we had no string. After demolishing most of the wine, I reluctantly called it a night.

The 'boudoir', as it was called, was cold, and the horrible green satin sheets felt damp, but I was so tired I climbed into bed. Despite my exhaustion and the many glasses of wine, I couldn't sleep. I turned on my transistor radio but could only get a German station and there was too much static to make the human voice comforting, even in a foreign language. At about three, the shaking started. It wasn't just the bed, it was the whole room, and it was terrifying. It lasted on and off for about twenty minutes. After it finally finished, I made fitful efforts at sleeping but without much success. At first light I made my way to the loo. It was next to the room and not one I'd visited before. It presented me with another shock. A large throne was balanced precariously on two floorboards either side, but in the front, there was a large hole. Peering down, I could see a long drop straight to the dungeons. I had visions of falling through and being impaled on one of the instruments of torture. Consequently, I was not at my best as I joined John for breakfast in the dining room. The caretaker inquired about my experiences in the haunted room and seemed very pleased when I recounted the violent shaking. He told me not everyone was so lucky. That was not how I would have put it.

I was thankful to leave Charleville Castle, and we made our way back to civilisation to stay at Leixlip Castle for our final performance. I reproached Desmond for our ordeal at

Charleville, but he found my description hilarious and was totally unrepentant, telling me the money we'd raised would go to restoring the Long Room. Our last performance was at nearby Kilcullen, and we had a wonderful dinner with Desmond and Penny afterwards. There was one postscript to this tour. When I was next down in Cumbrae Cottage, there were sudden strange noises which I hadn't heard before, loud, clonking sounds, and on two occasions I heard voices, although I was alone in the house.

Visitors heard the clunking noises too. I happened to mention this to Fenella, and she darkly remarked she wasn't at all surprised. I had brought the haunted spirits back with me from Charleville. I was sceptical, but it was odd and difficult to find a rational explanation. 'There are more things in Heaven and Earth, Horatio...'

My final tour of Ireland was with another Opera UK concert and as we neared the end something quite alarming happened. I woke in extreme pain affecting my whole body and could hardly move. I somehow made it back to England, where my doctor diagnosed polymyalgia rheumatica. I was put on a heavy dose of steroids. These had a miraculous effect on the pain which virtually disappeared, but the side effects were not so great. I put on weight again, my blood pressure went up and what I didn't know at the time was they also caused osteoporosis. I tried to ignore these problems and continued to work as hard as ever. Combining the job of artistic director and administrator of Opera UK took up most of my time and I was finding it increasingly difficult to get away to Cornwall. It was just too far for the odd night, and I finally bowed to the inevitable and reluctantly sold Cumbrae Cottage. It was a wrench to leave Cornwall, where I'd lived on and off all my life.

Finding it unbearable not to have a bolthole, on impulse I bought a houseboat, not listening to the various warnings from family and friends. It was a static boat, basically a floating wood and glass cabin on a beautiful mooring, between Shepperton and Chertsey. It looked out over the river to willow trees on the opposite bank, with not a building in sight. I named the houseboat The Windlass and moved in. The great joy of this escape was it took a mere forty minutes to make the journey from the London flat. I could therefore go down for a day, or even just an afternoon. The houseboat, newly built, had every modern gadget, including underfloor heating. It was heaven. I would wake up to swans sailing past my bedroom window, and the living room had sliding glass doors which opened on to a deck. Here I would sit and watch the coots, moorhens, and ducks. There was even a heron who stood for hours on one leg under the willow tree on the other side of the river. In the summer there was general traffic of river boats and holiday craft. But in the winter, it became hushed and peaceful. There were six other houseboats on this mooring, and one of the owners, Liz Murray, became a great friend. As I arrived for the weekend, she would totter down from her boat and join me for our gin and tonic time. Entertaining became a large part of the weekends as well, and every Sunday I would have visitors to lunch. The houseboat proved popular with everyone. Sometimes guests would drive down, others I would collect from Shepperton Station.

Living on water is never straightforward and I encountered many problems, all of which proved expensive to put right, but Liz was always on hand with advice. After the first year, I decided to invest in a roof garden with steps up the side of the boat. This proved a great joy, and I added a large box container for all the summer equipment, picnic stuff, cushions, and so on. One very hot summer day with the threat of a thunderstorm, I went to put the cushions away in the box. On opening the lid, I found a huge, white, lacey wasp nest in the wicker picnic basket. Some angry wasps were milling about, so I quickly shut the lid and rang Liz for advice. She told me the pest control people were expensive and could take days to come out and deal with it, so it would be best if I got rid of the wasp nest myself. Her next advice was to completely cover myself in protective clothing and then chuck the picnic basket, plus wasp nest, into the river. Nervously I covered myself with all the clothes I could find, including gloves, scarf, and sunglasses to protect my eyes. Bravely opening the lid, I picked up the basket and wasp nest and flung it into the river. It didn't sink but like a stately galleon floated down the Thames. Liz rang to tell me excitedly it was floating past her. I presumed it would eventually sink. One angry wasp had his revenge by stinging me in the neck, but apart from this, no damage was done, except I lost my lovely antique picnic basket.

Even with the relaxation on the houseboat, I was feeling overstretched. The constant strain of keeping Opera UK going, was fast becoming too much, but I was aware if I left, it would mean the demise of the company, so I just carried on. Then, in 2014, an unexpected incident made the decision for me, and closing Opera UK became inevitable.

Chapter Sixteen
SOMETHING'S GOTTA GIVE

IT HAS NEVER ceased to amaze me how, in a few seconds, everything can completely change. For me, it was an unexpected accident that was the cause. It occurred when I was returning home from rehearsals and walking up the steps at Waterloo Station towards the escalator. It was rush-hour, and hordes of people were rushing to get onto their trains. I suddenly felt something hit me violently in the middle of my back, and the force of the impact threw me to the ground. As I looked up, I saw a man walking away from me with a huge backpack worn precariously to one side, which must have been what hit me. I tried to get up but couldn't. My right ankle was at a very odd angle to my leg, and I now sat helplessly as people hurried past. Just as I was wondering what on earth I should do, a youngish woman stopped and asked me what had happened. I explained and pointed to my ankle. She calmly took out her mobile and efficiently organised my rescue.

Within minutes, help arrived. I was loaded onto a sort of bucket and taken up the escalator. At the top an ambulance was waiting to take me to St Thomas's Hospital. My good Samaritan came with me and asked if she could call someone. Bash was working in Pimlico at the time and on hearing about my accident came straight over to A & E. This amazing woman waited until Bash arrived and refused his offer of a cab to take her home. It is to my lasting regret I never found out her details and consequently couldn't thank her properly for her extraordinary kindness and care. There was so much going on, and by the time I was back from X-ray, she had gone.

I then had to digest the results of my fall, and they were pretty dire. The ankle bones were in pieces, and I needed an urgent operation. I also found out, in the most unpleasant way, I was allergic to morphine, which had me vomiting for two days. The surgeon who performed the operation said my fracture was complicated. Basically, the bones had fragmented due to my osteoporosis. This was the first I knew I had osteoporosis and arthritis was soon to follow, on top of the polymyalgia I already had. It was becoming obvious I'd inherited my mother's bad rheumatic gene. After the stay in hospital, I was returned home wearing a large boot, with an instruction to rest. Stupidly, I disregarded this. I had an opera tour due to start, which couldn't do without me. Unable to drive wearing the boot, I would climb into the car with the boot on, remove it and replace it with a shoe, then change back into the boot once I had reached my destination. Unsurprisingly, the pain began to kick in and the whole tour turned into something of an endurance test. Why are there always endless steps to reach the dressing rooms in most theatres? Not good after an ankle operation. Luckily it wasn't a long tour and I managed to get through it, but on returning to the surgeon there was further bad news. He told me the ankle urgently needed another operation and he was sending me to an ankle specialist at Guy's Hospital. This is how the brilliant Ali Abbasian came into my life.

Ali saved me from a probable future in a wheelchair. It is not necessary to go into all the details; suffice it to say he operated on my ankles four times. My left ankle had now become arthritic and to give me one good ankle, Ali gave me a replacement. Ankle replacements are highly complicated and not like knees or hips, both of which are performed regularly. I was lucky because Ali specialised in ankle replacements and was one of the few surgeons performing this procedure.

The result has been brilliant. I have absolutely no pain in my replaced ankle, unlike my poor right ankle which continued to give problems. It had been so badly shattered originally that a replacement ankle was out of the question. Ali tried to fuse it, but the fusion after the first operation didn't hold. He now decided to take more drastic action and as a last resort removed the fibula, replacing it with a metal rod which he somehow secured into the ankle. This meant there was now no movement possible between the base of the leg and the foot. It made stairs a problem, but at least the ankle was secure. This operation took place during the first summer of Covid, so I wasn't allowed visitors either in the hospital or at home. Although I was non-weight-bearing for months after each operation, I managed to cope by using a knee scooter with a basket on the front handlebars, enabling me to ferry myself to kitchen and bathroom.

I was just about managing when an unexpected complication occurred. Ali had made a large incision to insert the metal rod. This wound needed dressing every week at Guy's for six weeks, a lengthy procedure where the leg plaster would be taken off and, after new dressings were applied, replaced with another one. I think I went through every variation of plaster colour Guy's Hospital had. Each time this took up a whole day, with a lot of waiting, and the long ambulance journeys were hell. I was finally put in a boot which made access to the wound easier, but at this point Ali went down with Covid, and the state of my wound was neglected. To my alarm I noticed it had become inflamed and to my amateur eyes didn't look at all healthy. I rang my local medical practice, but as I couldn't get to see them, they asked for a photo of the wound, which I duly sent. After a couple of days some iodine patches arrived, but when I applied them, it made things worse. Thankfully, Ali was back, and I returned to Guy's. The wound was now horrible, putrid, and smelling. Ali went into immediate action, informing me I needed another operation urgently because the wound was badly infected.

Somehow, I'd managed to acquire three different varieties of infection, one of them being so rare it was difficult to find the right antibiotic. After this last operation, the operating room had to be deep-cleaned and I began to feel like a pariah. Put in a room on my own, I was to remain there for some time. A suction pump had been attached to the wound, which made alarming farting noises at intervals. On the first night, the pump kept coming detached and I was losing blood. All through the night a wonderfully kind Filipino nurse kept patiently re-attaching it, a long and complicated procedure, only for it to detach again an hour later. I apologised each time, but she just smiled sweetly and said, 'Please no worries, Jane. My job.'

By morning it was obvious a new pump was needed, and the doctors duly arrived and attached one. The complications from the wound were not over. Once released from hospital I had a PICC line (peripherally inserted central catheter) to deliver a strong cocktail of antibiotics to go straight into the bloodstream. Carers came in daily to administer the drugs, but one day they found the PICC line blocked. This meant there was some danger of a blood clot going straight to the heart. I was packed off to A & E and the line was removed. The antibiotics were now given by ordinary drip which the carers again administered. I was finally pronounced cleared, but this last operation had left me weak, anaemic, and with low blood pressure. My recovery was slow. We were in Covid, and I was still bedbound, but for my 80th birthday, Fran brilliantly managed to arrange a Skype. She rounded up so many of my family, friends, and relations, it was difficult to fit them all onto the screen.

My postponed birthday party eighteen months later was a wonderful event, taking place in the garden on a beautiful hot summer's day. I had survived all the operations and was now walking short distances and more importantly driving. There was still difficulty with stairs, and because my right leg was now shorter than the left, my balance had been affected and my back was often painful. But I am certainly not complaining. Thanks to Ali and the NHS, I can now do most of the things I want. My endless gratitude goes out to them. I just wish our hopeless government would pay the doctors and nurses properly and support our NHS, one of the few glories our country has left.

After spending five glorious years on the boat, the time came to sell it. There were two reasons for this. Firstly, the problems with my ankles meant long absences while recovering from the operations. The second reason was the crook of a landlord, who already charged astronomical fees for the mooring and kept putting them up. Owing to a dreadful one-sided lease, the landlord had all the power, while the boat owners had none, so any demands he made had to be met without question. I was warned about the dangers of this lease when I first purchased the boat, but was so excited about life on the river, I stupidly disregarded them. The lease contained a long list of rules which, if not obeyed, resulted in the boat owner being asked to leave, with only a month's notice. One boat was forced to leave while I was there, because the owner had painted it white, which was against the ridiculous rules. I have always hated injustice. I now made the mistake of questioning these decisions. I even wrote to my local MP, Kwasi Kwarteng (later the disgraced Chancellor) about the injustice of the lease and was outraged when it turned out Mr Kwarteng was a friend of the landlord and sent my letter on to him, which only aggravated the situation.

In the end, I had one disagreement too many. I was given a month's notice, telling me my lease was terminated and I was to remove my boat from the mooring. I was leaving anyway but would have liked more time. My houseboat was without an engine and the problem of removal was a complicated one. With a great deal of stress and difficulty, it was towed to a new mooring in Kent, where it was finally sold, but only after a lot of damage had been done to it. After five years my river adventure had come to an end, but despite the monetary loss, I had no regrets. It had been a wonderful experience and given immense pleasure, not just to me but to my many visitors. I now had to accept that living in two places was too demanding, which resulted in a drastic downsizing. Luckily, my London flat had recently been refurbished and enlarged. Even so, the cull was hard. I decided to look on it as a cathartic exercise, sorting out what I really needed to keep and what I didn't. The worst problem was the books. With great reluctance many of them went, including my *Punch* volumes. However, when finished, the choices I'd made were the right ones. My flat suited me perfectly, and still does.

While recovering from the operations and stranded for months on my bed, I decided to fill my time by writing fiction. This was something I had first started some years earlier. An idea for a novel had long been in my mind, about a mother/daughter relationship. I called it *Parallel Lines*. Previously I'd had an agent, Vernon Conway, but he'd retired some years back and I hadn't felt the need to replace him while working with the opera company. I now decided I would do without one. At the age of seventy-five, I wasn't prepared to search for another agent who would not necessarily take me on. It was the same with finding a publisher: the whole process would take far too long, with a possible rejection in the end. So, I went ahead and self-published, but I was lucky enough to find a great mentor in Dr Stephen Carver. He had been a lecturer in literature and creative writing at the University of East Anglia and now worked on projects of his own. He tutored me with enormous skill, making the transition from writing for theatre to writing a novel. I had no problem with dialogue, but the passages of prose were a greater challenge. Stephen's wife, Rachael, a talented artist, designed the cover. In 2015, I launched my first effort in fiction and thankfully it seemed to be enjoyed. Encouraged by the reviews and general reaction, I decided to make this novel the first book in a trilogy and followed it with *Triangles in Squares* and *Full Circle*.

I then moved away from family sagas to something completely different. I based the next novel on a notorious trial which had taken place in the States in the 1920s. Two Italian immigrants, Sacco and Vanzetti, were accused of robbery and murder. They protested their innocence to the end, but after many appeals were finally sent to the electric chair. This produced an angry reaction worldwide and the case became famous. I was fascinated by this story, although I decided to take a different angle. There had been a young boy, Beltrando Brini, who'd given evidence at the trial, evidence which should have given Vanzetti an alibi. But the jury, directed by the heavily biased judge, refused to believe him, being told the boy had learned his evidence by heart. My New York lawyer, Bob Montgomery, managed to find me transcripts of the trial, so I was able to use the exact words of Beltrando's cross-examination. I also used Vanzetti's letters and newspaper accounts. The research was intense. I even made a trip to Boston, where the library had a collection of Sacco and Vanzetti memorabilia. *The Brini Boy* is not an easy read, but for me it is the most important book I have written.

By now, I was hooked on writing fiction and consequently

soon embarked on another project, deciding again on a trilogy. Rather than self-publish this time, I approached a publisher, Jane Moffett, the founder of JJ Moffs. This was a small independent publishing house, and from the moment I met Jane I was convinced our collaboration would work. She loved my idea for the three books. The main character was to be a war correspondent, E G Rawlings, badly injured in Afghanistan and returning to England, suffering from PTSD. Once again, research was needed, not only about PTSD but also the life of a war correspondent and the wars Rawlings would be covering. The writing of these three books kept me happily occupied for the following three years, which meant I was little affected by Covid. After the

JM at book launch, 2020 (photo: Oscar Robertson)

operations I couldn't leave my room anyway. *The Strange Year of E G Rawlings* was followed by *A Year of Trials for E G Rawlings* and finally *Quo Vadis E G Rawlings?*, published in 2022. Jane Moffett found a great designer for the three book covers and the wonderful, and ever-supportive, Gyles Brandreth wrote suitably brilliant lines to go on the front, as well as making a witty speech at each launch party.

The books had great reviews and outwardly were a success, but the actual sales were disappointing. I think many factors contributed to this. During the launch of the first book, Boris Johnson was having his General Election, and then for the next two publications, Covid was with us, which meant nobody could get to bookshops. But the major reason was I just wasn't a famous or recognised name, which readers seem to require these days. Although money was spent on marketing, it wasn't enough to boost sales. Later I realised one further problem which I hadn't anticipated. JJ Moffs was a small publishing house and therefore didn't have general distribution into the bookshops. The books could be ordered from bookshops, or the publishers, or Amazon, but it seems the public need to see the books in front of them to want to buy them. Of course, it would have been perfect if the trilogy had been picked up and made into a television series. Many who read the books suggested it was an ideal subject, and Rawlings would be a perfect part for some actor. Being an optimist, I still live in hope this might happen.

In January 2020, Bash and I made a trip to watch a Test Match in South Africa. Our five days in Johannesburg were wonderful and one of the best experiences of my life. The weather was hot, the cricket exciting, and we managed a win. It had been perfect. A month later, the country went into lockdown. Thankfully, I never caught Covid. Some of the family did, but not too badly, although I know of people who were very ill, one or two still suffering with long Covid, and tragically my great friend Bridget lost her husband. Many mistakes were made by the Government, starting with Boris Johnson missing the first five Cobra meetings and going too late into lockdown. There was also a scandalous wastage on equipment and many millions going into the pockets of the wrong people. We did finally get the vaccines, but I fervently hope lessons have been learned, so we are more prepared for any pandemics that might hit us in the future.

While laid up after the operations, and when I wasn't writing, I listened to music or watched old films on television. I didn't read novels during this time, as my head was filled with my own material, and nervous about losing the thread. There were particular pieces of music which had special meaning. A few bars could take me straight back to a day, or significant moment. My tastes have always been mainly classical, but there were occasional pop songs, or numbers from musicals, which had the same effect. In the 'sixties it was the Beatles. In the 'seventies, under Don's influence, I listened to a great deal more pop. Rod Stewart was a definite favourite, and there was a song by Randy Edelman I particularly liked, for obvious reasons: 'I'm an Up Town, Up Tempo Woman, You're a Down Town, Down Beat Guy'. Apart from listening for pleasure, one of my favourite tasks when directing was picking out the appropriate music for each play. With *The Cherry Orchard*, Chopin's Prelude in E Minor set the tone of slight melancholy. In contrast, 'Putting on the Ritz' for Noel Coward's *Present Laughter* indicated to the audience they were in for a fun evening. If I hear the opening bars of any opera I directed, I'm taken back at once to remembering the exact staging I put in during the overtures. Going even further back, 'Take a pair of sparking eyes' from *The Gondoliers* immediately reminds me of my father, who would sing it in the bath. Of course, there are countless classical pieces that are special to me as well. Music has certainly helped me weather the storms, especially during the time after the operations when I was confined to my room for so long. It also remains one of the best remedies for pain I know.

The Final Chapter
WINTER

IF OUR LIVES follow the same pattern as the four seasons, then it follows I am now in winter, the last quarter of my allotted time. This is not one of discontent, quite the opposite. I am living an existence of quiet contentment. Thanks to Toby, who left me modestly provided for, I am without the financial worries which have plagued me all my life. Apart from the occasional purchase of another Pascin – a painter I love – I live very simply, and my wants are few. Even my picture extravagances will now cease as I have no further room on my walls. My days have fallen into a routine which gives me almost complacent satisfaction. Mornings are spent writing, after which I sometimes meet friends for lunch. If I don't go out to lunch it is a quick snack, and then there is gardening to be done, or a walk on Putney Common. Even my walks have a routine. I skirt the cricket pitch, avoiding out-of-control dogs and the odd flying cricket ball, and then follow a circuit through the woods back to my car. One result of all the operations means I can't sit in one position for too long before my back becomes painful, so I no longer go to concerts, theatre, or opera. I don't miss this, feeling I've had my fill of these pleasures. My evenings are now spent with music, old films or reading. This gives me a chance to work on one of my greatest hobbies, needlepoint. I have made over fifty cushions, which not only adorn my room but have been handed out to family and friends. This seemingly unexciting existence is punctuated with various events such as occasional parties and family reunions. I'm also a member of the Chelsea Physic Garden and Dulwich Picture Gallery, both of which are a delight.

My health is just about holding out, or at least as well as can be expected. The ageing body, like an old car, needs constant repair and replacement. I remember a quote from Sydney Smith as he approached the end of his life, saying each new symptom seemed like a knock on the door. He added that he had nine illnesses and his wife eight, and they passed the medicines from one to the other. Amusing, but it has an element of truth. The kind NHS find me endless remedies, but cannot stop the progress of old age, a process I accept without complaint. My one hope is I don't lose my wits. My greatest fear is I will become a burden to my children, and that I certainly don't want. The greatest sadness of getting older is the loss of so many relations and friends, some younger. Death seems an arbitrary affair. As to what happens afterwards, I have no idea. My personal faith I've always kept private, but I'm convinced mortal death cannot be the end.

Meanwhile, I'm perfectly content to discover the truth when the time comes. Although no longer a practising Christian, I still believe in Christian principles. Singing hymns and carols has always been a pleasure and there is glory to be found in religious music and paintings. I was brought up on a diet of the King James Bible and Book of Common Prayer with the beauty of the language. Not for me the ghastly modernising. My early years were full of trips to churches and cathedrals for services. As I reached adulthood, my dislike of religious dogma, and indeed all extreme religions, increased. So much damage in the world is done by the followers of doctrines and fanatical beliefs. Byron said he only believed in two things: 'a love of freedom and a detestation of cant.' I am happy with that. I would only add a continued loathing of man's inhumanity to man, resulting in so many dreadful wars and suffering.

Increasing age has inevitably meant travel, particularly the foreign variety, becoming more difficult. Many of my solo holidays abroad, even when younger, ended with accidents or illness: a fall in Montenegro, missing a marble step in Croatia, a bad attack of bronchitis during a visit to Boston, and in the last year, when visiting friends in North Carolina, I went down with a kidney infection. Even extensive travel in the UK has produced problems. Apart from limping – one leg now being shorter than the other – and loss of balance, the logistics of travel are problematic; wheelchairs at airports, an inability to climb stairs or mount the high steps onto coaches. I travelled so much in my earlier years I find I no longer have a wanderlust to see new places. Travel now is a means to see old friends, but in view of the difficulties, even these trips are lessening. Simplification is my answer to getting older. I wear no make-up but do take care of my skin, slapping on moisturiser morning and night. Being an almost fanatical sun-lover, I'm also careful to use suncream. Otherwise, my cosmetic needs are few. The same goes for my wardrobe. These days I have little need of clothes for smart occasions. When I'm asked to some fashionable event, I have an array of suitable attire, which otherwise sits in my wardrobe unused. I'm thinking of having a great purge and carting off these clothes to Oxfam, but so far have hesitated, regretting having thrown out my entire BIBA collection many years ago. Not only would this now be worth a fortune, but my granddaughters would have loved them!

Inevitably, spending so much time on my own, memories of the past come flooding back. Occasional visions float before me: the four small children in matching yellow sou'westers, macs and wellies stumping down the Port

Isaac beach, the large gatherings at Christmas, parties in the Spencer Park Garden and the family moments of pure joy and laughter. There is time, too, for critical self-examination. I've made many mistakes. What person hasn't? I can be hot-headed and impulsive, and sometimes I appear arrogant and impatient. The need to be the centre of attention paradoxically comes from my lack of confidence and low self-esteem. If I feel I've been treated unfairly, I tend to overreact. And certainly, as I get older my fuse gets shorter. Loathing confrontation as I do, the few people I dislike I now avoid. But there are positive thoughts too. I have revelled in good company and found I have a talent to amuse. It's wonderfully rewarding to make people laugh. I know I'm lucky to have experienced great passion, and one deep and lasting relationship as well. I have four wonderful children, ten equally wonderful grandchildren and many friends, too many to mention by name. I have enjoyed some success in my work and these successes have far outweighed the disappointments. I think I'm a survivor but have only managed this by keeping my innermost feelings private. My cheerful optimism masks well the heartbreak and hurt which I keep buried deep inside me. Those feelings will remain hidden and go with me to my grave.

And now? Now I will continue to live in my world of floribunda roses, tapestry cushions, J S Bach, listening to the cricket, occasional jam-making – marmalade and crab apple jelly – tending my pots on the terrace, and enjoying visits from children, grandchildren, and friends. Maybe I will even see the next generation with great-grandchildren. And who knows, there may yet be another novel in me. My father was right: it is far better to be born lucky than rich, and I have been lucky. There have been so many surprising incidents, adventures, and fascinating people I've met. A full and rich life.

So, until I make my final exit to the strains of Jessye

Norman singing, 'When you walk through a storm...' I will try and survive the latest horrors of our inadequate government, hope the terrible wars can cease, and live out my remaining years peacefully, content to leave the great questions without an answer.

> *What is Truth? What is Death?*
> *What happens with the Final Breath?*
> *What is Love?*
> *What is Hate?*
> *Who is God? And what is Fate?*
> *There are no answers, not a one,*
> *Just the rising moon and the setting sun.*

POSTSCRIPT

AT SOME POINT during Covid, a large package arrived. It contained all the letters I had written to Toby's cousin James Reeve, one of my very greatest friends, a painter and person 'extraordinaire'. While he'd lived in London, James had been a constant companion, and I relished his eccentricity and outrageous parties. But then he moved to Somerset, into a wonderful house with a large painting studio. I visited him on many occasions and was always given generous hospitality involving extremely rich meals and rather too much to drink. The house was as eccentric as James, crammed with antiques, some of them sinister, old religious relics, grotesque stuffed animals, bits of bones and skeletons, but also beautiful tapestries, pictures and *objets d'art*. Pervading the whole house was a whiff of turpentine and incense. The garden was another work of art, with stone pots overflowing with flowers, and urns, statues and wrought iron benches.

After a while, James began to spend half his year in Mexico, where his paintings were greatly admired. It was at this time we started our correspondence, and his letters were brilliant and entertaining. I think we both tried to outdo the other, with amusing anecdotes and observations. This kind of letter-writing is out of fashion now, so it was a delight to find someone who enjoyed it as much as I did. Even so, it came as a surprise to find he'd kept all my letters, and I was delighted to have them in my possession. Reading them brought back memories and incidents I'd quite forgotten, some of the descriptions making me laugh out loud. They turned the microscope onto the small moments in my life, somehow making them interesting. I was surprised how little had changed over the years; still the same anger at politicians, the sad state of the country, lack of money, worries over children, difficulty at work and problems with relationships. I think it was Truman Capote who said it was permissible when writing letters to give embellishment to the truth, and this is what I think I did.

Many of the descriptions were written with a good deal of hyperbole, but the element of truth was always there. They were also written in a rather racy style with an overload of dashes and exclamation marks, but so much of my life was vividly brought back to me.

I wanted these letters to somehow be included as part of this Memoir, but as the writing style is so very different, I decided against using these extracts in the main narrative, but to leave them for one section at the end. So here they are.

I'm starting with an account I wrote to James of my visit to New Zealand. This adventure began in the North Island, staying with my cousin Tania. I then flew to the South Island to start the long, solo journey back...

There is something glorious about driving alone. You can go as fast or slow as you like, stopping when you want, making detours when you feel like it and playing the same CD track over and over again. I had sensibly sorted out some ideal 'mood' music for every eventuality. I soared over mountain tops to the 'Ride of the Valkyries' or swept along the side of lakes to Bach's 'Preludes & Fugues'. The landscape is without doubt quite superb. I went in a tiny plane to visit Milford Sound (one of the Wonders of the World) and buzzed like a demented gnat over the Southern Alps – a quite terrifying experience which I will never repeat. So relieved to be back in my car. The only place I disliked in all my travels was Rotorua, back in the North, a hot tourist spot due to its volcanic activity. It stunk of rotten eggs, so I didn't stay but went off on a boat to visit the only live volcano in New Zealand – on White Island. This was exciting, with a distinct element of risk – hard hats and gas masks – a proper adventure. [Since my visit, White Island has been closed to all visitors after the volcano erupted, killing several tourists.] By the time I returned to Auckland I had driven over 2000 kilometres and for someone with a nervous disposition I felt a sense of triumph. The architecture was less spectacular than the landscapes which is, and the people of New Zealand a sort of nice middle class Essex community, but the accent is awful and often difficult to understand. All the 'e' sounds come out as 'i' sounds. For instance, 'Let the bell toll' would translate to 'Lit the bill toll'. Very muddling.

In the same letter I give a description of renovations I was making to my Cornwall cottage:

I drove down to Cumbrae a week ago to 'chill out' after my exhausting, but exciting, sojourn down under. I summoned my builder Mark and went up to my studio at the top of the garden – and to my horror found it full of water. 'We had a mighty lot of water when you were away,' Mark remarked laconically. It looked like the second flood, and I asked him to repair any holes in the roof immediately. He came back after five minutes inspection and said, 'The whole lot will have to come down. No point in patching it up. Best demolish it and start again.' Of course, I agreed. I was worried my Punch collection would turn to papier mâché. So today, I awoke at 8 am to the most fearful banging and crashing and on peering bleary-eyed through the window, found half the cowboys of North Cornwall with crowbars, taking down the building in what I can only term as a very aggressive way. By mid-morning there was a small group of onlookers and I have been ferrying an almost non-stop service of tea, coffee and biscuits for most of the day. One diminutive but wiry man, named Rambo, informed me it was going to take three days to rebuild the place. How much all this will cost I dread to think. Last night I rang Toby to tell him the studio was being rebuilt – thinking he'd be pleased as it would be an ideal place for him to paint – but he just remarked gloomily it all sounded very expensive and I shouldn't be so extravagant.

One of my great passions has always been cricket, and in one of my letters to James I described the famous Test Match when winning back the Ashes was at stake:

At this moment there are the most extraordinary scenes going on with the final Test Match. I realise this must be a distant event, tucked away as you are in darkest Mexico, and I know you are not the greatest cricket fan – but the fact is, for my sins, I am. You see, my grandfather was a famous cricketer, and I was brought up on a diet of cricket and Gilbert and Sullivan – and somehow both just stuck. Right now, the whole of England is on fire. This Series has been astonishing. Could we win back the Ashes? It hangs in the balance. So, at 10.25 today everything stopped as the crowd and anyone else who felt like it, sang a collective rendering of Jerusalem. Poor Blake must be turning in his grave and of course Joe Bloggs at the Oval hasn't a clue what the words really mean – but it's a great tune and the noise was mind-blowing, and I must reluctantly admit to finding it all very emotional. For the next five days I will be glued to my radio in the company of Aggers, Blowers and Jonner's, biting my nails and praying we can humble those horrible, hearty Australians.

We did win and I reported this to James in my next letter, although he never commented back on my cricket obsession.

By 2005 I'd acquired my small garden flat in St Simon's Avenue, Putney, making it my London base. Although I spent little time in the flat at this juncture, being either on tour or down in Cornwall, James delighted in hearing about the other six residents and always demanded more news of them:

Cleverly I managed to avoid the Soroptimist Garden Party, although it might have been amusing to see the summer frippery dragged from their wardrobes, draped and paraded for all to see at this annual outing. Although I missed the event, the rather terrible legacy was that the beautiful garden was now covered in horrid white plastic tables and chairs. I thought these would be taken away by Irish Paddy (caretaker) – but no – four days later they were still there. Then, the hooked nosed iron-grey lady from upstairs arrived at my door... 'my dear, I simply have to see your room – I hear it is absolutely splendid!' Nothing for it but to ask her in for a drink and poured us two large G & T's (mine very strong) and she sat for an hour putting me through nothing short of a third-degree interrogation which she punctuated with, 'Oh my dear, you are so clever...' 'Oh my dear, I do so admire you...' 'Oh my dear, how absolutely first class', etc., etc. Finally, with no let-up in the questioning, I changed the subject to the white tables and chairs, lamenting their ugliness. Well! Without more ado – she leapt to her feet, sailed down the garden and removed them all to the shed – came back red in the face with triumph and left soon afterwards no doubt to take a cold shower. Next morning there was a rude note in the hall from Mavis (House Manager) asking for an explanation as to where white tables etc had gone before she called in the FBI. I decided to keep a low profile and locked my door, but heard awful fracas in the hall between Iron Grey and M. I saw IG later and apologised for getting her into trouble, but she wouldn't hear of it and boomed she found them quite hideous as well. I'm definitely warming to her. All quiet on the Western Front since then.

James was actually Toby's cousin, not mine, I'd just adopted him, so many of my letters were taken up with the latest news of Toby:

My very good deed of the week was to take Toby to IKEA because he declared he needed a lot of things like ironing boards (how had he survived for so long without one?) IKEA is a nightmare at the best of times – but as long as you obey the system and follow the yellow brick road you can make the ordeal a brief affair. Not so with Toby – he doesn't understand systems and seemed oblivious of the signs and insisted on going in the wrong direction – making women swear, children howl, and men threaten violence. All lost on T. He didn't have in his hearing aids – so all this went over his head. I finally managed to get him, his trolley and all his goods though the check-out counter and into the car. On the way back he was positively triumphant, said he had dreaded it – but really enjoyed it hugely and would like to go again! Something to be avoided if possible. I then asked him if he wanted to accompany me to a SMART PARTY in the Oxo Tower – given by Keith Schilling, very successful showbiz lawyer, (who had just successfully won the libel case for Polanski.) Toby declined saying it sounded quite dreadful. I fully intend to go and drown myself in champagne to cover the huge cost of the cabs.

I did manage to take Toby to one of James's London exhibitions, this time of his portraits, a very smart affair, full of the London elite, including many of their joint relations:

Dearest James, WHAT A TRIUMPH. I am truly hugely pleased with your obvious success – and so well deserved. And what a fascinating bunch you gathered for the viewing – simply riveting – chattering classes with a dash of the cosmopolitan. I felt I was the youngest there – which of course I wasn't – but rather relieved to see a batch of young Packenham's arrive because some of your guests looked as if they were made out of paper and moth's wings. Toby revelled in it – I thought he would find it too much but not a bit of it. He found his perch and held court looking like a benevolent Mr Punch. He had some difficulty in remembering to whom he was related, which led to some quite hilarious mistakes as he claimed several relatives that were not his – two of them Mexican! Several people asked where your portrait of me was hanging, including Toby, and I had to admit to feelings of dejection – and rejection. It was rather like looking forward to a grand dinner party and then being told there was no place at the table! What will happen to me now? Will I be consigned to being stacked in a corner of your studio for ever? Or even worse – in the art gallery cellars.

James wrote back a contrite letter explaining to me my portrait had already been sold to a Mexican Gallery and he had forgotten to tell me. I would like to have bought it myself, but James Reeve is now an expensive and sought-after painter. Although he offered me a reduced price, I still couldn't afford him. I did ask Toby to buy it, but he declared he didn't think it was James's best portrait, didn't much like it and it didn't do me justice! I must be content with the fact that there is some far-off Mexican wall which I now adorn and is 'forever England'.

Toby's health wasn't the only family problem I wrote about. There was also Christopher:

My poor brother continues to be a major worry. He was taken to hospital having smashed his elbow after a fall. The doctors immediately put down his fall to his excessive alcohol intake, after he had told them, quite truthfully, the amount he drank daily. He pointed out – with his stammer which obviously takes him a long time to say anything and tries the patience of the hospital staff – he pointed out that he only drank the very finest wines. This is true – he is a complete gourmet and living out his old age by daily dining at his favourite restaurants (plenty to choose from, he lives in Chipping Camden) and indulging in rich dishes washed down with the very best claret. The consultant remarked rather acidly it wasn't the quality of the wines they were worried about but the amount. The real worry is he is now in a bad way. Deprived of his rich diet he has refused hospital food and become painfully thin. The combination of drugs they have poured into him, including morphine, has caused very erratic behaviour, delusions, and incipient madness. Confused from the start, he thought he was in his local hostelry and took the nurses for waitresses. 'Waitress where is my wine? The service here has really gone downhill, etc.' He also seems to be living out some sort of character from a John le Carré novel. One day he disappeared, and they had to call the police. He was eventually found sitting under shelves in the basement of the John Radcliffe, declaring he was defusing a bomb in the Australian parliament building! Another time he rang the police and said his house was being burgled and feared for his collection of fine wines and malt whisky. Things were getting out of hand and my poor niece, who is beautiful but somewhat shy, was at her wits end. The last straw was last week when his arm swelled up like a bolster and in true medieval fashion had to be drained of poison, only to find the infection was MRSA.

This finally drove me to action, and I called a meeting with consultants, physios etc.

The female consultant – a new one assigned to him – had done her homework. She explained Christopher was a complex case. It turns out part of his brain which affects his balance is atrophied, probably due to his drinking (what a terrible warning!) This had contributed to his frequent falls. He also had two faulty heart valves, resulting in swollen legs and general bad circulation, again due to alcohol intake. They would keep rubbing it in. They promised to take action on all fronts and once the MRSA had been treated, he could be moved into a nursing home. I can't see Christopher agreeing to that.

I was right: he didn't agree to it, but was finally returned home with carers coming in twice a day. He was now confined to his armchair, surrounded by his books, with a crate of claret on one side, and malt whisky on the other. As he could no longer get to the restaurants, they indulged him by delivering his favourite dishes to him. A year later he was diagnosed with lung cancer and months later gently drifted away.

At about the same time, Toby was also diagnosed with cancer in his liver, and I kept James abreast of the latest news, with frequent bulletins:

> *Toby a bit up and down. We thought he was doing pretty well, but then he was told he had to have a third bout of chemo, and this initially plunged him into gloom. It does make him feel awful for about six weeks. However, he has now cheered up and is planning two huge parties, one for thespians and the other for family and 'normal' friends! This reminded me that my father when up at Oxford sent out invitations stating 'I am giving two parties, one for those I like, and one for those I don't. You are invited on...' So, no-one, knew which party they were going to. However, he was 'hoist with his own petard' because the party for people he liked was dismal, whilst the other was a great success and he decided he liked all the people he disliked after all – and vice versa.*

In the same letter I added:

> *The children and grandchildren all thrive. Edie, Fran's eldest aged ten, is about to become a film star and has landed a big part in the next Jane Campion film (her of 'The Piano'). It's about the life of John Keats and to be called 'Bright Star'. Edie is playing Fanny's sister – Fanny being the poet's great love – and is in most of the scenes. I have seen some of the stills and she looks quite charming, I love that period for costumes. Yesterday she was joined by her sister Vita, and two of her cousins, Jess and Corinna – who were extras in a sewing circle.*

I continued with further accounts of London living:

> *The other day Irish Mary rushed up to me saying breathlessly, 'I am so glad to see you alive. I hadn't seen you for so long.' I explained patiently I had been working rather hard, but I might just as well have told her I'd been on Mars. She spends her days walking round the garden*

talking to the plants and doesn't have many marbles left poor thing. Iron Grey also met me one morning as I was going out and said in her booming voice, 'Don't you long to die? I just long to die.' Which is a bit unsettling when you are only departing for Sainsbury's.

A year later, Iron Grey did have her wish. I wrote to James:

Poor Iron Grey is gone, and I will miss her, but she did have a rather fascinating and unexpected funeral, of the 'humanist' variety. The coffin was a plain cardboard box – looked a bit precarious to me and gave me some anxiety when it was carried out. Strange friends and relations in hippy garb gathered and read ecofriendly messages and scattered the place with wildflowers, sadly gone limp in the heat – but as my great friend Bridget would have said, 'So beautifully ORGANIC.'

Irish Mary has now gone quite off her head, and they have been assessing her to see if she can stay. It is alarming how quickly dementia can take hold. She has taken to beating on people's doors – or on the floor – with her stick, demanding to know who she is, where she is and where is everyone. She has also taken to wandering off, leaving the front door wide open. I fished her back from St Simon's Church at the bottom of the road, and she declared she had gone to find God – which I thought a rather nice touch. Not so agreeable when she banged on my glass garden door at 6 am demanding attention. It took me some time to get her to her first-floor flat which she then declared wasn't hers. This morning I found her going round and round the hall in circles. After her usual, 'Who are you?' she said she was looking for the chickens. Chickens! Some throwback to her Irish childhood no doubt. Sad, but something will have to be done soon, for everyone's sanity, before a real disaster occurs...

She did leave soon after. Meanwhile news of Toby continued:

> *Glad to report Toby has yet again made a remarkable recovery from the chemo and hopes to be out of the hospital soon and off to Denville Hall for two weeks. I visited him in hospital yesterday and the place was mayhem. The man in the bed opposite was quite clearly demented. He looked like an axe murderer and walked up and down with his Zimmer frame claiming he had lost his bed. The other patients, except T, would shout out, 'It's behind you!' It was rather like an end of pier pantomime. At one point he lurched alarmingly towards Toby, who merely waived a wan hand and said, 'My dear old fellow, you're absolutely potty – your bed is not here but over there.' Toby's languid tones had a calming effect, but it won't last long, and the poor over-worked nurses can do little to help. The sooner we can get T to Denville Hall the better.*

In 2010, I packed up the Cornwall cottage and made the move to my houseboat on the Thames. James was of course given a full description:

> *Dearest James, The strain of moving onto the boat and unpacking the endless boxes has made my polymyalgia take a dive for the worse. I stuff down extra doses of steroids and keep all fairly under control. However, I wasn't prepared for an actual accident, and a fairly serious one. I don't know if you remember my bronze – of a curlew – with a massive, curved beak, like an iron spike? Well, I had put the bronze on the floor – and forgot I had, and then tripped over it. Result? The beak gashed my lower leg with a deep and nasty wound. Blood spurted out alarmingly, so I bound it tightly to stop the bleeding*

and thought that would be the end of it. A week later it was very red and inflamed and didn't look good at all. So, I went to the doctor who said I was dangerously near blood poisoning, and I was put on antibiotics and the wound was dressed.

That was last Friday.

Since then, I have had a fearful time. By Sunday night it was even more angry, swollen and bloody painful. I dragged myself to the surgery Monday and alarm bells went off. They took off the dressing and it was a ghastly sight. The poor nurse nearly passed out – let alone me. Another doctor came and decided I needed stronger antibiotics as it was badly infected, and I was still in danger of getting blood poisoning. Swabs were taken, the whole wound drained and cleaned, and new dressings put on. By which time I felt I had been in a field hospital in WW1. Daily dressings for the next week. It is slightly better but warned it will take a good while to fully heal...

Toby visited the houseboat for the first time – the weather was perfect, and he sat on the deck and smoked his way through a packet of cigarettes, drank the best part of a bottle of wine and declared it all a great success. I must admit, it was idyllic, with swans, the occasional boats passing – and the wind in the willows. When I have the boat a bit more sorted, I know I will be totally happy with it.

James had loved my description of the first meeting with Desmond Guinness in London, so I sent him an account of another encounter, this time in Oxford:

I had an amusing evening last week. I was invited down to Christ Church Oxford for another High Table dinner, after which, Desmond Guinness was to be the guest speaker. It was advertised he would be talking about

Irish Eccentrics. No Chance! From the moment he arrived it was obvious he was the worse for drink – you will remember I had experienced that very peculiar band of DG inebriation before! During the pre-dinner drinks and throughout dinner he just smiled that charming smile and of course everyone was mesmerised by those speedwell blue eyes. Then the moment came for him to speak. With some difficulty he got to his feet and looked at his audience with a rather bemused, benign expression. He told us – still smiling – he would NOT be telling us about Irish Eccentrics because he didn't know any! The Oxford matrons looked annoyed at this, but there was little they could do. Desmond proceeded to pull some crumpled sheets of paper from his pocket and announced he would tell us about what it was like to be a lecturer in America. He then picked up any sheet that came to hand – in no particular order – and read – with huge difficulty because he couldn't find his glasses – what was scribbled on that particular sheet. Unless a complete anecdote was entirely written on one page, all was lost – and most of it didn't make sense. In one of the longer moments, when he was puzzling over what he had written – someone lent forward and offered him their reading glasses. The pace picked up after that. I wish it had been filmed because it was a unique and totally eccentric performance. The most coherent part was when he at last put a bit together, and told how when broke, he had been lent an empty apartment just behind 5th Avenue in New York, where he existed on food parcels from kind friends – but was wary about the electricity supply as the butler and housemaid had recently been found dead in the lift after going missing for two days! Finally, he sat down – almost mid-sentence – declaring, 'I think that is all I have to say!' The Oxford ladies by this time had lips of string. I went and sat with D for quite a time afterwards. He was as charming as ever – at one point he asked how I thought it had gone. I told him that his audience had been riveted and were hanging on his every word. He seemed pleased with this.

The organiser of the event told me later Desmond had arrived at about 3 in the afternoon and said he needed to get a new shirt as he had spilled wine down the one he was wearing. Could he borrow some money? They obliged and he was pointed in the right direction to the shops and disappeared – only to appear in the same shirt, with no shopping packages, two hours later – obviously having spent his time in some watering hole!

It was a curious thing. When I saw Desmond in Ireland he always behaved impeccably, with never a sign of him being the worse for alcohol. It seems it was only in England he behaved like a wicked old reprobate, but he was never aggressive and however drunk always remained utterly charming.

James always showed an interest in my work, and it was therapeutic for me to have someone to moan to:

Dearest James – brief today – it is soooo hectic here. I am a victim of my own success (although I hasten to add NOT FINANCIALLY) – because since the Mitford/Waugh was such a Wow, I have been bombarded with requests for the production – and not only that production – but others on the ECT list. I had really let the English Chamber Theatre go, because one arts company is more than enough for anyone – and now? I am reeling, and it's not as if the Opera Company is easy either. What with the thieving administrator who has disappeared and the police unable to find him, now, for my sins I have formed a Gala committee of formidable do-gooder women, to help with a fundraising concert at the Cadogan Hall. Big mistake! They are horrors, one of them a complete

> *horror, and I am fed up with the lot of them. I may soon abandon them all and retreat to a soothing life on the boat, with my heron, coots, geese, (the Canadian variety,) ducks and swans my only companions.*

The boat was indeed restorative, and it had its occasional amusing moments as well:

> *There is great excitement along the river bank this weekend because a comedian called David Walliams has undertaken to swim the length of the Thames for some good cause. He is MAD.*
>
> *Forget the danger from swans, river boats etc – there is the horror of putrid water with sewage and bugs. Well – as expected, one day in and he already has the runs and is vomiting. All too grisly for words. He is due to pass this way Sunday afternoon and there is a forecast of a Force 9 gale. I really don't want him to drown in front of my houseboat – but I expect there to be a lot of safety boats – in fact a general circus! In view of the forecast, I have put away the garden tables and chairs. Too awful for him to be decked by a flying object from my roof garden!*

One of the perks of ECT were the many crossings of the Atlantic on the QE2. Because of the stars involved, Donald Sinden, Dorothy Tutin, Richard Griffiths etc., we were always put in first class and treated royally. But it was another QE2 trip I described in a letter to James:

> *The QE2 CRUISE was a different experience, not altogether a happy one and longer than the five-day Atlantic crossing. Trying to perform in very rough seas in the Bay of Biscay brought out the Dunkirk spirit if not the greatest of performances. The Grand Piano was thankfully screwed to the floor, but not so the piano stool, and the*

poor pianist found himself sliding from one end to the other, as each wave hit, with the singers clinging desperately to their lecterns. This cruise package took us to the Canary Islands and Madeira – the latter I rather enjoyed and brought back a bottle of Duke of Clarence Malmsey for Toby. Our fellow passengers were mainly British, a pretty ghastly bunch, very loud mouthed and vulgar, probably lottery winners. So different from those making the Atlantic crossings. Thankfully I was once again in First Class and removed from the general hoy polloi. The food was superb – perhaps not up to your Gulls Eggs souffle – but superb all the same. I started every meal with caviar and frozen vodka, followed with a variety of courses, i.e., bouillon followed by scallops and Chablis, followed by fillet steak and Chateau Margaux, followed by…you get the drift. Had to pay for the wine – my bar bill immense. Now back to bread and water.

There were many letters describing my various trips to the States, mainly when I was directing *The Lost Colony* in North Carolina:

I have just returned from the other side of the pond, having battled for two weeks with the elements, airlines, and an almost impossible workload. There was a snowstorm which seemed to follow me around. New York was terrible, complete white-out. They even had snow flurries in North Carolina, a rarity for them, sending the population into a panic, although the snow was less than an inch thick. It amused me because when in the summer it is boiling hot, steamy and nobody can think for the humidity and the flies, life carries on as normal. But with this minor interruption they closed the schools. I kept telling them –cold is healthy, think of dog's noses – but they obviously consider me mad. I somehow managed to survive the punishing schedule, auditions, not only in NC but a frantic three days in Florida, seeing thousands of kids auditioning – I was back in 'They Shoot Horses Don't They?' mode. I had to wear a VIP badge, which I told them severely stood for Very Imposed-upon Person on account of the fact I was giving a keynote speech and two workshops, as well as attending all the auditions and callbacks. They returned me to the UK Business Class; I think feeling guilty for over-working me! Toby sweetly came to meet me – but drove back so dangerously my blood pressure went zooming up for the first time in weeks! He'd forgotten to put in his hearing aid, so constantly turned to face me to understand what I was saying – which resulted in hysterical shrieks from me – 'Toby mind that car!' 'Toby! Look out!' Brakes Toby'! At one point he said, 'I feel very annoyed with those people you work for. They seem to have worn you to a complete frazzle! You're in a very nervous state!'

Next time, I will definitely take a hire car!

The last major opera production I directed was *La Traviata*. It opened for a short season in London and after that it went on a long tour, ending up in Truro:

As this was the last performance of La T., the chairman threw a party and of course everyone had far too much to drink. This resulted in three of the younger members of the company going on to various bars and picking up three others, before making their way back to their rooms. They must have made a good deal of racket because I was woken in the early hours by a furious landlord who demanded the company pay double for their rooms or he would go to the police! It took an hour to sort out irate landlord and settle the bill. I remember Toby having to do this sort of thing – especially on foreign tours – but this was the first time it had happened to me. To add to my ordeal, my own expensive hotel room was far from satisfactory. It had looked grand, a converted nunnery with turrets, which would have been a good location for a Dracula film. Because of the party, I arrived late, after midnight. There was an old bell rope which I pulled and waited a long time until an aged retainer finally arrived. He testily presented me with a key and told me to follow him. I had explained, when booking, about my damaged ankle and asked for as few stairs as possible. After the third flight I plaintively asked how much further. One more flight to the turret room, was the terse reply. This last flight was the steepest and worst – don't know how I made it – like the final ascent up Everest without the Oxygen mask. With some difficulty he turned the huge key in the lock, and I fell into a peculiar shaped room and immediately slept, only to be woken by the call from furious landlord. Unable to sleep after that, I decided to get up early and started the descent down to breakfast. I limped down the first set of steep stairs, slowly on account of my suffering ankle, and reached the next floor. Here I was faced by a long corridor, with doors either side, but no directions for the way out. It was a Kafka situation. I went up and down until I finally noticed one door with frosted glass at the top – nervously pushing it open – found to my great relief – it led to stairs down to the next floor. This had the same problem – only now with two doors with frosted glass. The first went into a billiard room, so I had to make my way back to the other frosted door. Finally reaching the ground floor I asked the receptionist the way to the dining room. I was the only person in a vast space. The aged retainer appeared, and I ordered bacon and eggs. It arrived. On a very large plate was the tiniest poached egg and the smallest rasher of bacon – nay half a rasher – but I was too exhausted to complain. As I paid the bill, I did mention the stairs to the receptionist. She was horrified and declared it must have been a mistake. Room 30 in the turret had more stairs than any other room. I blame aged retainer – revenge for late arrival. I also asked about lack of signs. She was again apologetic. The place was being re-decorated, and the signs wouldn't be replaced until the following week – I'd visions of guests wandering like ghosts up and down those corridors trying to find a way out. Sometime later I had a letter of profuse apology from the manager, offering me a night's free hospitality back in Dracula's Hotel. I politely declined!

There was a follow-up to this letter, with general family news:

I'm now having a necessary break from all things operatic until September. Meanwhile I am taking two of the grandsons – aged 12 – out to Canada for three weeks, to stay with my brother-in-law, for his family summer reunion and house party. Big event. It will be the first year without my sister and I feel I need to be there for moral support. He lives in the middle of Ontario on an old farm, with those interesting, shaped barns, and landscaped grounds. A lot of space and plenty of room to be on my own…

Josh's daughters are going to the Hamptons for the summer to stay with his wife Amanda's relatives. Jess (15) thinks it is all going to be very Scott Fitzgerald and is planning her wardrobe accordingly. I fear she will be quickly disillusioned. She and her sister Issy are both beautiful and willowy. I've told them to wear dark glasses at all times and they would cut a suitable dash…

The last few days on the houseboat have been glorious. It is worth every penny I can't afford! The children mutter about extravagance, but I can't give it up. It is my sanctuary.

After my ankle accident, the frequency of our letters lessened as there was little to report, apart from endless operations and trips to the hospital, and then there was Covid. I did write and tell James I was writing this Memoir, so he sent me the letters, thinking they might prove useful. And they have. But quite apart from that, this long correspondence, now in my possession, will always be treasured, occasionally to be dipped into, bringing back forgotten memories. Thank you, James, for the letters, and for our long friendship. My wonderful friend Bridget would always ask me, after I reported something to her, 'But darling, were you enriched?' I can safely say, about this long correspondence, 'Oh yes, I really was.'

INDEX OF NAMES

Abbasian, Ali 244–247
Adeane, Lady Helen 117–120
Adeane, Lord Michael 117, 120
Adeane, Philip 109
Adrian Boult, Sir 138
Alexander, Michael 106
Allen, Pat 102
Allen, Penny 102, 109, 117
Allen, Sir Thomas 181
Anthony, Nigel 235–236, 238
Archer, Robin 117
Arias, Enrique 70–74, 89, 101–103, 184
Arias, Mary 103
Arias, Roberto 184–185, 187
Ashcroft, Dame Peggy 157
Ashe, Michael 87
Ashton, Sir Frederick 185
Athol, Duke of 83
Atkins, Eileen 92, 139, 231
Ball, Peter Eugene 140
Barnsley, Edward 24
Baylis, Lilian 157, 184
Beresford, Elizabeth 106

Berlin, Donna 223
Bernstein, Leonard 171
Betjeman, John 67
Blair, Isla 116, 146–147, 187–188, 212
Blenkinsop, Guy 51
Bolam, James 75, 213–214
Boulanger, Nadia 138
Brandreth, Gyles 211, 251
Brook, Peter 87
Brown, Georgia 165
Brown, Harold 110
Burton, Richard 62, 121
Cahill, Teresa 157–158
Carlton, Timothy 79
Carpenter, Edward 92, 153, 156, 200
Carreras, Jose 171
Carver, Dr Stephen 249
Carver, Rachael 249
Cash, Tony 181
Charteris, Hugo 88
Christie, Julie 75, 79
Conway, Vernon 248
Cook, Peter 145
Cope, Jonathan 181
Cosby, Bill 194

Coward, Noël 80, 88, 213
Cox, Brian 132, 135–136
Cripps, Sir Stafford 19
Cronshaw, Bill 176, 184
Cumberbatch, Benedict 79
Curnutte, Carl 216, 218–219
Dalton, Timothy 160
Dankworth, Jacqui 206
Davis, Carl 117, 128, 131, 134, 136–138
Davis, Jane 33
Dawson, Basil ('B') 88
de Cormier, Bob 171–172
Dench, Judi 145, 157–158, 200, 204
de Valois, Ninette 184–185
Douglas, Felicity 88, 103–104, 111
Douglas Home, Lady Margaret 13
Drabble, Margaret 145
Durdin-Robertson, Moira 236
Durdin-Robertson, Olivia 237

280

Elizabeth, HM the Queen 117–120, 185, 214
Elizabeth, HM the Queen Mother 156–157
Evans, Joni 108
Fazan, Eleanor 87
Feldman, Lauretta 165–166
Ferrier, Kathleen 52
Fielding, Fenella 233, 235–238, 240
Fisher, Doug 160–161
Fontaine, Joan 61
Fonteyn, Margot 183–187
Forbes Adam, Colin (father-in-law by marriage) 88–89
Forbes Adam, Nigel (brother-in-law by marriage) 88–89, 98, 117
Forbes Adam, Toppet (sister-in-law) 87–89, 98, 117
Fox, James 106
Frangcon-Davies, Gwen 40
Fraser, Donald (Don) 22, 81, 134–138, 140–143, 146, 149–150, 155–156, 158, 163, 165, 167, 169–171, 180–181, 187, 190–191, 197–198, 203–211, 221, 233, 252, 269, 276
Garcia Flores, Juan 101
Georgiadis, Nico 150
Gibson, Sir Alexander 151
Gielgud, John 40, 94

Gillingham, Canon F H (Gilly) (grandfather) 23, 35–37, 58, 90, 262
Gimmy, Mrs (great-aunt by marriage) 23–24
Gladstone, Kitty 90
Glenconner, Lord 95
Glover, Julian 116, 129, 146, 231
Grace, Nickolas 158
Griffith, Andy 219
Griffiths, Richard 274
Guinness, Desmond 233–237, 239–240, 271–273
Guinness, Penny 234–235, 240
Gummer, John 28
Haggard, Stephen 40
Hannen, Nicholas 'Beau' 91
Hardy, Robert 181
Hastings, Max 106
Hazleton, Julia 160
Heath, Edward 73, 118, 120
Helpmann, Robert 183–187
Hepburn, Audrey 185
Heslewood, Jennie 79
Hobson, Harold 116–117, 128
Hobson, Valerie 40, 52, 61, 65–66, 74, 99
Hodge, Patricia 181
Holst, Gustav 39, 52
Hootkins, William 162, 164
Hornby, Edward 67
Hose, Stephen 222
Houston, lebame 215–216

Innocent, Harold 158–159
Ivey Long, William 217
Jacobi, Derek 115–117, 126, 128–129, 139, 146, 160, 187–188, 195
Jefford, Barbara 233
Jellicoe, Ann 75
Johnson, Boris 251–252
Jones, Freddie 79
Jones, Paul 135
Kaye, Danny 52
Keaton, Eleanor 165–166
Kempson, Rachel 40, 74
Kennedy Onassis, Jackie 189–193
Kettel, Gary 141
Korda, David 87
Kunz, Charlie 83
Kwarteng, Kwasi 247
Lambert, Verity 97, 138
Lavender, Ian 206
Leigh Hunt, Barbara 158
le Mesurier, John 146
Leventon, Annabel 137
Logue, Christopher 140–141
Louther, Bill 140
Macleod, George 49–50
Mares, Mary 20
Marquand, Richard 87
Marsh, Jean 156
Martin, Trevor 160

McClure, John 171–172, 189
McClure, Susan 171
McCowan, Alec 139
McCulloch, Betty (née Gillingham) (mother) 13, 15–16, 22, 25–27, 29, 36–44, 48–50, 53–58, 61–63, 65–66, 70–71, 73–74, 77–79, 86, 89–90, 92, 94, 101–103, 119–120, 129–130, 145, 152–153, 202–203, 244
McCulloch, Joseph (father) 14–15, 19–20, 22, 25–26, 28–29, 31, 33–34, 36–38, 40–46, 48, 50–55, 59–67, 69–71, 73, 75, 77–81, 86, 89–94, 124, 144–145, 152–153, 183, 197–198, 200–202, 252, 257, 268
McEnery, Cindy 229
McKellen, Ian 113, 115
Menuhin, Yehudi 145
Moffett, Jane 250–251
Mongomery, Bill 235
Mongomery, Daphne 235
Montague, Lee 116, 160
Montgomery, Robert (Bob) 191, 193, 195, 249
Moody, Ron 181
Moore, Harry 75
More, Julian 87
More, Sheila 87
Muir, Thomas 84

Mullis, John 223
Newson, Gillian 146
Nicholas, Jeremy 91, 136, 160–161
Nicholas, Paul 136
Norman, Jessye 167–181, 187, 191–193, 198, 222, 257
Norman, Monty 87
Norris, Dan 225
O'Connor, Michael 223
Olivier, Laurence 62, 145
Panovs (Russian dancers) 126
Parry, Natasha 87
Patrick, Anna 106
Patrick, Beth 106
Patrick, Victor 106
Pesante, Scheherazade 223, 225
Phillips, Colwyn 20
Phillips, Jestyn, Viscount St Davids 20
Phillips, Myfanwy 20
Phillips, Rowena 20
Pierce Higgins, Ben 76
Powell, Roger 24
Quayle, Anthony 40, 62, 156–157
Quinn, Anthony 193–196
Rawlings, Ann 69, 250–251
Redgrave, Lynn 74, 217–218
Redgrave, Michael 40
Redington, Michael 73, 79, 146, 149

Reeve, James 259–260, 262–267, 269–271, 273–274, 279
Richardson, Ian 150
Rigg, Diana 200
Robertson, David 62, 76, 81, 87, 116, 121, 128, 230, 250
Robertson, Toby (Sholto David Maurice) (husband) 28, 62, 68, 76, 81–107, 109–119, 121, 123–128, 130–131, 133–134, 136–141, 143–144, 148, 150–153, 155–156, 165, 168–169, 183, 185, 196, 205–206, 208–209, 221–222, 228–233, 254, 259, 262, 264–268, 270–271, 275–276
Rostropovich, Mstislav 125
Rowe, John 235, 238–239
Rudin, Jack 197–199
Rudin, Susan 199
Scales, Prunella 87, 107, 158
Schilling, Keith 138, 264
Schlesinger, John 94, 104
Scott, John 181, 278
Seyler, Athene 91, 99
Sherman, Bob 162, 164
Sinden, Donald 274
Spacey, Kevin 228
Spain, Nancy 52, 76–77, 80, 91
Straker, Peter 136

Streuli, Peter 79, 81, 84
Syms, Sylvia 129
Tarrant, Margaret 25
Temple, William (Archbishop of Canterbury) 20, 34
Thatcher, Margaret 29, 145
Thomas, Mike 110
Thomas, Peggy 66
Thurburn, Gwynneth 74
Tutin, Dorothy 139, 274
Vallone, Raf 115
Walker, Fiona 79
Walker, Lillias 83
Walliams, David 274
Wall, Max 106, 142–144, 206
Waters, Jan 113, 126, 130–131, 142, 160, 162, 221
Werner Laurie, Joan 52, 80, 91
West, Joe 107
West, Sam 107
West, Timothy 107, 116, 125, 128, 131, 139, 141, 146, 150–151
Whately, Kevin 181
Williams, Michael 158
Wise, Herbert 79
Woolard, Rear Admiral Sir Robert 214–215
Woolford, Tim 180
Zeffirelli, Franco 115

Printed in Great Britain
by Amazon